Healthy Human Life

Healthy Human Life

A Biblical Witness

James K. Bruckner

CASCADE *Books* · Eugene, Oregon

HEALTHY HUMAN LIFE
A Biblical Witness

Cascade Books
An Imprint of Wipf and Stock Publishers
199 W. 8th Ave., Suite 3
Eugene, OR 97401

www.wipfandstock.com

ISBN 13: 978-1-61097-947-4

Cataloging-in-Publication data:

Bruckner, James K.

    Healthy human life : a biblical witness / James K. Bruckner.

    xviii + 238 p. ; 23 cm. —Includes bibliographical references.

    ISBN 13: 978-1-61097-947-4

    1. Health—Biblical teaching. 2. Pastoral theology—Biblical teaching. I. Title.

BS680.H4 B7 2012

Manufactured in the U.S.A.

For all who have striven for health within illness;

for Donald and Eunice

"I am the Lord who healeth thee."
Exodus 15:26

Contents

Foreword by Mary Chase-Ziolek ix
Preface and Acknowledgments xiii

Part One—Primary Biblical Narrative

Chapter One
What is a Healthy Human Being? Claims from the Book of Genesis 3

Chapter Two
What is a Healthy Community? God Shapes His People in
Exodus—Deuteronomy 27

Chapter Three
What is Human Wholeness? Descriptive Content from
Deuteronomy 58

Part Two—Primary Word-Concepts

Chapter Four
Levav: What is a Whole Heart? 79

Chapter Five
Nefesh: What is a Soul? 104

Chapter Six
Me'od: What Are the Elements of Strength? 131

Part Three—Primary Traditions of Restoration

Chapter Seven
Face to Face with God 157

Chapter Eight
Telling the Truth in Suffering 180

Chapter Nine
Remembering God: Testimonies of Healing and Health 205

Bibliography 229

Foreword

Healthy Human Life: A Biblical Witness

IT HAS BEEN MY pleasure to witness the development of Jim Bruckner's work on the Bible and health through our work as colleagues at North Park Theological Seminary. I have been impressed with the scholarship, passion, and respect with which he has approached healthy human life as understood in Scripture. His ability to speak across disciplines is impressive, from his first class on Biblical Perspectives on Health and Healing to lectures given, workshops led together and now in this book. While much has been written about the healing stories in the Gospels, far less has been written about the Hebrew Scripture's foundational understanding of health and wholeness that people of faith have pondered throughout the ages.

This text comes at an important time when more and more congregations are engaging in ministries of health and partnering in neighborhood health initiatives; research on religion and health is growing and health professionals are eager to have their faith undergird their care. Bruckner begins his work describing a healthy human being, a healthy community, and human wholeness. These images from the biblical witness are central to the work of health professionals and church alike.

One of this text's unique contributions is articulating the distinctively communal and relational understanding of health and wholeness found in the Hebrew Bible. Our health care system focuses on the individual, yet health is not only the result of personal choice, it is also shaped by communities that provide or limit opportunities for well-being. In an age when the individual pursuit of health can become a god, Bruckner brings to our attention the Scriptural challenge to create communities where health for all might be possible. You will never read the Ten Commandments the same after considering his interpretation of these "ten words" as a charter of freedom protecting community and individual well-being.

Long before the contemporary language of holistic health recognizing the integration of body, mind, and spirit came into being, the people of Israel were challenged to love God with heart, soul, and strength (Deut 6:5). Bruckner explores each of these word-concepts from the Shema, bringing to light their contemporary significance. Today's faith and health movement has much to gain from Bruckner's scholarship. Those engaged in faith and health partnerships bringing together congregations, community organizations, and government agencies to improve the health of neighborhoods will find the communal aspects of health characteristic of the Hebrew Bible consistent with public health practice. The discussion of justice considered in characteristics of a whole heart, resonates with the contemporary issue of disparities affecting health that require a communal response. Bruckner argues that a healthy human life as described in the Bible is one lived in community and who better than congregations to participate in nurturing the well-being of their neighborhoods?

A growing number of congregations are taking on the challenge to promote health, healing, and wholeness developing wellness activities such as walking challenges, healthy eating initiatives or health fairs, services of healing, lay caregiver programs, or support groups. Pastors will find in Bruckner's work rich material for challenging their congregations to be places of health and healing. Those engaged in congregationally-based health ministries such as faith community nurses will find in this text foundational material to undergird their ministry of health.

The third section of the book explores traditions of restoration highlighting the relational nature of health, so foundational to the healing arts. Health professionals and chaplains rooted in the Judeo-Christian tradition will find in this text a biblical perspective that gives voice to the faith-based significance of the care they provide. Bruckner considers the significance of presence, lament as an expression of suffering, and the role of remembering God's acts as resources to renew well-being. Within the health professions, research on religion and health abounds, most often explored from a medical or psychological perspective with little attention given to the influence of Scripture on this connection. Bruckner's work provides a biblical perspective that would enrich this research.

The biblical witness of a multicultural healing community described in the Book of Revelation brings this text to a close. It is a vision with which public health professionals can identify, whether or not they are people of faith, which resonates with the goals of the Healthy People 2020 national initiative to "achieve health equity, eliminate disparities, and improve the health of all groups, and create social and physical environments that promote good health for all." Christians trying to live into the challenge of what healthy human life means today will recognize that the health of each of us is related to the health of all of us.

May this biblical witness to a healthy human life enrich your life, the lives of those with whom you live and for whom you care.

Mary Chase-Ziolek, PhD, RN
Professor of Health Ministries and Nursing
North Park University and Seminary
Chicago, Illinois
January 1, 2012

Preface and Acknowledgments

EUNICE ERICSON WENT TO the northwest coast of Alaska in 1953. She had just graduated from the Royal Academy of Nursing in Edmonton, Alberta and answered a plea for nurses for the Maynard McDougal Memorial Hospital in Nome. On a staff of three, she was the E.R. nurse and did everything else including obstetrics, surgery, and hospice. She cared for victims of abuse, malnutrition, and bear attack. The local radio station provided her a venue for a regular short home health and nutrition broadcast. When a patient in one of the dozens of villages that the hospital served needed a medical evacuation, she traveled with them in a small plane. She did this for little more than room and board in the midst of an Eskimo culture that she came to love during her forty-five years in Alaska. She was my mother.

This book originated in a conversation that started in a hallway with Mary Chase-Ziolek, PhD in nursing. She asked me to think about teaching a course on the Bible and health, for the then-new certificate program in Faith and Health. I thought about Eunice and how her ideas about healthy human life flowed from her love of Scripture. "Biblical Perspectives on Health and Healing" was born. The initial questions were basic: What should we know about the biblical witness that will transform the way we practice healing arts? What does Scripture say about the body and about the soul? What does a loving God have to do with human health?

This was to be a master's degree level seminary course, so I expected seminary students, but something unexpected happened. The class kept filling up with health care professionals from diverse backgrounds. Over the last seven years, my classroom has been filled with nurses (mostly in the master's nursing programs) and other health care professionals, including a public health official, a psychiatrist, a veterinarian, a dentist, a tai chi instructor, and a massage therapist. The dialogue in the classroom and in the online version of the course has been interesting, poignant, and always thought provoking. As a result, this book is written with health care professionals and those preparing for health care professions in mind.

Spirituality and Health

The renewed interest in *spirituality* of all kinds in relation to human health calls for an articulation of a biblical spirituality in relation to human health. Until we know our own traditions, we cannot enter dialogues with others about their own. I hope that this book will serve to further that dialogue that we might all learn to live healthy and whole lives before God. It is my hope especially that those preparing for or engaged in health care professions will find this book to be a good reference for understanding the biblical sources of Christian spirituality and religious practice.

The well-known epidemiologist Jeff Levin has demonstrated that the "theosomatic triunity" (which he defines as body, mind, and spirit) of a human being is changing medical practice, research, and education.[1] He concludes, "The weight of published evidence overwhelmingly confirms that our spiritual life influences our health. This can no longer be ignored."[2] The term "spiritual life" and "spirituality" can be, however, shapeless, amorphous terms. The great irony is that, in Scripture, when you look for spirituality, you find real and embodied relationships. Human spirituality and human "spirit" are *never* disembodied. Human reality and health in the Bible are body-based and deeply integrated in a relationship with God's creating Spirit.

Contents

This book is organized by three sections with three chapters each. The first section engages portions of the primary ancient biblical narratives of Genesis (chapter one), Exodus (chapter two), and Deuteronomy

1. Jeff Levin, *God, Faith, and Health: Exploring the Spirituality-Healing Connection*, 215.

2. Ibid., 223.

(chapter three), as they bear relevance for understanding human health and wholeness. Human lives are made of stories about relationships; these biblical stories provide a storied narrative basis for understanding human health.

Chapter one interprets the story of relationships in Genesis. In these key texts, healthy, whole relationships between man, woman, God, and animals are gained and lost. Deception disintegrates toward death. Alienation becomes part of the human reality. Chapter two considers the narrative of delivered slaves in Exodus, who embark upon a new holistic sociality at Sinai. It surveys the six-hundred and thirteen commandments of the Torah to demonstrate the variety of concerns for community health. The third chapter engages the book of Deuteronomy and its definition of human health. The narrative is grounded in choosing to love the God who has demonstrated his love for a broken people. The *Shema* (Deut 6:5) and its injunction: "You shall love the Lord your God with all your *heart*, all your *soul*, and all your *strength*" centers this choice and establishes a paradigm for section two.

The second section (chapters four through six) engages the *Shema's* words "heart," "soul," and "strength" as critical aspects of human wholeness. Each chapter examines one of these Hebrew word-concepts. The three Hebrew words and their New Testament Greek counterparts appear frequently in Scripture. The range of use offers a theological and substantive look at healthy, whole human life and, by contrast, a *heart*, *soul*, or *strength* that is sick, broken, dysfunctional, or misused. In the canonical and narrative context, these three word-concepts give deep descriptive background of healthy relationships and behaviors that result in a whole life.[3] Such a life has integrity and is fundamentally relational toward God and the community.

Section three engages three aspects of contemporary healing practice by presenting biblical traditions of the restoration of human health. Chapter seven describes the ways the "face" and the *presence* of others and of God are used in Scripture, and how these can create a healing environment. Chapter eight discusses the honesty of *lament* as the seedbed of hope, and claims that healing often begins with a truthful account of

3. These three words do not form a technical definition of ancient biblical human anthropology. They are not composite parts of a person, but aspects of a person in relation to personal growth in relationships and actions. See Joel Green, *Body Soul and Human Life: the Nature of Humanity in the Bible*, 14; Green has a helpful summary and critique of Old Testament scholarship on biblical anthropology, 3–16.

suffering, trauma, or sickness. Chapter nine focuses on testimonies and narratives that create an environment conducive to healing; specifically that telling the story of God's past, present, and future deliverance is a transforming practice. In the biblical tradition, these three practices are necessary elements in restoring health to individuals and a community.

God's intention is to restore or to give added or transformed strength to the one who suffers.[4] God seeks partnership with human beings, who use the power of the "dominion" given in Genesis to bring blessing and restoration to the whole creation. God "empowers" people to comfort those "in affliction" as the apostle writes to the Corinthians: "Blessed be . . . the God of all consolation who consoles us in all our affliction, so that we may be able to console those who are in any affliction with the consolation with which we ourselves are consoled by God" (2 Cor 1:3–4).

Perspective

The ancient text of the Bible has been used in many ways, some better than others, over many millennia. It is "the most difficult writing men [sic] can read."[5] This is due, in part, to its incredible array of literary forms, written over a period of more than one thousand years. Moreover, it is a canonical text that bears the marks of editing and canon formation over the same time period. To complicate matters, Jews and Christians claim that it is a living word that bears instruction for our lives today (Deut 5:3; 30:14).

I write from the perspective of a professor of Old Testament in a protestant seminary. In this book, I refer to the Hebrew Bible, in part for clarity (*"Tanak"* is a relatively unknown Hebrew acronym) and to avoid the notion that it is old and outdated in relation to the "New" Testament. The Christian confession is that the Hebrew Bible is the living Word of God and "is useful for teaching, for reproof, for correction, and for training in righteousness" (2 Tim 3:16). I incorporate the perspectives of linguistics,[6] textual criticism, cultural anthropology, and a

4. For example see Ps 103:3; Ezek 18:31–32.

5. Mortimer Adler and Charles Van Doren, *How To Read a Book,* 294. This classic on "intelligent reading" has been a staple in graduate programs for over 50 years.

6. This book often refers to the original words and concepts behind English Bible translations. Where Hebrew or Greek words are used, the word root rather than the

Protestant theology that relies on the insights of both Jewish interpreters and the fathers of the church. I dare to think that I primarily write as a human being who has seen the effects of unhealthy living in both the two-thirds world and American cultural contexts.

Thanks

A special thanks is due to the Lilly Foundation and the Association of Theological Schools and their generous Theological Scholar's Grant. I am certain that this book would not have been written without it. It allowed me the time and financial help that were necessary to complete an interdisciplinary enterprise. Moreover, the discussion with other scholars in Pittsburgh, midway through the project, was exceedingly valuable to my work. Thanks especially to Frances Pacienza and Stephen Graham for their excellent support.

I am thankful for many other people: for Mary for that first of many conversations in the hallway about human health and the Bible; for my many students and their interaction with this material; for my research assistants: Jen, Adam, Luke, and Cathy; for Ben, Nick, and Luke who thought and commented; for my colleagues at North Park Theological Seminary who consulted at numerous points; for David Templin, MD, a life-long mentor and selfless practitioner throughout Alaska, who offered many helpful suggestions; and for Karin and Paul for providing, yet again, a place to write. I am thankful also for Wendell, Byron, Carolyn, and Julie, who always asked, then listened, and asked again. The place of honor is for my wife, Kris, who, in addition to continual love, support, dialogue, and companionship, applied her professional skills as an editor to the first draft of the manuscript.

---

specific form is used to aid the general reader in seeing the intra-biblical connections between words. My purpose is that a reader without knowledge of the ancient languages may still understand the ideas they communicate.

Part One

Primary Biblical Narratives

Chapter One

What is a Healthy Human Being?

Claims from the Book of Genesis

Introduction: What is a Human Being?

CULTURAL, RELIGIOUS, AND SCIENTIFIC traditions differ in their view of the substance of a human being, with corresponding assumptions concerning daily life and health. The way a society treats women, children, those with disabilities, criminals, and the elderly is based on the degree to which they are regarded as more or less human. The practical matter of how a health care professional views and treats patients to heal or maintain their health is related to her or his assumption of what a person *is*. Is the patient simply a sick mammal? Is she a lost soul? Or someone with unreached potential? Is this patient as important as the person in the next room?

Science and modern medicine have generally focused on human beings as biological complexities, but the ancient narrative of the Judeo-Christian traditions has a richer and more substantive view. The biblical narrative makes claims about human origins and human relationship to God, while corroborating much of what science and philosophy have learned about people. Its deeper perspective engages the human imagination about the past, provides perspective for restoring human health in the present, and gives hope for what we can be in the future.

Chapter one will engage and interpret the ancient narrative of Genesis, which provides a look at human beings in their original relationship to God, animals, the environment and themselves. In these key texts, healthy, whole relationships between man, woman, God, and animals are gained and lost. Death and alienation become part of the human reality.

The chapter will focus on five central points of the biblical witness: 1) all human beings are made of the same common clay; 2) all receive God's breath; 3) all human beings are made in the image of God, the Creator of all things; 4) all humans are given dominion, which can be used for good or ill; 5) all human beings are capable of deception of self and others to their own and others' detriment, and to the detriment of our shared, vulnerable environment. Created from clay and God's breath and made in God's image, human beings are constantly at risk of twisting or rationalizing the nature of their created reality. Awareness of this factor is an important component of maintaining a healthy life.

Common Clay: God Formed

Several years ago, I gave a guest lecture in a "Nursing and Spirituality" course. Among the future nurses were agnostics, orthodox Jews, a Muslim immigrant, and an African Christian student. The Christian asked, "When I am giving primary care to someone who does not share my faith, how can I communicate with them beyond the medical care? They don't even believe in God!" The answer I gave is rooted in a claim made by the biblical text of Genesis. Before Judaism, before Christianity, before Islam or any other faith system, God created humanity from the same clay. All people, all human beings were made from the ground, and share the same created ancestor.

Genesis one's account of creation makes a remarkably *universal* claim about the origins of human beings. Most creation stories worldwide focus on the creation of the ethnographic group that tells the story. Most are ethnocentric etiologies. This is true among indigenous peoples today and was also the case in the ancient world. The Canaanite myth describes the creation of the Canaanites.[1] The Babylonian *Enuma Elish* describes the ascendance of their god Marduk over the other gods and describes the order he sustained for the sake of the Babylonians.

---

1. The Canaanite god Baal defeats Yam, the god of the Sea, to gain superior position in the "Baal Cycle" discovered at Tell Ras Shamra (Ugarit).

In contrast, the origins of Israel do not come into focus until the twelfth chapter of Genesis, after the formation of all other cultures and languages is described. The creation described in Genesis includes *all people*. We are all made of common clay.

> Then the LORD God formed the human (*ha-adam*), . . . dust (*'aphar*) of the ground (*ha-adamah*) and breathed into his nostrils the breath of life; and the human (*ha-adam*) became a living being" (Gen 2:7; my translation).

A Hebrew play on words drives the point home: "*ha-adam* was formed from *ha-adamah*." A comparable English word play would say: "*the human* was formed from *the humus*." This reminds us of our humility in relation to one another, and that our "common ground" extends to all living creatures.[2] The text claims that all life originally came *from the earth's soil:* plants (Gen 2:9); amphibians and mammals (Gen 1:24); and birds (Gen 2:19).

The formative "raw material" of the first human is the *dust of the ground*.[3] Later in the narrative we are also reminded that human beings are originally mortal. Only access to the tree of life provided the conditional immortality of the garden. In our created form, we are not built to live forever. Once humans gain the knowledge of good and evil and lose access to the tree of life, death becomes the norm.

> By the sweat of your face you shall eat bread until you return to the *ground* (*ha-adamah*), for out of it you were taken; you are *dust* (*'aphar*), and to *dust* (*'aphar*) you shall return. (Gen 3:19)

Our capacity to treat all people as equals regardless of their personal histories is given in the very act of creation. All are created by God, made from the same clay, and will suffer the return to the dust. To be human and to meet others on this common ground is deeply imbedded even in the linguistics of the ancient narrative. Christian belief in the bodily resurrection is a conditional understanding of immortality, and does not negate the shared experience of the human condition.

The texts also gives humans commonality with all living creatures, both plant and animal life. They are not created in exactly the same way,

---

2. The word play works in English because the Latin source of humus (organic matter in soil) and humility are the same. "Human" was differentiated in early Latin as *homo-huminis,* but seems to have shared the *hum-* before written sources.

3. See J. R. Levinson, *Filled with the Spirit*, 14.

but we are given a point of relationship in the biblical text. All living things are made from the ground and are given life by God.[4] We recognize this interdependence in the web of life that creates health between persons and all aspects of their environment.[5]

Common Breath: God's Breath of Life

Breath serves as a primary indicator of health for doctors and nurses. Attention to breathing by a delivering mother can manage pain in childbirth. Hospice nurses can recognize the approaching end of life by the sound of a patient's breathing. God is the source of the newborn's first breaths and the each breath taken thereafter. Genesis 1 and 2 tell us that God gave the breath of life to all creatures, and breathed his own breath into the nostrils of human beings in order to give them life.

"Breath of life" is expressed in three ways in biblical Hebrew, each with its own nuance. In Genesis 1:30, the words translated "breath of life" are *nephesh khayyah*. "And to every beast of the earth . . . to everything that has the *breath of life* I have given every green plant for food." *Nephesh* indicates the body-based reality of created life. In its basic forms it can mean "throat" or "neck," or even jugular vein or "trachea," where the blood and breath passes through.[6]

To be a living being is to have the breath of life in your throat and lungs. In Genesis, this exact Hebrew expression is translated "living creatures" to describe animals (Gen 1:24) and "living being" (or erroneously "living soul") to describe human life (Gen 2:7).[7] "Everything that has the breath of life" in Genesis 1:30 could well be translated "everything that is a *living life*."

The second Hebrew phrase translated as "breath of life" is *nishmat khayyim*. "Then the LORD God formed man from the dust of the

4. The Sinai law provides for the protection of the non-human creation and the theology of new creation provides for their restoration (Rom 8; Rev 21).

5. The prophets called God's people to recognize that this kind of "healthy materiality . . . is the first principle of a biblical ecology." On human relationship to the earth see Ellen Davis, *Getting Involved with God*, 188–90.

6. L. Koehler and W. Baumgartner, *The Hebrew and Aramaic Lexicon on the Old Testament*. Study Edition, vol. 1, 711–13. The rabbinic tradition is that the Nephesh is the blood that flows in the veins, citing Deuteronomy 12:23. See Abraham Cohen, *Everyman's Talmud*, 77.

7. See discussion of "soul" in chapter five.

ground, and breathed into his nostrils the *breath of life*" (Gen 2:7). Its basic meaning is "pant," focusing on the mechanics of inhaling and exhaling as in the expression, "catching my breath." It implies the transitory nature of life and the millions of breaths a person needs to sustain his or her life. Life is dependent on the ability to breathe clean and unobstructed air. We have this "breath of life" in common with the animals. The book of Job describes the *borrowed* nature of breathing. If God were to gather back his "spirit" (*ruakh*) and "breath" (*nishmat*) "all flesh would perish together, and all mortals return to dust (Job 34:14–15; see also Job 33:4).

The third Hebrew word expressed in English as "breath of life" is *ruakh khayyim*. "For my part, I am going to bring a flood of waters on the earth, to destroy from under heaven all flesh in which is the *breath of life* everything that is on the earth shall die" (also at Gen 7:15). *Ruakh* means "breeze," "wind," "breath," and "spirit." Genesis 1:3 indicates its creative source, "a wind from God swept over the face of the waters" (NRSV; most other translations have "the Spirit of God"). The interchangeable uses of "spirit" and "breath" in Hebrew can be seen clearly in the parallel occurrence in Psalm 104:29–30.

> When you hide your face, they are dismayed; when you take away their breath (*ruakh*) they die and return to their dust. When you send forth your spirit (*ruakh*) they are created; and you renew the face of the ground."

All breath and all spirit, all human and animal life, are part of God's active creative work. Everything breathes *in relation to* the Giver of life, whether they recognize this continuing providential action or not.

The challenge for those in healing professions is the capacity to combine the humility of our "common clay" and dependence on God for our every breath with responsible and effective use of our strength in relation to others. The biblical grounding of our shared createdness provides a conceptual framework for identifying with a patient or a client, regardless of any differences in social, religious, economic, or educational status. We are all made of dust and must return to it. At the same time, we have been given constructive strength and power to wield for one another. The psalmist recognizes the humility of human life in relation to the whole universe as well as the power we have in relation to the physical world.

> When I look at your heavens, the work of your fingers, the moon and the stars that you have established; what are human beings that you are mindful of them, mortals that you care for them? Yet you have made them a little lower than God, and crowned them with glory and honor. You have given them dominion over the works of your hands; you have put all things under their feet (Ps 8:3–6).

We live between both truths. We are as humble as dust, yet honored above the rest of creation in some unique ways. It is the second chapter of creation which describes God's anthropomorphic action, "the LORD God formed man from the dust of the ground, and breathed into his nostrils the breath of life" (Gen 2:7). The personal attention of forming and breathing indicates that God has a unique interest in the human aspect of creation, for male and female are made in God's own image.

The Image of God in the Human Creation[8]

The image of God is the universal value that Scripture places on human existence, as the innate dignity of being human in relation to the Creator. The child with Down's syndrome and the child prodigy both bear the image of the Creator by virtue of their human existence. The image persists without regard to intelligence, wealth, virtue, particular mystical gifts, or beauty.[9]

The image of God is also the created capacity of any person either to manifest the glory of God or to divert that glory for their own purposes. This is what we experience as the ability to make genuine decisions. Animals make decisions too; but typically they make decisions which are instinctive and predictable.[10]

---

8. For the image of God as a theme especially see C. Westermann, *Genesis 1–11: A Continental Commentary*; P. Bird, "Male and Female He Created Them: Genesis 1:27 on the Context of the Priestly Account of Creation," 129–59; and J. Barr, "The Image of God in the Book of Genesis—A Study in Terminology," 11–26.

9. For a good articulation of this universal value perspective see the World Council of Churches Faith and Order Paper 199 published as *Christian Perspectives on Theological Anthropology*, 11–12.

10. K. Barth describes a related two-fold capacity given in the image as "addressable" (related to God and others) and "responsible" (differentiated from God and others). K. Barth, *Church Dogmatics*. III.1.48, 196.

Universal Value and Genuine Choices

The inherent value of all life is established in Scripture by the simple claim that God made it and "saw that it was good" (declared seven times in Genesis 1). All life wears the label, "creatures, well-made by God." The ancient narrative also claims that each human being is "made in the image of God" (three times in Genesis 1). Genesis 1:26–27 is one of the most discussed passages in the Bible. What does it mean to claim that God made us in the "image of God"?

> Then God said, "Let us make humankind in our *image*, according to our likeness; and let them have dominion over the fish of the sea, and over the birds of the air, and over the cattle, and over all the wild animals of the earth, and over every creeping thing that creeps upon the earth." So God created humankind in his *image*, in the *image of God* he created them; male and female he created them. (Gen 1:26–27)[11]

The first implication of this claim is that everyone is made in the image of God, therefore imbued with dignity, deserving of respect and of love as an image-bearer of God. The Bible claims that God's concern is especially tilted toward the helpless and powerless of the world. Those who faithfully bear God's image accept that the image of God is indiscriminately present in all persons.

The second implication involves human choice. Everyone has the potential to bear God's image as it was intended, that is, to be a blessing to others and give honor to its Source. The image is given in relationship, by God, to be borne by us within that created relationship. It is possible, of course, to refuse or misuse that relationship. Human beings may use the image of God for self-aggrandizement, promoting themselves at God's expense.

The two options can be found in the Hebrew root behind the word "image" (*tselem*) which may mean "idol" or "icon." The word for "image" is *tselem*, and there are only four verses in the Bible where "image" refers to God (Gen 1:26–27; 5:3; 9:6). In the biblical books that follow Genesis, the word *tselem* always means "idol."[12] Idolatry is the

---

11. For a discussion of the history of interpretation of "male and female" in relation to "image of God" see M. A. Gonzalez, *Created in God's Image*.

12. See Num 33:52; 1Sam 6; 2 Kgs 11:18; 2 Chron 23:17; Ps 73:20; Ezek 7:20, 16:17, 23:14; Amos 5:26; and fourteen times in Daniel. Ten other more specific words for idols are used in Hebrew. The language of the "image of god" in humanity surfaces

perversion of the image of God through the worship of created things in place of God. It describes the practice of giving glory to the created rather than to God. The positive human capacity of the image of God is described in terms of manifesting God's glory in right relation to God.[13] This is also how the New Testament describes the life and work of Jesus and the life of the Christian.

Every person, created in God's image, is a particular manifestation of God's glory with the capacity to usurp that glory. The vulnerability of the sick, weak, or injured may keep them from usurping that glory to the common degree. They may therefore more fully reflect God's glory, as they recognize their helplessness.[14]

Earlier Interpretations of "Image of God"

The phrase "image of God" has been subject to many differing interpretations because relatively little is said about it in Scripture. The history of interpretation falls into two major categories.[15] The first is the *structural view*, rooted in the Greek philosophy of Aristotle and held through Augustine, the church fathers, and Aquinas. This view argues that the "image" is an inherent human capacity that mirrors one of God's best capacities: the will to the good or pure reason.[16] This tradition became deeply rooted in Christian interpretation.[17] It formed, perhaps inadvertently, the basis of centuries of slavery, colonialism, and oppression of those deemed "less reasonable" by virtue of social class, race, or age. The structural view renders anyone who has diminished rational capacities, *for any reason,* a correspondingly diminished image of God.

---

again in the Christian Scripture to explain the phenomenon of Jesus.

13. See S. Grenz, *The Social God*, 204–12.

14. See chapter six on "all your might."

15. S. Grenz, *The Social God*, 141–82. He notes with D. J. Hall and H. Berkhof that "by studying how systematic theologies have poured meaning into Genesis 1:26, one could write a piece of Europe's cultural history." Berkhof, quoted in Grenz, 143. Hendrikus Berkhof, *Christian Faith*, 179; see also Douglas J. Hall, *Imaging God*, 91. For a survey of contemporary models of theological anthropology including progressive liberal, postliberal, feminist, black liberation, womanist, Hispanic/Latino, Asian American, and native American, see D. N. Hopkins, *Being Human*, 13–52.

16. See Grenz, *The Social God*, 144–48.

17. Ibid., 152–62.

The second major interpretive tradition is the *relational view*, born during the Reformation, particularly in the writings of Martin Luther.[18] The image of God is described as a mirror in the created person reflecting the will of the Creator in their life.[19] The image is the result of the relationship between the creature and the Creator. Luther argued that the capacity for the image and likeness of God were lost to humanity through sin. The "lost image" could be restored for the believer through the Word and the Holy Spirit, so that the person could grow in conformity to God's image, to "feel, think, and want exactly what God does."[20] The image in this view depends on how a person responds to God. John Calvin followed a similar line of thought.[21]

Christian theologians interpreted the "image" as an ideal to which some may be able to ascend (soteriologically) in order to account for the serious problem of sinful human decisions (e.g., Gen 3:11, 4:10, 6:11–13). But the issue is not that the image is "lost" or "marred" in sin. It is an *ipso facto* created human power. Rather, it is used, but used idolatrously. To bear the image is to be a particular manifestation of the glory of God. Idols also are a particular manifestation of one aspect of creation which manifests God's glory. So Romans 1:23 says, "they exchanged the glory of the immortal God for images (*eikonos*) resembling a mortal human being or birds or four-footed animals or reptiles."

Scripture does not corroborate that the image of God was lost in the "fall" (Gen. 3).[22] Relationships were broken (see "Original Sin" be-

18. Summarized in ibid., 162–76.

19. The mirror terminology is from Paul Ramsey, *Basic Christian Ethics*, 254. The relational view is described also by Phillip J. Hefner in "The Human Being," 1:323–40. Biblical scholar J. Muilenburg demonstrated this view from the Hebrew Bible over against the structural view. See J. Muilenburg, "Imago Dei," 392–406.

20. M. Luther, "Lectures on Galatians," in *Luther's Works*, 26:431. Quoted in Grenz, *The Social God*, 165.

21. See summary in Grenz, *The Social God*, 166–70.

22. Much of the Christian tradition of interpretation of Genesis 1:26–27 has treated the "image of God" in humanity as an ideal that was lost or marred in the "fall" of Genesis 3, but the "image" is present after Genesis 3 in 5:1 and 9:6. In the Catholic mystical tradition, the image is said to be regained through the process of purgation, illumination, and possible union with God, climbing the ladder through personal experience with God. In Protestant traditions, justification through conversion initiates the process of regaining the image. It is followed by a life of sanctification, growing closer and closer to God and the originally intended "image of God." In a recent treatment of OT theology, the Christian humanist tradition version of regaining the lost image is described as an ascent to becoming more humane (see John Rogerson, *A*

low), but the existence of God's basic creation remained intact. While the relational view is too confident about managing the Christian's will and its results, it does point toward a revised relational understanding of the image beyond a built-in structure of human rationality. It points to human agency in relationship.

Image is the capacity to be self-determining or self-transcendent; "image" (*tselem*) in people provides the capacity to do what is "right in your own eyes." It is the agency to will to cross the boundaries established by God. Tillich notes that the image of God provides the possibility for people to reject God; to use one's "image of God" in an idolatrous way. [23]

Image of God in the New Testament

In the New Testament the concept of bearing the image of God is both sustained and further developed. New Testament texts do not focus on the universal presence of the image of God, but elevate Jesus as the image of God. The data of the NT therefore, is centered on human relationship to the Christ. By extension, a new humanity is formed around this newly revealed Christocentric anthropology. [24] A theological construction of the image for Christians may be called an eschatological

---

Theology of the Old Testament: Cultural Memory, Communication, and Being Human, 174. All these traditions of *ascending* to the image lost in the fall share the same assumption: that human beings living after Genesis 3 are *not* created bearing the fullness of the true image of God. We are born, at best, as a damaged or marred image from which we may climb to the true image of God in life. The problem for the exegete, however, is that the Bible never describes this marring of or this climbing to the image. In fact, expression "the image of God" is presented, *ipso facto,* in Genesis 1 and does not appear again until the NT. After the "falling out" of Genesis 3 and the further slide into sin described in Genesis 4–11, Adam and Eve and subsequent human beings are not said to have lost the image in which they were originally made. Certainly their relationship with God is described as radically altered. The text goes to great length to describe exactly how it is altered; but the image of God is never mentioned. Rather, every human being since then has also been created in the image of God. As we shall see, the "image" is not a soteriological ladder to climb. The biblical text claims that it is a basic reality of created human existence.

23. "Only he who is in the image of God has the power of separating himself from God. His greatness and his weakness are identical." P. Tillich, *Systematic Theology,* 2:32–33. Quoted in M. Gonzalez, *Created in God's Image,* 76. Soren Kierkegaard notes that the freedom the image of God gives a person, even to reject God, creates tremendous anxiety that leads people into all kinds of destructive and self-destructive behavior (sin). See S. Kierkegaard, *Gospel of Our Suffering.*

24. Grenz, *The Social God,* 204.

view of the new humanity.[25] Christ is called the "image of God" and believers are called to participate in the image of God in Jesus Christ by putting on or "wearing" that image in anticipation of the new creation.[26]

This New Testament focus allows the universal value of human life in relation to God's image. It embraces both possibilities: "Just as we have borne the image of the man of dust, we will also bear the image of the man of heaven" (1 Cor 15:49). All people are, by the fact of their creation, bearers of the image of God, even as they are animated dust from the earth.

Most recent biblical commentators suggest that the "image of God" has a primarily functional significance.[27] If the first implication of this claim is that everyone is made in the image of God, the second implication is that each one has the potential to bear God's image as it was intended; to be a blessing to others and give honor to its Source. The primary data for understanding this functionality in Scripture is the concept of dominion.[28]

Human Dominion

God has sought human beings to be in partnership with their Creator to bring blessing to the world. The Bible describes this use of the image

25. Ibid., 223–66.

26. Christian Scripture draws upon this claim in Colossians 3:10–16 with a call to all cultures and ethnicities (Gentiles) to renew their knowledge of Genesis 1. There are to be no cultural divisions among God's creation; rather kindness, forgiveness, and peace. Grenz calls this "the indicative as the source of the imperative." Jesus image-bearing is the indicative; Christian discipleship is the imperative." Grenz, *The Social God*, 252–64. Christian theologians have begun to move to a wider biblical view of the image, as Grenz does. While previous generations have worked christocentrically, recent work has broadened the relational view of the image in humanity through a Trinitarian lens. Especially see M. Gonzales and S. Grenz.

27. For a brief survey of OT scholars including Clines, Wenham, and the dissenting Barr, see Grenz, *The Social God*, 188–89.

28. For dominion as a calling by God to life vocation see J. Green, *Body, Soul and Human Life*, 61–65. Green cites Christopher Wright, "OT Ethics: A Missiological Perspective," 5–8; and Fancisco J. Ayala, "Biological Evolution and Human Nature," 46–64.

of God as *dominion*.[29] According to the ancient narrative, we were made for this relationship.[30]

> Then God said, "Let us make humankind in our image, according to our likeness; and let them have *dominion* over the fish of the sea, and over the birds of the air, and over the cattle, and over all the wild animals of the earth, and over every creeping thing that creeps upon the earth." (Gen 1:26)
>
> God blessed them, and God said to them, "Be fruitful and multiply, and fill the earth and *subdue it*; and have *dominion* over the fish of the sea and over the birds of the air and over every living thing that moves upon the earth." (Gen 1:28)

The Babylonian narrative of creation tells a very different story. In the *Enuma Elish*, man was made for the purpose of serving all the gods, especially Marduk and his human rulers in Babylon. Israel's story declares that the Creator of all peoples made "male and female" in God's own image for freedom and ruling, not for slavish service to the gods of power. He gave everyone dominion.

In recent years, the English word "dominion" has acquired negative connotations, due to the overwhelmingly *bad dominion* exercised over the environment and powerless peoples in the last centuries. In Hebrew, dominion (*radah*) is a value free word, but the contrast between *good* and *bad* dominion is a major theme of the Bible. The overarching narrative goes to great lengths to identify and to distinguish between them.

Caregivers and people in the healing professions have dominion over others. Whether a client has a sick animal that they love, a problem they want to discuss, or a sickness to be healed, even the status of credentials is a sign of power. Scripture puts this power in the perspective of our own createdness. We did not create our own intelligence, health, or opportunities, but simply made good use of them. This is *good dominion* over our knowledge, expertise, and care of others.

---

29. For the relationship between the image of God and dominion see P. Bird, "Male and Female," 137–38; H. W. Wolff, *Anthropology of the Old Testament*, 162–64; D. J. A. Clines, "The Image of God in Man," 97; S. Grenz, *The Social God*, 196–97.

30. "Subdue" (*kabash*) and "dominion" (*radah*) are used primarily in Scripture to describe the rule of kings and queens. Regents are assessed as either good or bad.

What is Good Dominion?

The first demonstration of good dominion and subduing in Genesis is a partnership between God and humans in caring for the well-being of a garden. The deeper background for this "subduing" dominion is in the myths and poetry of the ancient east.[31] Scripture bears the marks of this cultural milieu in the theme of bringing order out of chaos.[32] Human "subduing" follows the model of God's creating order by "subduing" any chaos that would disturb or destroy human life. It is diametrically opposed to destroying the natural order and ecosystems that make healthy human life possible. That kind of bad dominion and subduing would *re-introduce* chaos.[33]

Good dominion as management of and care for the non-human creation is codified in the Sinai legislation:

> When you see the donkey, even of one who hates you, lying under its burden and you would rather hold back from setting it free, you must help to set it free (Exod 23:5; Deut 22:4); The food of the land every seventh year shall be only for your livestock and for the wild animals in your land (Lev 25:7); If you come across a bird's nest beside the road, either in a tree or on the ground, and the mother is sitting on the young or on the eggs, do not take the mother with the eggs. You may take the young, but be sure to let the mother go, so that it may go well with you and you may have a long life (Deut 22:6–7); You shall not muzzle an ox while it is treading out the grain (Deut 25:4).

31. In the beginning, "the earth was without form, and void; and darkness was upon the face of the deep" (KJV; Gen 1:2). "The deep" (*tehom*; "formlessness" *tohu*, is from the same word root) represented chaos across the ancient east. Chaos itself is represented in Scripture as "Leviathan" or "Rahab." See texts and discussion in J. Bruckner, *Exodus*, 142–43.

32. "Subdue" is also a value free word. In the ancient socio-ecology subdue had three major contexts:

1) Subduing dangerous animals for safety of children in the encampment. For example bears or wolves at the edge of the camp; 2) Subduing domestic animals. For example, herding livestock to safe pasturage, training and bridling camels and horses; 3) Subduing the ground for agriculture. This subduing included cutting and digging trees, extracting rocks, plowing soil, pulling weeds, cutting during harvest. Most of these activities are regulated by the commandments given at Sinai to insure that the "subduing" was good and not misused.

33. For the ironic history of Christian misinterpretation of this concept see Lynn White Jr., "The Historical Roots of Our Ecological Crisis," 15–31.

God is concerned about the long-term viability of the land, over against the shortsighted goals of people: If you do not give the land a Sabbath rest (let it lie fallow every seventh year) the land will enjoy the rest without you (Lev 26:45; cf. Hos 4:1–4). The implication is that God will remove Israel and send them into exile in order to protect the land. When good dominion is not practiced in Jerusalem, Jeremiah warns, God will cast the people out of the land (Jer 7:4–16). God speaks directly to the earth as he declares the exile of the people from the land for their failure to practice good dominion (Isa 1:2; Jer 6:19). The protection of the land is necessary for the future feeding of animals and humans.

People who bear God's image in relationship are instructed to exercise good dominion over all aspects of creation. If such goodness is learned in relation to the voiceless non-human creation, it may be practiced in relation to people who have need by those who have the power to help them.

Beyond the Torah in Scripture, the language of human dominion is cause for assessment and reflection in the ancient narrative. In the book of Kings, the Deuteronomist declares which rulers did and which did not exercise good dominion in Judah and Israel. The psalmist celebrates and describes the nature of good dominion in royal songs that hope for rulers who will lead as God intended from the beginning. A king's good dominion will be expressed in a servant leadership, bringing justice for the poor, thriving cities, and care for earth so that all will flourish.

> May he have dominion from sea to sea, and from the River to the ends of the earth . . . For he delivers the needy when they call, the poor and those who have no helper. He has pity on the weak and the needy, and saves the lives of the needy. From oppression and violence he redeems their life; and precious is their blood in his sight . . . May there be abundance of grain in the land; may it wave on the tops of the mountains; may its fruit be like Lebanon, and may people blossom in the cities like the grass of the field. (Ps 72:8, 12–14, 16; see also Ps 97)

The attachment of the language of dominion to the highly profiled king of Israel ought not to distract from the essential qualities and measures of good dominion. The servant-ruler language in the Hebrew Scripture culminates in Isaiah 53. Here the people confess that they did not recognize at first the leader who brought them healing. He was too humble in their eyes, suffering in his leadership on their behalf.[34]

> Surely he has borne our infirmities and carried our diseases; yet
> we accounted him stricken, struck down by God, and afflicted.
> But he was wounded for our transgressions, crushed for our in-
> iquities; upon him was the punishment that made us whole, and
> by his bruises we are healed. (Isa 53:4–5)

This faithful development of good dominion is expressed in God's vindication of the servant-leader: "See, my servant shall prosper, he shall be exalted and lifted up and shall be very high . . . so he shall startle many nations; Kings shall shut their mouths because of him" (Isa 52:13, 15). This expression of good dominion is a natural conclusion if we consider its beginning in the garden with the first humans tending and protecting the garden that God had planted. Ideally, the earth is ever viewed as a garden to be cared for as God's special creation, in partnership with humanity. This partnership is the primary metaphor for dominion in the Bible.[35]

Dominion in the New Testament

In the New Testament, the language of Jesus' good dominion is developed in two main ways. The first is through his teaching about the "kingdom of God," typified by the Sermon on the Mount.[36] The theme permeates Gospels.[37] The tenor of Jesus teaching on good dominion in this kingdom may be best illustrated in his conflict with his own disciples concerning children. The disciples tried to stop children from reaching him to be blessed by speaking sternly to them.

> But when Jesus saw this, he was indignant and said to them,
> "Let the little children come to me; do not stop them; for it is
> to such as these that the kingdom of God belongs. Truly I tell

34. See also Isaiah 42:1–4, which includes "a bruised reed he will not break, and a dimly burning wick he will not quench, he will faithfully bring forth justice."

35. See W. Brueggemann, "The Human Person as Yahweh's Partner" in *Theology of the Old Testament*, 450ff.

36. See Matthew 5–7 where it is referred to as the "kingdom of heaven."

37. For a full delineation of kingdom-dominion language see "basileus" and "basileia" in *Theological Dictionary of the New Testament*, 97–102; and C. Caragounis, "Kingdom of God/Kingdom of Heaven" in *Dictionary of Jesus and the Gospels*, 417–30.

> you, whoever does not receive the *kingdom* of God as a little
> child will never enter it." And he took them up in his arms, laid
> his hands on them, and blessed them. (Mark 10:14–16; Matt
> 19:13–14; Luke 18:15–17)

The second major New Testament development of good dominion follows Isaiah's vindicated suffering servant as a means of describing the work of Jesus as a dying and rising king. The ultimate act of dominion and rule was to bear the sins of the world, defeating sin and death and inaugurating hope in a new creation. The apostles quoted Isaiah 53 as a way of explaining the rootedness of Jesus death and vindicating resurrection in the tradition of servant-dominion.[38] The paradigm for a wounded healer is established. So also people in healing ministries often bear their good dominion in their own suffering on behalf of others.

To be made in the "image of God" and to exercise "dominion" in Scripture does not mean an ascent to God or ascendency of pure reason. It means that every created human being, from the person with limiting disabilities to the most capable savant, is made in the image of God and related to God through their createdness. This reality is present even in those who are ignorant or who reject this revealed relationship. According to the ancient narrative, all people and every person share this dignity, regardless of their cultural or personal assent. For the person in the healing arts, this provides an understanding of the imbued dignity of every wounded person as an image-bearer of God.

Human Rationalization and Self-Deception

A primary claim of the Hebrew Scriptures is established when the narrative says that God made the human body and declared that it was good.[39] It is echoed by the psalmist: "For you did create my vitals; you did weave me in the womb of my mother . . . thy works are wonderful." (See Ps 139:13–15; see also Job 10:1–18). The earth, the human body, and all creation are declared good, not a limitation from which we long to escape. Scripture describes sin, not as the failing of bodily flesh or the physical creation, but of a good human creation that has twisted or

---

38. Acts 8:30–35; 1 Pet 2:22–25; Rom 4:25, 5:18; 1 Cor 15:3

39. That God fashions the body (Gen 2:7) and declares that it is good is germane to all Hebrew thought. "The idea of an evil body is utterly alien to the whole OT." J. Muilenburg, "Imago Dei," 393.

forgotten who it is. The root of this self-deception, the ancient narrative shows, is the rejection of the Creator that gives and sustains its life.

If we look around, it is clear that something has gone terribly wrong with basic goodness, God's image in human beings, and with human dominion. Bad personal and public decisions abound. Health professionals see it daily: high risk behaviors, chronic abuse of children, spouses, and the elderly, and addictions of all kinds. In the public forum, bad dominion is even more devastating: unacceptable statistics of violent crime—murder, rape, and assault; avoidable starvation and malnutrition world-wide; and the many genocides of the twentieth and twenty-first centuries. The earth also suffers increasing degradation through human abuse. Bad dominion abounds. What is wrong with humanity?

The ancient narrative uses the word "sin" to describe these kinds of behaviors. "Sin" in Scripture is not an arbitrary religious category. Sin is sin because it destroys or degrades God's good creation. "Sin denies the worth and dignity of human beings, disrupts the community and hampers the flow of love and justice."[40] The narrative describing the "original" sin of Adam and Eve is instructive for understanding the root of life-denying behavior. Genesis 3 sets the stage for the rest of Scripture and its polemical call to humanity to return to good relation with the Creator and a partnership in good dominion to sustain the goodness of the earth through life-affirming behaviors and acts of healing. The world needs people in healing professions of all kinds.

The Original "Sin"

The poetic narrative drips with the imagery of deception:

> Now the serpent was more crafty than any other wild animal that the LORD God had made. He said to the woman, "Did God say, 'You shall not eat from any tree in the garden'? . . . For God knows that when you eat of it your eyes will be opened, and you will be like God, knowing good and evil." So when the woman saw that the tree was good for food, and that it was a delight to the eyes, and that the tree was to be desired to make one wise,

---

40. World Council of Churches, *Christian Perspectives on Theological Anthropology*, 11.

> she took of its fruit and ate; and she also gave some to her hus-
> band, who was with her, and he ate. (Gen 3:1, 5–6).

At first glance it appears that the woman is deceived by the "crafty" serpent, as she claims when confronted later by God in the garden. She has made her decision, however, with eyes wide shut. The serpent asked questions and spoke a version of the truth about what would happen.[41] She decided to eat from the tree knowing that God had restricted it, for what she guessed she might gain for her and her husband. The husband later claims that this was the woman's fault, but he also knew enough to make a good decision. The point is that they were both fully aware of what would bring health and life in relation to their Maker, but casually chose otherwise. This narrative is paradigmatic for understanding two basic human barriers to the goodness, health, and wholeness God intended for the good creation and his partnership with humanity.[42]

The first metaphorical barrier is illustrated in the *reaching* for the fruit and grasping what was not intended for them. This was an attempt to live as if they were autonomous. They pretended to be creatures with no limitations. Over-estimating human capacities in relation to God: not to praise or thank God; not to live by the limitations God established for human life is sometimes summarized as the sin of *pride*. That is an adequate word if we mean "pride in relation to the limits" that God has set for a healthy and good life.[43]

The second metaphorical barrier to the "good" God intended is *curving in on oneself* to enjoy and eat the fruit in isolation. Adam and Eve turned their backs to God, in order to focus on the fruit, which had another purpose in God's creation. They pretended that God had not made them to be free to enjoy the whole creation.[44] This barrier under-

---

41. R.W.L. Moberly, "Did the Serpent Get It Right?"

42. R. Niebuhr articulates these two forms of original sin as pride and idolatry. They are rooted in human anxiety about our mammalian existence. *The Nature and Destiny of Man* (New York: Charles Scribner's Sons, 1943) 178–79.

43. This is really a false pride. It is a failure to take our body and createdness seriously. Some Christian traditions denigrate the human body (usually as a strategy to avoid sinful behavior) and focus on "spiritual" aspects of life. Sometimes this error leads to the "spiritual" individual's neglect of their own body and sometimes to the physical neglect of others for whom they are responsible.

44. This really a false humility established in our minds by means of a strict materialistic view of our bodies and the world. It involves taking our bodies too seriously by reducing life to just our bodies rather than living as embodied creatures made by

estimates or "under-reaches" our capacities in relation to God and the world.[45] It means losing one's self in some aspect of the created world. It is called "sin" because it is tells a lie with a life. The image of God is intentionally turned away from God as its reference toward a good aspect of creation, and is re-established as a person's self-referential power. God's glory, created in the human being, is mis-directed by being redirected to the creation itself.[46] Self-deception has taken root.

Both over-reaching and under-reaching are unhealthy responses to God's good creation. Neither is the ideal possibility of trusting God for both our limitations and our freedom. Each form of the "fall" is an attempt to live *sui generis* ("of his/her own kind"), i.e. as author of one's own story, living and acting without reference to God.[47]

If we interpret the forbidden Tree of Knowledge of Good and Evil with the background of the image of God in mind, we see that the basic relationship of trust between the Creator and the human creation was lost in the exchange in the Garden.

> And the LORD God commanded the human, "You may freely eat of every tree of the garden; but of the tree of the knowledge of good and evil you shall not eat, for in the day that you eat of it you shall die." (Gen 2:16–17)

Not eating from the tree was the means God gave for acknowledging God as the Creator; It was the opportunity for humanity to use their dominion to give glory to God through a simple act of restraint. In a sense, their restraint was the first form of worship.[48] Eating from the tree, on the other hand, was an exercise of the agency of the image of God to cross the boundary established by God and to commandeer God's godness for oneself. Over-reaching is an attempt to use dominion

---

a creating God who calls us into a transcendent relationship. Under-estimating our value in relation to God leads, in its worst form, makes the human form an object of worship and service.

45. Increased emphasis on sin as under-estimating human value is provided by several women theologians. See Judith Plaskow, *Sex, Sin and Grace*. Niebuhr called this sensuality, in the broad sense. It is the impulse that leads to idolatry. See Niebuhr, *Nature and Destiny*, 178–79.

46. For a good primer on the sin of pride as one of the seven deadly sins see Karl Clifton-Soderstrom, "When Self Takes Center Stage." See also Michael E. Dyson, *Pride*.

47. See S. Hauerwas, *The Peaceable Kingdom*, 30–34; see also J. Bruckner, "Boundary and Freedom: Blessings in the Garden of Eden."

48. See M. Luther, Luther's Works, vol. 1, 94–95.

in relation to God, beyond the boundary established for dominion. It is a grasp at power over God.

The human impulse behind this grasp is self-trust and mistrust. Can people trust God, while pursuing truth about God, that God has their best interest at heart, even though he keeps his plan for us partly secret? Can they trust, even though God keeps something back, especially what exactly happens in death? As long as Adam and Eve did not eat from the tree they were acknowledging, "God knows, and we don't; we will trust him today." One day they turn to the "possibility" of the Tree. It leads to knowledge, even if that means knowledge without trust in God. In eating, they do gain knowledge: of their nakedness, of their vulnerability, and of their mortality. This makes trust more difficult.

Regardless of one's religious convictions, this narrative is instructive for understanding the predominance of self-deception in risky life-denying human habits, illness, broken relationships, and death issues.

Consequences of Self-Deception: Heavy Relational Losses

The situation at the end of Genesis 3 is the loss of the ultimate healthy situation. Four relationships of mutual trust are broken: Creator-human, human-human, human-animal, and even Adam and Eve's self-identity suffers in the experience of shame and anxious hiding. Blaming someone else takes the place of mutual trust (Gen 3:12, 13).

The first set of consequences is revealed when God comes down looking for two naked people who are hiding from him in the leafy trees (Gen 3:7–14). The almighty God asks, "Where are you?" not to discover their location, but to discover the relational loss in their own words. They express their fear ("I was afraid"). Their consequences of mistrust have led to alienation from God. It has also led to self-alienation in shame over their nakedness ("I was naked and hid myself"). The human-human trust is broken as Adam blames Eve, blaming God while he is at it. ("The woman whom you gave to be with me, she gave me fruit from the tree and I ate.") The tenuous human-animal relationship ends as Eve blames the serpent for her decision to eat. With blame, there is always plenty to go around. Everyone in the story is alienated from everyone else.[49]

49. This alienation leads to increasing violence later in the narrative by Cain (Gen 4:1–16), by Lamech (4:23–24), and among all people (6:11–12).

Anyone who works in the healing arts has echoes of the themes of this story, even if this particular story is unknown. The characters have changed, but the blame game happens every day wherever brokenness is uncovered. Moving beyond blame to the restoration of mutual trust is the work of many counselors, therapists, and loving friends. God discovers the truth simply by asking questions. Facing the truth about broken trust is the first step in healing and recovering health.

A description of the second set of enduring consequences bearing on the actions of Adam, Eve, and the serpent follows in the subsequent verses (3:14–19).[50] Anxious labor is increased for all three participants. The man goes from caring for the garden God planted to the hard-sweat life of a farmer (3:17–19): "in toil you shall eat of it all the days of your life." The Hebrew word for "toil" is (*'atsav*) means "anxious labor." This is exactly the same word used for the woman's enduring consequence: "in anxious labor (*'atsav*) you will give birth to children" (3:16). Oddly English translations do not reflect this important similarity. Each of them will find their labor more difficult because of their broken relationships.

The consequences of sin are not irreversible.[51] Genesis 3 is not the end of the story, but the beginning; the results of sin were not God's original intention for creation. Through restored relationship with God and with each other, these consequences of "sin" can be lessened.

The narrative moves the reader in this mitigating direction before the end of chapter three. The "fall" was not a total break from relationship with God. In verse 20, the woman is called "the mother of all living" or "Eve" (Ms. "living"). In verse 21, although they already had fig

---

50. These verses have been called "God's curse." Most biblical scholars argue that these are not curses. The text is not in the literary style of a curse and does not use the typical language of biblical curses. The word "curse" appears in a passive participle form in 3:17, as a description of the natural consequence of the serpent's involvement ("because you have done this you are cursed") and Adam's action ("the ground is cursed because of you"). God is, of course, involved and the text recognizes God's role in declaring the curse. When it is mentioned again in Genesis 5:29 at the birth of Noah, God is working to counteract and undo the curse on the land. It is lifted in Genesis 8:21–9:3. The language of God's blessing surrounds this text from the blessing of animals, humans, and Sabbath rest before it (Gen 1:22, 28; 2:3) to the blessing of people and life after it (over seventy-five times in Genesis; e.g., 5:2; 9:1, 26; 12:2–3; 24:35; 27:28; 39:5; and especially Gen 49:25–26.

51. Women have known from the beginning how to control birthing pain and anxiety with techniques to reduce the "anxious" part of labor.

leaf clothing, God made skin clothing for them. Later the narrative tells us that God speaks directly to Cain who is angry about Abel's success. God is still in close fellowship with his human creation. Enoch, whose relationship with God was more trusting, "walked with God" as the first humans had in the garden. Apparently relationship with God was still possible for everyone, even after the "falling out."

Yet, there are some things that cannot be reversed. The Genesis narrative is particularly interested in longevity.[52] In the garden, the Tree of Life (2:9; 3:22–24) was the source of their longevity. They were not prohibited from eating from it and it gave them a conditional immortality based on their access to it.[53] When God drove them from the garden, it was precisely to limit their access to this tree and limit their days to no more than 120 years (Gen 6:3).

The Problem of Violence

One other vital narrative in the book of Genesis bears on outcomes in human health. The problem of violent men was an ancient as well as a contemporary concern. A catastrophic escalation of violence in Noah's day raised the question of God's response to the power of violent people. In the flood narrative (Genesis 6–9) the deterioration of human life through relationally destructive human behavior became unbearable.

> The LORD saw that the wickedness of humankind was great in the earth, and that every inclination of the thoughts of their hearts was only evil continually and the LORD was sorry that he had made human kind on the earth and it grieved ('atsav) him to his heart. (Gen 6.5)

52. Diminishing life spans noted in Genesis 4–11 have the function of demonstrating the increasing slide into a lack of health: "My spirit shall not abide in man forever for he is flesh, but his days shall be one hundred and twenty years" (Gen 6.3). While the amazing numbers cannot be explained medically, the ancient narrative is intent on illustrating the debilitating effect of human sin on the created order in the declining ages: Adam 930, Seth 912, Enosh 905, Mahalel 895, Enoch 365. (Methuselah is a famous exception to the pattern of decline at 969). In Genesis 11 the decline continues: Shem 600, Arpachshad 438, Shelah, 433, Eber 464, Peleg 239, Reu 239, Serug 230, Nahor 148, Terah 205, Abraham 175, and Joseph 110 years.

53. A discussion of conditional immortality will follow in chapter five. The next time that the Tree of Life is mentioned in Scripture is in the last book of the NT (Rev 22:2) where it stands next to the River of Life and its leaves are for the healing of the cultures of the world.

Many people who personally encounter horrific suffering or violence have a similar overwhelming response of sorrow and grief, without the power to do anything about it. Often the human response is to ask the question, "How could a good God, if he exists, allow such horror in the world?" This question may stand in the way of a person's reconciliation with God. The flood text functions as the Bible's first *theodicy* in narrative form.[54] So why doesn't God wipe out all the evil people and perpetrators of suffering in the world? The narrative demonstrates for the questioner what indeed happened when God used that as a solution. It pushes the reader to consider how God now works in the world in partnership with those who are willing to bring health and healing to a good creation.

The narrative begins with God's identification with the consequences of sin. God was "grieved" in his heart. The verb root is identical to the word used to describe a woman's "anxious labor" in childbirth and man's "anxious labor" to produce food from the earth. God shares in consequences of human sin. This is not an impassible god from Greek mythology, but a God who loves and struggles with the complexity of loving people who are often not interested in a loving relationship.

The decision is made to destroy all but one family in a flood in order to begin again with a less violent family. The results are predictable. The members of Noah's surviving family can make choices of their own that lead to more broken relationships. It did not put an end to violence or bad choices. God makes a momentous decision: never again to destroy everything because of the rootedness of the tendency to evil in all people.

> The Lord said in his heart, "I will never again curse the ground because of humankind, *for the inclination of the human heart is evil from youth*; nor will I ever again destroy every living creature as I have done; as long as the earth endures, seedtime and harvest, cold and heat, summer and winter day and night shall not cease." (Gen 8.21–22)

Amazingly, and for the reader's benefit, the reason for the flood is the *same reason* given for the promise that there will be no more floods. It is remarkable that God chooses to take a new course of action; a new way of relating to a wicked world. God's interaction with the world will be

---

54. "Theodicy" means an explanation of why a good God allows the persistence of evil in the world.

different. The flood narrative concludes with God entering into a covenant with the *world*, in spite of human wickedness. More, God makes this promise, not *in spite of* human failure, *but because of it.*

This means, of course, that evil will persist in the world with a good God and with people who will have to make choices. They will need to be taught, however, because of their tendency to lean toward their evil inclination,[55] their handicap of self-deception, false pride, and false humility. Human decision making is imperfect and impaired.[56] Practices of good dominion will have to be inculcated by those who believe the divine promises made in the ancient narrative and who choose to partner with the Creator to bring healing and wholeness to a broken world.[57]

55. In the Jewish tradition, this point of decision, repeated thousands of times in a person's life, is described as an "inclination to good; inclination to evil" (yester tov; yester ra'a; see Gen 6:5; 8:21). Each person has both and must learn to lean to the good; to choose life-affirming behavior. The 613 commands given at Sinai have exactly this purpose: to instruct people in choosing life over death (Deut 30).

56. Genesis has another poignant narrative of impaired decision involving the murder of Abel by his brother Cain (Gen 4). God enters into conversation with Cain to help him deal with his anger and learn to use the power (dominion) he has for good rather than to kill Abel. God fails.

57. On the need to learn and acquire practical knowledge of our common and individual good and on suspending one's own good for the sake of another see ethicist Alasdair MacIntyre, *Dependent Rational Animals,*135.

Chapter Two

What is a Healthy Community?

God Shapes His People in Exodus—Deuteronomy

THE EXTRAORDINARY SEQUEL TO the creation story of Genesis is the deliverance of the Hebrew people from slavery and the legislation given in the Sinai narrative. The narrative of Exodus is a story about a rescued community embarking upon a new holistic sociality: community, God at work, a developing plot, and public health regulations adapted to new situations. This amazing combination of law and narrative is unique in ancient eastern literature.[1] The expressed purpose of the biblical regulations is the longevity and thriving of the formerly oppressed community.[2] The laws provide protection for this fledgling people from

1. None of the other seven known legal codes of the ancient east share these features. They exist simply as law codes. Some have formulaic introductions (Hittite), but none have the extensive and continuing saga of the health of a community at heart. The seven law codes are from Sumer, Ur-nammu (c. 2100 BCE) and Lipit-Istar (c. 1800 BCE); Eshunna (from Akkad, c. 1700 BCE); Hammurabi (from Babylonia, c. 1700); Hittite (Asia monor, c. 1300 BCE); middle Assyrian (c. 1100 BCE); and Neo-Babylonian (c. 600 BCE). The interests and power behind other codes can be somewhat determined by scholars who study the cultures behind the documents. The most explicit protect the interests of the king, promising blessing if the law of the land is kept. Exodus begins in a diametrically different way: the people are freed from the rule of a dictatorial king who had the kingdom's interest, but not the people's good, at heart.

2. This is historically significant since the only community to survive from the ancient world with its legal code intact is the Jewish community. All the others were discovered in the last two hundred years by archeologists. The holistic embedding of health regulation in a broad historiography provided a vehicle of interpretation for the law. As the socio-historical context changed, it was possible to amend the laws in relation to the new context. The socio-historical shift can be observed even in the second

the internal and external forces that threaten to undo any vulnerable society. This chapter begins with the narrative setting of the community health laws and a discussion of God's promise that the delivered people would have "none of the diseases of Egypt." The focus then turns to the Ten Commandments and their implications for public health. Finally, a survey of the six-hundred and thirteen total commandments of the Torah demonstrates the variety of concerns for community health.

Narrative Paradigm for Community Health Laws

Laws that regulate healthy public practice are presented in Exodus within the context of a narrative of deliverance by God. The deliverance from slavery alone would be only an interesting story, however, if the new sociality given in the form of commandments had not functioned to hold a disparate and desperate people together as a community. In Genesis, God had declared that the creation was "good." When people turned away from their Creator, God pursued his commitment to the physical world of human beings by clothing them (Gen 3:21), by giving Eve children (Gen 4:1), and by blessing and making promises to the survivors of the flood. Most significantly, God repeated promises to Sarah and Abraham that all cultures of the world will be blessed through their descendents.[3] This promise is continually endangered in

---

account of the Ten Commandments in Deuteronomy. For example, the earlier account of the command against covetousness in Exodus 20:17 reflects the semi-nomadic life of the Hebrews. The later recounting of the same command in Deuteronomy 5:21 reflects a more settled agrarian setting. This pattern of amendment is established by God as a legal precedent early in the narrative in conversation with Zelophad's daughters and Moses. See Numbers 27:1–11 and 36:1–13 where the divine precedent of legal amendment is repeated and firmly established in the narrative.

3. See God's sustaining promises at Gen 9:1–17; Gen 12:1–3; 15:1–5; 17:1–8; 22:15–1; 26:2–5; 28:13–15. The repetition of these promises generation after generation function to hold the uneven narrative together. The prequel to Exodus goes like this. In Genesis 12, the Lord began a new initiative, calling Sarai and Abram "in order to bring blessing to all the nations of the earth." He worked by means of a specific culture of the world, promising to bring flourishing to all cultures of the world. From the beginning, however, this promise of thriving health is endangered, usually by community health-related issues. In the narrative, the challenging systemic issues are addressed and resolved in a variety of ways. In Genesis 12, Abram's fear of violence in Egypt, where he had gone because of famine, led to the endangerment of "Sarah of the promise." In Genesis 18–19, the systemic violence of Sodom is contrasted with Abraham's hospitality to strangers. In Genesis 20, Abraham's fear of Abimelech

the story. In Exodus, the giving of the Torah established, among other things, a structural standard of human health and thriving for a common people who would otherwise have disappeared into the sands of time. This is the way the story goes in Exodus.[4]

In the early chapters of Genesis, the boundaries of the garden give us the essential characteristics of human life, including God's intention for thriving and the human compromise of that blessing. The balance of Genesis provides the story of the patriarchs, through whom God promised to bless the nations of the world. This promise is in constant danger from the many contrary actions of the principal characters, culminating with Jacob's family left in Egypt where "a king arose who did not know [their protector] Joseph." This ominous narrative hook at the end of Genesis leads us to Exodus, where God must intervene in a dramatic way to assure the safety and well being of his suffering slave-people, and thus his promise to Abraham.

---

and lack of trust in God resulted in Sarah living in Abimelech's tent. God exposed Abraham's breach of trust through widespread sickness and the closing of all wombs, and communicating with Abimelech in a dream. This innocent "outsider" became the agent of blessing for Sarah and Abraham and restored health to his own community through the integrity of his conversation with Abraham. In Genesis 26, the restriction of rights to necessary water supplies endangered the promises made for a flourishing community. Isaac, however, persevered peacefully. What began at wells named Esek ("contention") and Sitnah ("quarrel") was resolved by agreements with local herders at Rehoboth ("a broad place") and Beer-sheba ("well of oaths"). The promise was again endangered by internal threats in a dysfunctional family (Genesis 37–50) Jacob fled from his brother Esau after stealing from him. In the far country of Haran, God worked to restore Jacob by means of his wives. Through the vitality of Rachel, Leah, Zilpah, and Bilhah, the patriarchs of twelve tribes of Israel were born. With a large family in front of him, Jacob was emboldened to return to face Esau, who welcomed him. When Rachel's eldest, Joseph, was sold into slavery by his oldest brothers, the promise of a thriving community and the blessing of the world was again at great risk. Joseph, however, rose through his ability in Potiphar's house, was thrown into prison for his integrity, but released through the use of God's gifts and grace. He personally flourished in Egypt as advisor to the Pharaoh. In Egypt, the reunited and reconciled family was fruitful, especially because of Joseph's administration of grain. The family multiplied into a numerous people. The fulfillment of the promise of their thriving seemed in view in the land of Goshen.

4. Critical scholarship notes that the Sinaitic code was probably completed around the time of the Babylonian exile. Nonetheless, the narrative context provided by the canonizing community implores the reader to understand that the torah of Sinai was given by God for the purpose of establishing a way of living previously unknown to those delivered from bondage. Rhetorically, this placement and theological origin is necessary if the law is to remain a living word for subsequent generations, as it has.

The midwives of Exodus 1 signal that the health of the Hebrew community will be a major theme. The promise of a flourishing community is endangered as they are put into slavery under a new Pharaoh "who did not know [their protector] Joseph" (Exod 1:8). The midwives demonstrate great tenacity in opposing Pharaoh's policy of infanticide (Exod 1:15–22). Shiphrah and Puah "feared God and did not do as the king of Egypt command them, but they let the boys live" (Exod 1:17). The irony was that Pharaoh thought the males were the threat to his power. The women, however, were the agency of God's work to bring health and healing and overcome the Pharaoh's oppression. The midwives, Miriam, Moses' mother Jochebed and Pharaoh's daughter all were used by God to ensure the promise to the nations.

God secured the freedom of the Hebrew slaves. The outlines of the story are fairly well known: God called Moses at the burning bush to represent God to the Pharaoh to demand the release of the Hebrew slaves, that they might worship the Lord in the wilderness; Moses and Aaron confronted the Pharaoh, who increased their quota of bricks per day; the ten catastrophic signs of the Lord's power (commonly known as the "plagues") struck Egypt; the Pharaoh relented and let the people go; then he changed his mind and pursued them with chariots, trapping them at the Sea; the Lord parted the water with a strong east wind; the people escaped through the Sea on dry land; the Sea closed in over the chariots, leaving the people safe and free in the wilderness; the people sang and danced, as Miriam led with the tambourine.

On the heels of this great celebration of deliverance from slavery, the narrative immediately turns to the human reality of the new social situation: they are all refugees, camped in a desolate place. After three days journey with no water they came to Marah ("bitter") but the water-source was polluted. The first concern named after the dancing was over was a public health matter. The water was undrinkable. "The LORD showed [Moses] a piece of wood; he threw it into the water, and the water became sweet" (Exod 15:25).[5] Then Lord said,

> If you will listen carefully to the voice of the LORD your God, and do what is right in his sight, and give heed to his commandments and keep all his statutes, I will not bring upon you *any*

5. Rosner suggests that this may be an "early instance of desalination." Fred Rosner, *Medicine in the Bible and Talmud*, 9.

> *of the diseases that I brought upon the Egyptians;* for I am the
> LORD who heals you (*Yahweh Roph'eka*; Exod 15:26).[6]

After Marah, the Lord took them to the healing oasis at Elim, where there were twelve springs and seventy palm trees (Exod 15:27). They camped there near the water. The text does not describe the community repair done in the several weeks they stayed there.

"None of These Diseases" (Exod 15:26)

God's promise that the people will have "none of the diseases" of Egypt is more than a promise of protection from illness. It is a promise to protect the community from the oppressive structures of Egypt through the creation of a new sociality at Sinai.[7] Following the dramatic release from the systemic life-denying policies of the Pharaoh, this promise is nothing less than God's declaration to oppose "large social systems that produce disability before which individual persona are completely helpless."[8]

One tradition interprets "these diseases" as the systemic oppressions of Pharaoh's forceful rule. Pharaoh's self-proclaimed deity (son of the sun-god Re) established the systemic disease of slavery with huge quotas, and a seven day work-week. A system of taskmasters employed from within the slave-community carried out beatings to serve royal profits. The beatings and killings served to keep fear, desperation, and hopelessness as common currency in the enslaved community.

"None of these diseases" in this context implies that the Lord, the Creator of all things, is offering a new kind of sociality to the delivered slaves. They have not been delivered simply to be free, but to serve a God who created them and called them "good" and who made them in the "image of God." God now seeks to reveal a new way of living in relation to each other. One of the many markers of this new sociality is the biblical preoccupation with the treatment of the poor, the widow, and the orphan. The Torah and the prophets mention care for these, the most helpless and hopeless in any society, over four hundred times.

---

6. Cf. Pss 103:3; 147:3.

7. Identifying the "diseases of Egypt" has a significant interpretive history. For a discussion, see John Wilkinson, *The Bible and Healing*, 32–41.

8. W. Brueggemann, "Healing and Its Opponents," 3.

This transformation is social and systemic, as well as for individuals. Though individual health is also a necessary good, the biblical vision is of a healthy and whole community. Recent research in neurobiological systems corroborates that "our autobiographical selves are formed within a nest of relationships, a community."[9] God's declaration is a new social creation to transform specific systems of oppression and legislate against their return.[10]

A second interpretation of the promise concerning Egypt's diseases is offered when it is repeated in the book of Deuteronomy.

> The LORD will turn away from you every illness; all the dread diseases of Egypt that you experienced, he will not inflict on you, but he will lay them on all who hate you. (Deut 7:15)

This repetition comes forty years later in the narrative, after the wandering in the wilderness, just before the entrance to the land of Canaan. Subsequent texts in Deuteronomy focus on specific physical ailments experienced in Egypt.[11] These texts insist the prevention of these diseases is tied to keeping the Sinaitic regulations. A partial list is given in Deuteronomy 28.

> The LORD will afflict you with consumption, fever, inflammation, with fiery heat and drought, and with blight and mildew; they shall pursue you until you perish . . . The LORD will afflict you with the boils of Egypt, with ulcers, scurvy, and itch, of which you cannot be healed . . . The LORD will afflict you with madness, blindness, and confusion of mind; . . . The LORD will strike you on the knees and on the legs with grievous boils of which you cannot be healed, from the sole of your foot to the crown of your head. (Deut 28:22, 27, 28, 35)

---

9. J. Green, *Body, Soul, and Human Life*, 116.

10. The biblical laws against oppression of the poor are not Pollyannaish. The Torah does not pretend that the institution of slavery did not continue as a basic cultural establishment in the ancient east, and even among the Israelites. The law, rather, provided the strongest slave protection and release legislative formulations among all of the seven extant legal codes of the ancient east.

11. Rabbi Samuel ben Meir (Rashbam) suggests the diseases refer to water-borne illness, as the context of Exodus 15:22–27 implies. The diseases of Egypt are a reference to the bloody Nile. "Healer" (*rophe'*) is the root behind "wholesome" water in 2 Kings 2 and Ezekiel 47. See Brown, *Israel's Divine Healer*, 75.

As if this is not enough, the list above is broadened to include all diseases mentioned in the Torah and all those not mentioned, but known in Egypt.[12]

> If you do not diligently observe all the words of this law that are written in this book, fearing this glorious and awesome name, the LORD your God, then the LORD will overwhelm both you and your offspring with severe and lasting afflictions and grievous and lasting maladies. He will bring back upon you all the diseases of Egypt, of which you were in dread, and they shall cling to you. Every other malady and affliction, even though not recorded in the book of this law, the LORD will inflict on you until you are destroyed. (Deut 28:58–61; see 7:11–15)[13]

Two conclusions may be drawn from this interpretation. First, freedom from disease is not presented as a magical gift that God gives his chosen faithful people. The diseases are avoided by a community's commitment to its own wholeness through observing the laws provided for the health of the community. Second, God wants to be known, through the covenanting of public law, as the one who brings health and healing.[14] He claims this positive self-identification of God, "I am the LORD, who heals you."[15] The practice of faithfulness to God's law is the means by

12. Exod 15:26 itself leans forward toward the language of laws given at Sinai. It does not speak of specifics, but of fostering an observant relationship with the LORD. "If you will listen carefully to the voice of the LORD your God, and do what is right in his sight, and give heed to his commandments and keep all his statutes, I will not bring upon you any of the diseases that I brought upon the Egyptians; for I am the LORD who heals you."

13. Later in the wilderness the LORD did bring plague upon the Israelites when they turned away to worship the golden calf (32:35) and engaged in pagan sexuality at Baal-peor (Num 25:8–9; cf. Num 16:46–50). This is the counterpoint. God's intention is to work with people who will promote the general welfare and health of the people in relationship. When the covenantal relationship is broken, illness is rampant.

14. Deut 32:39 "See now that I, even I, am he; there is no god besides me. I kill and I make alive; I wound and I heal; and no one can deliver from my hand." Brown's distinction between God as the agent of "supernatural" healing versus the "prophylactic" benefits of keeping the law (Brown, 77) is a modern distinction imposed anachronistically on the text. The distinction of "supernatural" from "natural" was made first by Descartes. It is a distinction without a difference in the ancient worldview. How God brought divine healing was exactly through the covenantal law that he required the people to follow. Perhaps that they agreed to and ever followed it was a miracle.

15. As M. Brown notes this means, "I am your healer, not those other gods of Egypt." This reassertion of monotheism (or henotheism) is a repeated theme in Exodus and beyond. See Exod 12:12; 15:10–11; 18:11; 20:1–6; 22:19; 34:6–17 and discussion in

which God bestows the blessing of health to his people: e.g., various situations for washing, quarantine for contagious disease, guidelines for sexual practice. The protection and promise are covenantal. They are not "magical," but are tied to the practices described in the Sinaitic legislation, which constitute the healthiest diet, lifestyle, and social standards among the ancient eastern law codes.

Community Structures

God's intervention is not limited to a one-time rescue. Exodus through Deuteronomy set forth the necessary elements of healthy life together *in community*. The rescued Hebrew slaves are formed into the people of Israel as God establishes laws and systems that will provide safety, order, healthy patterns, and food for their daily lives. God shapes the health of the community through the creation of a new sociality, public health legislation, Sabbath rest, purity laws, and worship practices. While many of the specific laws are antiquated by cultural differences, the principles are established. God cares about every aspect of human health and life: what you eat, what you wear, who you sleep with, what you do with your wealth, how you treat animals and trees and your neighbor; even public sanitation.

The foundations of any healthy society are found in its community structures. God inaugurates the new wilderness community by announcing that they will have "none of the diseases" of Egypt. After some time in the wilderness, God gives the Hebrew people "ten commands" (literally "ten words") which function as a charter of emancipation and protection against their re-enslavement. The Torah also provides six-hundred and thirteen commands, given at Sinai, many of which bear on sustaining public health within a community. While some of these laws still have direct influence in the twenty-first century, the weight of their genius is in the prevention of debilitating communal diseases and the inculcation of practices and behaviors that make possible a healthy and thriving community.

Brown, *Israel's Divine Healer*, 67–75.

The Ten Words and a Healthy Community:
Preventative Measures

The "Ten Commandments" are a familiar concept in the Jewish and Christian communities and sometimes in the society that surrounds them,[16] though few people can name more than three or four. Often they are viewed as an arbitrary list of prohibitions from an ancient time. In recent biblical studies and public discourse the "ten" have been making a comeback.[17] They are an important resource for understanding healthy human society and community, especially when viewed through their purpose in their original context.[18]

The ten commands were given by God at Sinai as a charter of freedom for the recently freed slaves,[19] to ensure a new and healthy society

16. These commandments are the "top ten" list of the charter of freedom God gave in the Sinai wilderness. Traditionally they are called "the Ten Commandments" although the Bible calls them "the ten words." A similar distinction can be made for the word "torah" which is often translated "law," but has "instruction" as its basic meaning. The humorous comment that these are "suggestions" rather than commandments is rather off the point. The "words" and "instruction" indicate a close relationship with the God who gives them, not primarily as "command" and "law" but as words of guidance given by a Creator and liberator who cares about what happens to the people under guidance.

17. See D. Brent Laytham, "Keeping the Commandments in Their Place." The literature on the commandments is extensive. Important recent works include Carl E. Braaten and Christopher R. Seitz, eds. *I Am the Lord Your God: Christian Reflections on the Ten Commandments*; William P. Brown, ed., *The Ten Commandments: The Reciprocity of Faithfulness*; and Roger Van Harn, ed., *The Ten Commandments for Jews, Christians, and Others*. For a selected bibliography see J. Bruckner, *Exodus*.

18. The Ten Commandments hold a special place among the six hundred and thirteen laws in the Tanak (Hebrew Bible). They were the only commands the LORD spoke directly to the people from the mountain (Exod 19:7–19, 25; 20:1; Deut 5:22). At their request, God stopped his direct speech and communicated thereafter through Moses (Exod 20:19-21). They were the first commands given at Sinai and were separated from those that follow by narrative discourse (Exod 20:18–22). They were written by God on tablets of stone (Exod 31:18; 34:1, 28; Deut 5:22). The Ten were given the title "The Ten Words" (Exod 34:28; Deut 4:13; cf. Deut 5:22; 9:10) and were later placed in the Ark of the Covenant with a second title, "The Testimony" (Exod 40:20; Deut 10:4–5). These commands were repeated as a group in Deuteronomy 5:6–21 with little alteration, just before the crossing of the Jordan. They were also repeated at other critical junctures, as in Josiah's reform in the seventh century BCE (2 Kgs 22). Miller suggests this makes them similar to constitutional law; Miller, *Interpretation* 43 (1989) 231; also Wright, *Deuteronomy*, 63. Jesus referred to the ten as a group in his conversation with the rich young ruler (Mark 10:18–20; cf. Matt 19:17–20; Luke 18:19–20).

19. For a fuller discussion of the Ten Commandments as a bill of rights that

that would develop in the wilderness and into their years in the land of Canaan.[20] The commands function in the narrative as a charter of perpetual emancipation and as a protection against the re-enslavement of the Hebrew people. They stand as paradigmatic pillars of a new sociality, offering a means to freedom from bondage to others, sin, and a culture of death. Participation in this covenant was by unanimous agreement: "The people all answered as one: 'Everything that the LORD has spoken we will do'" (Exod 19:8a).[21]

The commandments can be validated as a constitution of freedom by the external evidence that neighborhoods where these commandments are kept are good places to live.[22] A community that embraces these commands today will certainly be counter-cultural, as the foundation is complete trust in and love of God, rather than the assumption that God does not exist. Membership in this neighborhood depends on

---

establishes and sustains a liberated people see Harrelson, *Ten Commandments and Human Rights*; and Wright, *Deuteronomy*, 64–66. Harrelson uses the term "charter of human freedom" especially in reference to the negative form of the commandments. "Without such crisp prohibitions that point unmistakably to the path that leads to death, who can hold fast to the freedom under God that these bonds entail?"(186). His language of rights, as he notes (xv), is not from the biblical setting. The original setting is a voluntary charter or covenant between the people and the Lord who has delivered them, and wants to keep them out of slavery of all kinds, not a declaration of rights over against others.

20. The rabbis noted that the commandments were God's second act of creation. The first creation separated chaos and order. The second act created a people by revealing the separation of right and wrong. (G. Plaut, *The Torah*, 521). Fretheim demonstrates the prevailing theme of creation in Exodus, not least in the legal material. "The law is given to the people of God as a vehicle in and through which Egypt will not be repeated among them. The law is a means . . . whereby God's cosmic victory can be realized in all spheres of human interaction." (Fretheim, *Exodus*, 204).

21. The relationship is based on the metaphor of "eagle's wings." "Thus you shall say to the house of Jacob, and tell the Israelites: You have seen what I did to the Egyptians, and how I bore you on eagles' wings and brought you to myself. Now therefore, if you obey my voice and keep my covenant, you shall be my treasured possession out of all the peoples. Indeed, the whole earth is mine, but you shall be for me a priestly kingdom and a holy nation. These are the words that you shall speak to the Israelites." So Moses came, summoned the elders of the people, and set before them all these words that the LORD had commanded him. The people all answered as one: "Everything that the LORD has spoken we will do." Exod 19:3b–8a. See also 2 Kings 22:3.

22. See Patrick D. Miller, "The Good Neighborhood: Identity and Community through the Commandments." In *Character and Scripture: Moral Formation, Community, and Biblical Interpretation.*

your willingness to be moral, not on genetic ties.[23] Willingness to live as a person redeemed by God and to remember God's acts of deliverance in worship are primary elements of its true freedom with boundaries.[24]

The first command protects against bondage to abusive people and relationships. The charter of freedom can be stated, "You are set free from fear of multiple false gods."

> Then God spoke all these words: "I am the LORD your God, who brought you out of the land of Egypt, out of the house of slavery; you shall have no other gods before me." (Exod 20:1–3)

This first word about no other gods before the LORD contrasts directly with the "land of Egypt . . . house of slavery." They are free from the Pharaoh's abusive system. Its purpose is to prevent the common human inclination to return to complicity in systems of bondage or abuse.[25] These life-denying tendencies of slavery are the venue of "other gods." The redeeming God of Scripture, however, calls his newly delivered people to acknowledge only the Creator, who made them in his image and has personally delivered them from bondage. This is only possible if they continue to recognize and name the LORD as the only true God worth having. The authority that an abuser seizes and misuses rightly belongs to a loving God. Abuse of power is a "sin" because of its effect on another, but also because it usurps God's rule and destroys the deliverance and blessing God intended.

The second command protects against bondage to man-made things.

> You shall not make for yourself an idol, whether in the form of anything that is in heaven above, or that is on the earth beneath, or that is in the water under the earth. You shall not bow down

---

23. Ibid., 57–60.

24. See J. Bruckner, "Boundary and Freedom: Blessings in the Garden of Eden."

25. The first example of the people's inclination to return to the bondage of a false god came in Exodus 32 in the golden calf incident. See the final section of this chapter for a discussion of the outcome. The second example came in Numbers 25 when "Israel yoked itself to Baal-Peor" in the Moab. Their entrance into the religion based in cultic prostitution was a serious threat to their survival as a healthy community, free to serve the Creator of all that is. God struck them with a plague, likely related to their newly engaged sexual practices, in order to get their attention and to save the people, as a people.

> to them or worship them; for I the LORD your God am a jealous
> God . . . (Exod 20:4–5a)[26]

This second word of the ten insists that the character of God the Creator of all things cannot be captured in a physical representation. The Lord of Scripture is free of the bounds of nature and of time, although free to act through nature and in historical relationships with human beings.[27]

Healthy communities are not beholden to false or man-made absolutes. Contemporary images of power, wealth and possessions are everywhere in the media, with the insistent message that they are of ultimate value. Those who make absolutes of themselves, their own interests, their success, their own bodies or their own lives become their own idols. This was the first impulse of the falling-out in the garden: seeking independence from the Creator; making a break from our relationality, the source of our story, and our createdness by elevating our physical and psychological whims.

The bondage to self emerges in the modern world in full force with common appropriations of Rene Descartes' proposition, "I think therefore I am." Even religion and biblical doctrine can become an idol when a limited understanding of God is confused with God's own self.[28] A contemporary ethicist has said, "We tie ourselves to a fixed, predictable, tame substitute for God instead of linking arms with the untamed energy of the living God."[29]

The third command protects against the bondage and mistrust of living in a community of curses and false oaths.

> You shall not make wrongful use of the name of the LORD your
> God, for the LORD will not acquit anyone who misuses his
> name. (Exod 20:7)[30]

26. For a commentary on "jealous God" and on "visiting the iniquity of the parents on the children" that follows in this command, see J. Bruckner, *Exodus*, 182–84 and especially 302–8.

27. Cf. Brevard Childs, *The Book of Exodus*, 406–9.

28. So P. Tillich's "object of ultimate concern" cited in Daniel Polish, 33. See Polish, "No Other Gods" in Roger E. Van Harn, ed. *The Ten Commandments for Jews, Christians, and Others*, 23–39.

29. D. Gill, *Doing Right*, 105; see also p. 110.

30. "Misuse" is literally, "lift up in vain." The "Name of the LORD" is the unpronounceable four consonant ("tetragrammaton") Hebrew word rendered "Yahweh" given to Moses at Sinai (Exod 3:1–15). Jewish tradition "fences" the Name, which alternatively is articulated *hash-shem* or *adonai*, so that it was never spoken. The

This third word of the ten bears on the health of a community in two ways. First, it discerns attitudes of the heart as revealed through speech patterns. Flippancy and a disrespectful attitude toward the Lord who is the Creator of all that is, will certainly be paralleled by a disregard for the human and non-human creation. An ethical corollary to this command is to use all names with respect, never mocking or intentionally misusing them.[31]

The second bondage it signals is the problem of false oaths. The LORD's Name was used in swearing to tell the truth in court. A specific violation of this command would be corrupting the legal process by lying (Lev 19:12; Deut 6:13; 10:20; cf. Lev 6:3–5). The prophets also exposed the misuse of the Name of the LORD in a community that exploited others for profit and met to praise the LORD (Amos 5:21–24; Isa 1:11–17). This meant that a devout person, by the measure of prayer and regular worship, could lift up the Name in vain. This command protects the truth, and works to eliminate hypocrisy by the healthy practice of "practicing what you preach."

The fourth command protects against bondage to taskmasters. The charter of freedom could be stated, "You are set free from slaving work without a day of rest." Few would argue that a day of rest is not a critical component of human health in the western world.

> Remember the Sabbath day, and keep it holy. Six days you shall labor and do all your work. But the seventh day is a Sabbath to the LORD your God; you shall not do any work—you, your son or your daughter, your male or female slave, your livestock, or the alien resident in your towns. For in six days the LORD made heaven and earth, the sea, and all that is in them, but rested the seventh day; therefore the LORD blessed the Sabbath day and consecrated it. (Exod 20:8–11)

A seven day "week" still forms the structure of our working world. The "weekend" was created by this ancient narrative.[32] No weekend was observed in Mesopotamia, Canaan, or Egypt. No one took (or gave) a "day

---

continued protection of this specific name in Christian tradition is discussed in J. Bruckner, *Exodus*, 44–45.

31. Gill, *Doing Right*, 323.

32. The dual day weekend came into being only recently, with the combination of Jewish (and Seventh-Day Adventist) Sabbath and the Christian "Lord's Day" on Sunday.

off" every seven days. It required trust in the Creator that they would prosper without working every day. The seven day week was provided by God, the owner of all of time. It gave the former slaves the gift of rest and rest in the God who gave it. It is pure gift, implying that to rest is to share in the life of God, who also rested.

Sabbath commands do not begin or end with this text. Many others preserve life and foster health for the environment, economic health of a community, and protection for the weakest members. Scripture has Sabbath commands for fields to rest, lying fallow; the release of debt slaves every seventh year; the required rest of working animals and the return of land to those who have lost it every forty-nine years.[33] Rest for enslaved workers is a special concern in Scripture, as the injunction is twice repeated in the deuteronomic decalogue. Israel's God was for oppressed workers in a way that Egyptian, Mesopotamian, and Canaanite gods were not. It was the "greatest worker protection act in history."[34]

Jesus gave a radical interpretation of Sabbath rest when he declared that it was "made for man."[35] He healed on the Sabbath, giving rest and respite from disease, rather than following a strict observance of the gift as an unbending law.[36]

The fifth command's charter of freedom can be stated, "You are set free from a community that neglects its elders."

> Honor your father and your mother, so that your days may be long in the land that the LORD your God is giving you. (Exod 20:12)[37]

God asked the newly formed community to honor parents who were no longer an economic asset in the family.[38] The original context addresses

---

33. Among the Ten Commandments, the sabbath is the most broadly represented. See Exod 21:2; 23:10–12; 31:12–17; 34:21; 35:1–3; Lev 19:3; 23:3; 25:1–55; 26:2; Num 15:32–36; Deut 15:1–18.

34. Wright, *Deuteronomy*, 76.

35. See Mk 2:23–3:5; Matt 12:1–13; Luke 6:1–10; cf. John 9.

36. Rabbinic law allows for breaking observance in order to save a life.

37. Both mother and father were mentioned (mother first in Lev 19:3), in contrast to the Akkadian Code of Hammurabi (1750 BCE), which only expressed concern for the father.

38. Extended families are deemed vital for the ongoing health and vitality of a community.

the adult children in the community (Deut 27:20). Honoring parents is learned by children watching their parents honor the elderly.

The commandment instructs that honor (or "weight" *kavod*) be given, simply because they are one's mother and father.[39] This is not a question of subordination, but of giving serious weight to parents' concerns and needs. Leviticus 19:3 adds that "respect" (*yara'*) should be given. The elder, on the other hand, was also liable before God for keeping the commands. The abuse of parental authority is addressed by extension of the commands against killing (physical abuse), adultery (sexual abuse), and false witness (verbal abuse).[40]

This fifth word names *longevity* as a health related benefit of honoring parents. In the interpretive tradition this has always been understood to refer to family systems and the honoring of elders in a community. Alienation of individuals from family networks is detrimental to the whole community. Western values of individualism and our tendency to be very mobile for employment advancement has made this a difficult command to keep well. The negative consequences of neglecting this positive command include the loss of family wisdom concerning personal health. Within Jewish and Christian communities the concept of "family" includes the possibility that individuals from dysfunctional families may find an extended family of support and honor within the worshiping neighborhood.[41]

The sixth command protects against a community's bondage to violence. The charter of freedom can be stated, "You are set free from living with systems of disregard for human life and legalized murder."

You shall not murder. (Exod 20:13)[42]

39. Specific laws prohibit the radical dishonor of mother and father. Parents should not be attacked or cursed (Exod 21:15, 17; Lev 20:9; Deut 21:18–21; 27:16).

40. The role of the father with child is described in Proverbs 4:1–27, especially guiding the child to a life of wisdom (cf. Prov 10:1; 13:1; 15:5; 19:18). The New Testament specifically links good parenting and the command to honor parents when it quotes the fifth command (Eph 6:1–4; Col 3:20–21).

41. Gill expands the scope of family this way: "Honor and care for those who are God's agents and representatives in your life." He also offers this corollary: "Show love to others by giving care and honor to their significant others, their agents." David Gill, *Doing Right*, 323.

42. The verb translated "murder" (*rasakh*) is sometimes translated generically as "kill." The generic Hebrew word for "kill" is *harag*. English does not have one word that clearly suffices. "Murder" is too specific and "kill" is too general. The word means *unauthorized killing*. It is defined by its relation to the context of illegal action, or killing

The sixth through tenth commandments most directly address the question of the world as a "good neighborhood." Community order and safety are public health issues (as seen in any emergency room). The issue is addressed in five negative commands: "You shall not kill, you shall not steal, you shall not bear false witness, and you shall not covet." These commands, when kept, obviously improve the safety of a community.

No one wants to live and die in a community where citizens or an unjust government kill, yet even in the last century, many millions have. The malicious "spilling of blood" is viewed in Scripture as an anti-creational act (a sin against the Creator) that affects even the *earth*. Bloodshed "pollutes" the land (Gen 4:10–12; Num 35:33–34; Deut 21:1–9).

God's community also had to respond to unlawful death through a legal system. An individual homicide can easily debilitate a community, especially when the perpetrator was not called to account by an honest system of justice. Violent persons were to be held responsible for the results of their actions, regardless of their social position (Num 35:31; Lev 19:15). The "eye for an eye" principle was given to the courts and God's law to decide.

At the same time, God called the new community to practice better justice: "I am the LORD. Do not hate your brother in your heart . . . Do not seek revenge or bear a grudge against one of your people, but love your neighbor as yourself. I am the LORD" (Lev 19:16b–18). The underlying principle was theological: "Life belongs to God" (Lev 17:11; Gen 9:6). Individuals and the community were admonished not to seek revenge for bloodshed themselves, since this too destroyed the community. To this end, cities of refuge were established so that the accused could find refuge from personal blood revenge until justice could be administered by proper authorities (Num 35:6–37).

Modern ethics follows a long tradition of teaching this commandment as a very broad principle. "Never do anything that threatens or harms the life and health of another person. Rather, regarding it as

---

outside of God's law. In the Old Testament it refers to a range of unacceptable killing, including high-handed killing (premeditated murder), homicide of various kinds, and manslaughter through various levels of negligence (intentional and unintentional). These differences are specified by numerous laws given at Sinai (Exod 21:12–14; Num 35:30–34; Deut 19:1–13).

God's own creation, do whatever you can to protect that person's life and health and to promote peace and reconciliation."[43]

The seventh command protects against bondage to the false idea that uncommitted sexual relationships will bring you satisfaction and freedom. The charter of freedom can be stated, "You are set free from a culture that accepts adultery and its collateral damage."

> You shall not commit adultery. (Exod 20:14; also in Deut 5:18; 22:22; Lev 18:20; 20:10)[44]

Sexuality was not a purely private matter, but constitutional of the good of the newly created community of God. The promise to bless the nations of the world through Israel could be fulfilled only if the integrity of marriages, families, and thus the community of faith, would be sustained over millennia. Laws regulating sexuality are common in the ancient east, but the death penalty for adultery in Israel was especially severe (e.g., Deut 22:22).[45] Adultery was considered a high-handed sin against God (Gen 39:9).

The prohibition of adultery is generally a protection of the integrity and emotional stability of the family for the sake of the children, wife, and husband. It preserves the trust which is foundational to healthy familial relationships. The integrity of the family protects the most vulnerable in society, the children, whose emotional security is always at

---

43. Gill, *Doing Right*, 323. Luther's *Small Catechism* explains, "We are to fear and love God so that we do not hurt our neighbor in any way, but help him in all his physical needs."

44. In a limited sense, "no adultery" meant sexual fidelity within marriage. In the most limited sense it meant that no one except her husband was to have sexual relations with a married woman. Whatever the primary social structure in Israel at a given time (polygamy or monogamy), the bond of marriage was limiting.

45. Jesus removed the penalty of stoning for adultery, (John 8:1–11) but did not soften the demand of the law, clearly labeling it as sin. At many points he intensified and internalized the command, suggesting that hell was the end result: "You have heard that it was said, 'Do not commit adultery.' But I tell you that anyone who looks at a woman lustfully has already committed adultery with her in his heart . . . It is better for you to lose one part of your body than for your whole body to go into hell" (Matt 5:27–28, 30b). Here Jesus' interpretation of the Sinai law was more radical than the law itself. Jesus also criticized the legal loopholes provided in the Sinai law for divorce, equating it with the faithlessness of adultery. (Matt 5:31–32, continuing the trajectory of Mal 2:16.). Jesus allowed for the possibility of divorce only in the case of the unfaithfulness of a spouse (Matt 19:3–9). The devastating effects of adultery are spelled out in the father's warnings to the son in Proverbs 5:1–23; 6:23–35; 7:7–27.

risk.[46] The Hebrew prophets attacked adultery as evil and detestable, because it brought external devastation to the individual and the community.[47] Maslow's hierarchy of need reflects a similar concern. The second most basic need (after breathing, food, water, etc.) is "safety" meaning the security of body, morality, the family, and health. The prohibition against adultery protects these very basic human needs.[48]

The eighth command protects against bondage to a culture that steals from the poor to sustain itself and creates an incentive for the poor to steal to sustain their lives. This summary reflects the biblical context of Hebrew slaves who had been delivered from exactly such a society. God did not want them ever to return to or be complicit in such a society again. Theft was life-denying for the wealthy and for the poor.

> You shall not steal. (Exod 20:15)[49]

The law against stealing is common in many cultures. The remarkable feature of Sinai law was the even-handed penalties for the thief who was caught. The destructive effects of stealing in a community were primarily countered not by violent suppression but by restitution.[50] In other ancient cultures the loss of a hand could result, and penalties for theft were most severe for lower economic classes. In biblical law, if restitution was not possible, the severest penalty was debt slavery, until the debt was paid, or for seven years. There was no penalty for stealing

---

46. The rabbis taught that in avoiding adultery with Potiphar's wife, Joseph kept all the commandments. He honored God by keeping his law, made no idol of pleasure, did not blaspheme by damaging the LORD's reputation, honored his parents, did not steal what was not his, did not bear false witness with his body, and did not covet what belonged to another.

47. Jer 23:10; Ezek 18:10–13; Hos 4:2; Mal 3:5.

48. A. H. Maslow, "A Theory of Human Motivation."

49. Theft was prohibited in order to protect the goods and livelihood of the people and to sustain freedom and trust. It is incompatible with living under God's protection (Ps 50:16–18) and is a kind of blasphemy (Prov 30:9). Stealing marks a city as corrupt (Isa 1:10:23) and brings a curse on the thief and the one who protects him (Zech 5:3–4; Prov 29:24).

50. Exodus 22:1–12 establishes case law to deal with restitution in specific cases of theft. It provided guidance for the loss of property through theft: if a sheep or an ox were stolen and found either dead or alive; if a thief were to be killed while breaking into a home, either during the day or night; if an ox grazed in someone's field; if a set fire consumed someone's property; and what to do if loaned items were stolen. See Bruckner, *Exodus*, 209–12.

bread, because even the poor were not supposed to be hungry. Ample grain was to be left in the fields for them to glean for bread.[51]

Culturally systemic theft is prohibited further in Deuteronomy, broadening to laws against moving property landmarks, exploiting workers or resident aliens, false weights and measures, bribery, preventing gleaning by the poor, loan-sharking, vandalism, and withholding the sabbatical forgiveness of debt.[52] This inner-biblical expansion of the law against stealing created a trajectory that shifted the burden to every level of society. The poor must not steal, but the privileged should make sure it was not necessary for them to steal by "stealing" hope. It was also possible to correlate this move with the exercise of generosity (Job 31:16–40; Ps 112:1–9).[53]

The ninth command protects against bondage to a culture where lying is a way of life and false witnesses are easily bought.

> You shall not bear false witness against your neighbor. (Exod 20:1–3)[54]

The ancient narrative is concerned with the adverse effects of both private and public courtroom lying. The original context of courtroom law is reflected in the command itself, literally translated, "You will not answer against your neighbor with a false testimony." In Egypt they had been victims of exactly this crime. Pharaoh's false testimony against them was that they wanted to worship God because they were too "lazy" to work. He accused them of lying and offered his own version of the situation. His powerful "false witness" led to the law of increased labor.[55] God's new community was to be a place where the truth was told.

---

51. E.g., see Deut 24:18–22 which reminds the secure of their origins in slavery.

52. See Wright, *Deuteronomy*, 83.

53. Jesus corroborated this expansion and intensified it by putting the weight of the final judgment on whether or not one cared for the poor materially in Matthew 25:32–46.

54. The Sinai law addressed the perpetual problem of false witnesses in court and the vetting of suspect witnesses before both priests and judges with an extreme penalty for perjury. The sentence that *would* have been given for a guilty verdict of the accused was to be transferred to the perjured witness (Deut 19:16–21). The problem of giving false witness as a means of profit was attacked by the eighth- and seventh-century prophets. The intimidation of truthful witnesses, giving false witness against the poor for gain, bribe taking, and manipulation of property law was a serious problem (Amos 5:10–15; Isa 5:23–24; 10:1–2; cf. Hos 4:1–3; Jer 5:1, 26–28; 7:5–10).

55. See Bruckner, *Exodus*, 57–60.

The commandment against false witness is made more specific later in Sinai law with detailed instruction concerning conduct in public court. It is broadened to include gossip and slander against one's neighbor in general. You must not lie about your neighbor, in or out of court. Leviticus 19:11–12 combines the public courtroom and private deceit contexts: "Do not lie. Do not deceive one another. Do not swear falsely by my name and so profane the name of your God. I am the LORD." The broader problems of deceit, gossip, slander, and lying about members of the community were also addressed in the law (Lev 19:11, 16). They are summed up in the succinct, "Do not spread false reports" (Exod 23:1). The perpetual problem of spreading false reports is also lamented by the Psalmist.[56]

For a healthy community, an ethical summary principle is helpful: "Never communicate false or irrelevant information in a way that could harm someone's life or reputation. Rather, regarding truthfulness as an essential, core attribute of God's character and presence, communicate truthful information and wisdom that helps people and situations."[57]

The tenth command protects against bondage to a culture of coveting, materialism, and acquisition.

> You shall not covet your neighbor's house; you shall not covet your neighbor's wife, or male or female slave, or ox, or donkey, or anything that belongs to your neighbor. (Exod 20:17)[58]

---

56. Ps 5:8–10; see Ps 27:12–14; Ps 50:19–22; Ps 15:2–3. The book of Proverbs is also replete with admonitions against the wrongful and destructive use of the tongue. The New Testament reinforces the necessity of telling the truth in every case. See Jas 3:1–18; 4:11–12; 1 Pet 3:10.

57. Gill, *Doing Right*, 324. It is stated positively in M. Luther, *Small Catechism*: "You must defend your neighbor, speak well of him, and explain his actions in the kindest way."

58. Already this command is radical, internal, and very broad. Inner-biblical development, interpreted by the rabbinic and New Testament traditions, pushed its meaning into the public and observable realm. No one could be sure to keep this command if "coveting" was not also an observable offense. This move was made first in Leviticus by specifying examples of observable coveting. The sequence of Leviticus 19:11 recites and expands on the eighth (v. 11a), ninth (v. 11b–12), and tenth (v. 13) commandments. The text reports and expands the tenth command as follows: "Do not defraud your neighbor or rob him. Do not hold back the wages of a hired man overnight. For an accounting of this development see Bruckner, "On the One Hand . . .On the Other: The Two-fold Law Against Coveting,"

This tenth word warns that a preoccupation with material success and material measures of life will distort relationships with others. Most commentary on this commandment notes its unique internal and radical nature. Covet means "desire" or "to take pleasure."[59] This focus on internal desires is sometimes seen as an extension of the law against stealing, false witness, or adultery. The prohibition stands against the internal source of all sin: longing for things that cannot be rightfully yours. Conversely, guard your attitudes and foster gratitude.[60]

The ten commands provided a way for the liberated slaves to maintain order and guaranteed the benefits of their freedom. The command against *idols* prevented the false bondage of Egypt's prolific statuary. *Sabbath rest* provided respite for all workers. *Honoring parents* protected the integrity of extended families, intentionally broken in slave economies. No *stealing* and no *false witness* worked against economic exploitation. The purpose of the commands was to restrict the forces and tendencies that would diminish healthy freedoms in human society. To that end systemic structures were commanded to establish that freedom. Contemporary society has reversed and inverted the commands. Coveting is our priority, sexual license is expected, extended family is ignored, and God is irrelevant. The commands provide for God, family, faithful sexuality, and property protection, in that order.[61]

The Six-hundred and Thirteen Commandments

Many more laws than the *ten* have a significant bearing on sustaining public health within Jewish and Christian communities. Many of these laws have influenced western medical practice. Many describe practices and behaviors that can still make communities around the world healthier. Close to one-third of the "613" biblical commandments address public health issues.[62] I have identified about one hundred and seventy-five laws for the categories below.

59. The same as the word translated "covet" in Deuteronomic law (*'avah*; Gen 3:6; Deut 5:21) is used about Eve, who saw that the fruit was "pleasing" (*'avah*) and took and ate. The synonym used in Exodus is *khamed*. In its extreme form, coveting becomes a consuming appetite that is never satisfied.

60. Gill, *Doing Right*, 324.

61. Wright, *Deuteronomy*, 66.

62. Fred Rosner counts 213 of 613 as health related commands. Fred Rosner,

The list of 613 commandments is a compendium of biblical law that allows the interpreter to reasonably work with the vast amount of material in the Sinaitic law. The thousands of sentences of instruction in the Torah (Genesis-Deuteronomy) were analyzed, vetted, and summarized by Rabbi Maimonides in the twelfth century into 613 commandments.[63] Maimonides' list forms the basis for most subsequent lists used in Judaism. This summary form of 613 was possible and helpful because many of the "laws" are repeated two or three times. In addition, numerous detailed instructions, for example, concerning handling a corpse, could be summarized under one law, "Carry out the law of the impurity of the dead" (Num 19:14; Maimonides #443).

The deliverance of the slaves from Egypt grounds the laws in a real narrative. The people coming out of Egypt needed real help if they were to survive and thrive. This included a worldview shift and new behaviors, including better health practices. Historically, these laws came into their present form in the Torah during the Second Temple period, following the Babylonian exile. During this time of external pressure on another re-start of the Jewish community, the laws formed the basis for an enduring, healthy, and thriving community, at home and in the Diaspora.

No one advocates a return to keeping all 613 commandments.[64] Most Jews do not eat lamb at Passover in part because of the strange cooking instructions.[65] The laws are more than twenty-six hundred years old. Many are archaic or alien to common sensibilities: don't wear clothing with wool and cotton blends; don't boil a kid in its mother's milk; and don't eat shellfish.[66] Especially offensive are the laws about the treatment of slaves which assume the institution of slavery, or harsh punishments such as stoning for adultery. It is an alien world for most

---

Medicine in the Bible & Talmud, 9. For valuable resources in rabbinic interpretation of the commandments and their bearing on human health see Rosner as well as: Julius Preuss, *Biblical and Talmudic Medicine* and R. William Cutter, ed. *Healing and the Jewish Imagination*.

63. Rabbi Moses ben Maimonidies (died 1204 CE) is also known as Rambam. He worked primarily in North Africa (present day Egypt and Morocco).

64. The formal Ashkenazi and Sephardic codes of present day practice in Judaism were developed through centuries of rabbinic interpretation of the 613.

65. Exodus 12:9.

66. All of these examples do make sense in their contexts. See J. Bruckner, *Exodus*.

readers. Most commentators are also troubled by the link sometimes made between sin and illness.[67]

Why turn to the 613 at all? These laws and principles have stood for thousands of years as the source of wisdom for practice and conduct of Jewish and many Christian people. Not every law has been equally valuable and all of the laws have been subject to interpretation. The best traditions have included drawing comparative wisdom from the text within an interpretive community for the health and well-being of communities of faith. The worst interpretations and enforced practices have been severely critiqued and reinterpreted. No simple reading of the enduring text is free from the power of the reader. The purpose here is to identify general patterns within the 613 laws that bear on contemporary health and welfare issues. The commands, interpreted through lenses of historical cultural anthropology, yield a wide concern for the health of the public and the environment.[68]

In addition, the principle of community systems and holistic context in religious communities is far from obsolete. Many of these commands continue to bear relevance among readers of the Bible. The medical community has engaged the question of spirituality as a health resource in thousands of studies, with the result that attention to spirituality is becoming a standard part of medical educations. Moreover, religious communities that practice and teach behavioral restraint based on biblical laws contain *ipso facto* healthier people.[69]

67. The link between a person's sin and their illness is not the only possibility provided in Scripture. It may be the result of someone else's sin, unrelated to sin (random), the work of a hidden enemy, etc. For a helpful taxonomy of sources of illness in the Bible see Daniel Simundson, "Health and Healing in the Bible," 330–39. Carol Meyer names the Job narrative as an important counterpoint to the equation of sin=illness, reminding the reader that Scripture must be read as a whole. Carol Meyer, "Wellness and Holiness in the Bible."

68. This is a modern medical perspective on the text. The original historical context has been elucidated as "pollution and taboo" by Mary Douglas, in *Purity and Danger.*

69. See J. D. Fawver and R. Larry Overstreet, "Moses and Preventative Medicine." Fawver and Overstreet comment, "[God] knew that His world is filled with bacteria, viruses, fungi, and parasites, and He provided medical information that has withstood the test of time, continuing to be valid thousands of years after first being revealed" (270).

Categories of Biblical Laws Pertaining to Public Health

Reading within a contemporary perspective,[70] the many laws that bear on community and public health can be divided into seven general categories of disease and injury prevention: laws pertaining to *1) handling meat, 2) prevention of illness and infection, 3) washing, 4) sexual behavior, 5) violence, 6) resting and eating, and 7) protection for women, the poor, or the weak.* The health benefits of most of these laws will be seen as self-evident to people in health related professions.

1. *Forty two laws concern handling meat.*[71] Examples of instruction for the preparation and disposal of food include the following:

- The one butchering animals and handling meat must wash his hands and feet before service. (Exod 30:19)

- Cover the blood of a slaughtered beast/fowl with earth. (Lev 17:13)

- Remove all blood from the meat. (Deut 12:21–24)[72]

- Salt all freshly slaughtered meat. (Lev 2:13)

- Don't leave the fat overnight. (Exod 23:18)

- Burn and do not eat meat which has become unfit or blemished. (Deut 14:3; Lev 7:19)[73]

- Burn and do not leave meat past the time allowed for eating it. (Lev 22:30; Lev 19:7; Exod 12:10, Num 9:12, Deut 16:4)

---

70. Biblical scholars, working only as historians of the text, will insist that reading the commands in this way ignores their cultic context and other *sitz im leben*. I acknowledge the gap, understanding the cultic context, but consider the exercises of demonstrating the health related benefits of these laws in any context and historical moment to have merit nonetheless.

71. Obviously these were given in a time that did not have refrigeration.

72. Blood could not be examined for disease (as meat generally could) to guarantee healthy consumption. "Clean" (kosher) killing of animals for the removal of all the blood was required. Talmudic law insured this in part by insisting on a razor sharp knife that needed no pressure for cutting cleanly and quickly. See Julius Preuss, *Biblical and Talmudic Medicine*, 503–5.

73. The majority of meat was offered as a "sacrifice" to comply with the clean and human butchering policies of the law (Deut 12:21). Eating meat was never taken for granted. God was always acknowledged as the blood and fat portions belonged to God.

2. *Prevention of illness, infection, and infectious diseases is found in twenty-two laws.* Examples include the following:

- Prepare latrines for public sanitation wherever you live. (Deut 23:13–14)[74]

- Anyone who has suffered genital discharge due to illness (e.g., venereal disease), or discharge of blood, or a contagious skin disease must go to the priest for clearance (with an offering), after bathing. (Lev 15: 25, 28–29; Lev 15:3, 13–14; Lev 14:10)

- The one with a contagious skin disease (*metzorah*) must not remove his signs of impurity. (Deut 24:8)

- Clothing that has been in contact with contagious diseases should be burned. (Lev 13:52)

- Everyone who is in contact with a corpse (by the deathbed or otherwise) shall remain apart from those who have not, for seven days. They must cleanse with water and ash (soap) and take a ritual bath on the seventh day to become "clean." (Num 19:14–22)

- Do not delay burial of the dead. (Deut 21:23)

- Do not cut your skin when mourning. (Deut 14:1)

Specific instructions for the covenant of circumcision, required for all Hebrew males, are also beneficial. The command is to circumcise males on the eighth day after birth (Lev 12:3). The eighth day is now widely recognized as the optimal time for circumcision since the level of vitamin K/prothrombin-clotting agent is at 110% in the child. The knife of flint is recognized for its sterility (chipped from hard stone; Exod 4:25; Josh 5:2–3).[75]

3. *Washing in order to be declared "clean" is found in fourteen laws.* The result of washing, of course, is the elimination of bacteria and improved hygiene.[76] The saying, "cleanliness is next to godliness" is

74. The motive given for this in Scripture is that God is present and does not want to see anything filthy (Deut 23:14).

75. For a summary of medical journal evidence for circumcision as preventer of penile cancer see Fawver and Overstreet, 276–77.

76. The purpose of the purity laws are not primarily about "cleanliness" but about preparation for approaching God in worship (holiness). To call this "hygienic washing" is an anachronism that the original context does not know. So Carol Meyer, "Wellness

not from Scripture, but it could be. The so-called "purity" laws are set in a continuum of holiness in Scripture, as a preparation and precondition of approaching the Lord God in worship. To be "next to" God in the tabernacle, you had to be declared "clean." Examples include the following:

- If you touch any dead vermin (mice, lizards, etc.) or move any dead animal you must wash and wash your clothes; if anything else touches dead vermin, you must wash it. (Lev 11:29–39)[77]

- Every "unclean" person must immerse himself in a bath (*mikveh*) to become clean (Lev 15:16). A person becomes unclean routinely. It includes every time a man has an emission of semen (Lev 15:16); a woman finishes her menstrual period (Lev 15:19); a woman gives birth (Lev 12:6); contact with unclean animals; the end of a contagious disease; and contact with human corpses or dead animals (as above). Any fabric involved in any unclean situation is also to be washed.[78]

- Once a year you must clean your home spotlessly. You must not see any (*chametz*; lit. "yeast") dust for seven days. (At the festival of Passover; Exod 12:19; 13:7)

4. Twenty four Laws pertain to sexual and marital behavior, preventing genetic isolation (incest), disease, and encouraging fecundity.[79]

---

and Holiness in the Bible," 127–33. On the other hand, "holiness" in Scripture is not simply a religious category of an arbitrary God while "cleanliness" is a physical concern. Interpreters after Descartes have been held hostage to this erroneous idea, one we must be delivered from for our own health. The biblical narrative of deliverance grounds the laws in the reality that the people coming out of Egypt needed *real* help if they were to survive and thrive. This included a worldview shift that included new behaviors that provided better health practices. Whether or not contemporary interpreters accept it as purposeful, the hygienic result of washing for "holiness" was accomplished. The obvious benefits of these laws were not applied in European medicine until the nineteenth century. Freeman and Abrams include a medical anthropologist's telling description of the ritual of "scrubbing" before surgery.

77. Washing your hands before you eat was a rabbinic extension of the laws of washing for everyone. See the history of hand and foot washing in rabbinical literature in Preuss, *Biblical and Talmudic Medicine*, 524–25.

78. See the history of the various laws of bathing (full body washing) in rabbinical interpretation in Preuss, *Biblical and Talmudic Medicine*, 526–44.

79. The medical community knows the epidemic of STDs in the last thirty years. We have now come to the point of giving the HPV vaccine to fifth-grade girls as a necessary step in prevention. The ancient world also knew about STDs but had another

- Have children with your wife. (Gen 1:28; cf. Gen 2:24)

- Do not let your family become involved with female or male prostitution. (Deut 23:18; Lev 18:6) A woman was expected to be a virgin when she married. (Deut 22:13–21)[80]

- Forbidden sexual relations: sixteen laws concerning incest; five prohibiting bestiality and homosexual intercourse. (Lev 18:1–30; 20:10–23; Deut 22:23–29)[81]

- Do not castrate any male. (Lev 22:24; this was a common practice in other cultures of the ancient east).

5. *Public safety and preventing the potential for domestic violence is found in nineteen laws.* These include responding to physical assault, murder, kidnapping, and rape as well as six laws addressing festering anger and cycles of vengeance (preventing domestic violence and feuds).

- The creditor must not forcibly take collateral. (Deut 24:10)

- The judge must not fear a violent man in judgment. (Deut 1:17)

- The court must implement laws against the one who assaults another or damages another's property. (Exod 21:18)

- Eight laws concern breaking up violence and prohibiting murder. (Exod 20:13; Num 35:12, 25, 31, 32; Deut 25:12; Lev 19:16)

- Do not take revenge. (Lev 19:18)

6. *Resting and Eating.* Forty-five laws pertain to healthy habits of resting for the whole community (eighteen) and of not eating certain foods (twenty-seven). Examples include the following:

- Rest from labor for everyone and everything on the seventh day. (Exod 20:10; 23:12)[82]

---

kind of prevention in mind. Abstinence/monogamy still forms a basis for the healthier sub-groups in our society, as measured by insurance actuaries. See data in Jeff Levin, *God, Faith, and Health*, 19–44; see discussion also in Brown, *Israel's Divine Healer*, 76–77.

80. This, with the law against adultery and prostitution, also removed the option of promiscuity from a young man.

81. The motive given for these prohibitions is quite plain: If you do this, you will be healthier longer. "You shall keep my statutes and my ordinances; *by doing so one shall live*"(Lev 18:5).

82. See Sabbath command in comment on the Ten Commandments above.

- Fourteen laws of rest during special days of remembering the acts of God's deliverance and forgiveness. (Lev 23:7, 8, 21, 24, 25, 32, 35, 36)[83]

- Those who are newly married should be exempt from public or military service for one year. (Deut 24:5)

Concerning foods, not all prohibitions can be demonstrated to have health benefits, but many can, especially in a hot climate without refrigeration.[84]

- Do not eat the blood of any animal.[85]

- Do not eat any of the fat of cattle, sheep, or goats. (Lev 7:23)[86]

- You may eat any animal that has a split hoof completely divided and that chews the cud (Lev 11:2–3). This excludes swine, which carry parasitic trichina larvae, and other named meat-eating parasite-laden animals and birds (rats, skunks, snakes, eagles, vultures, buzzards, ravens, seagulls, etc.; see Lev 11).

- You may eat fish that have fins and scales (Lev 11:9). These move in flowing water. This excludes many bottom feeders and shellfish.

7. *Protection, provision, and safety for the poor, young, or vulnerable are found in thirty-two laws.* Examples include the following:

- Thirteen "laws of gifts to the poor." (Lev 19:9–10; Deut 14:28, 15:7, 8; 24:19)

- The hired worker may eat from unharvested crops where he works. (Deut 23:25)

- Do not demand as collateral utensils needed for preparing

---

83. Passover, Yom Kippur, Shavuot, Rosh Hashanah, Sukkot, Shmini Atzeret. See chapter nine for the theme of remembering deliverance and salvation as a practice of health and healing.

84. See commentary of specific dietary laws in Fawver and Overstreet, 272–75.

85. Exsanguinated meat lasts longer. The original motive for this is that all life belongs to God, not to people and the life is in the life-blood. In not eating the blood, the eater acknowledges that the meat is a gift from God. See Deut 12:16, 23–25; Lev 3:17; 7:26; 17:14; Gen 9:4. The first Christians upheld these statutes, even for Gentiles. See Acts 15:20, 29. See discussion in Preuss, *Biblical and Talmudic Medicine*, 503–5.

86. See extensive commentary on health benefits in R. K. Harrison, *Leviticus: An Introduction and Commentary*, 58.

food. (Deut 24:6)

- Return collateral to the debtor when needed. (Deut 24:13)
- Do not oppress the weak (Exod 21:22); Do not put a stumbling block before a blind man or give him harmful advice. (Lev. 19:14)

Protection of the young and vulnerable:

- Do not pass your children through the fire to Molech (a Canaanite God requiring child sacrifice in exchange for the prosperity of the parents; prohibited but practiced in Israel; Lev. 18:21).
- The court must fine one who seduces a maiden. (Exod 22:15–16)
- A seducer or rapist must marry a maiden (if she chooses) and never divorce her. (Deut 22:29)
- The slanderer who falsely accuses his wife of adultery may not divorce her. (Deut 22:19)

Protection for those accused of murder:[87]

- Designate cities of refuge and prepare routes of access. (Deut. 19:3)

General public safety:

- Do not allow pitfalls and obstacles to remain on your property. (Deut 22:8)
- Make a guard rail around flat roofs. (Deut 22:8)
- The court must judge the damages incurred by a goring ox (Exod 21:28); incurred by a pit (Exod 21:33); or by a fire. (Exod 22:5)

Protection of animals:

- Help another remove a load from a beast that can no longer carry it. (Exod 23:5)
- Help others load their beasts. (Deut 22:4)

---

87. The Sinai laws are also full of legal procedures with extensive instruction on how to keep a just court. These laws established an early ancient system of rule by law rather than by force. See James K. Bruckner, *Implied Law in the Abraham Narrative*.

- Do not leave others distraught with their burdens (but help to either load or unload). (Deut 22:4)

- Do not take a mother bird when taking eggs from her nest. (Deut 22:6–7)

"Forgiveness" may be the most important single factor for effecting health in the Torah. Exodus ends with forgiveness. The laws are not simply a list of commands. They are deeply embedded in a storied and dynamic relational setting. The people's resolve to "have no other gods" before their Creator and redeemer was tested almost immediately. While Moses was on the mountain for forty days, they took their leadership into their own hands and demanded that Aaron build a golden calf for them from the gold the Egyptians had given them as the left.[88] They had been enslaved under the lordship of the false Egyptian god of the sun, Re, and his regent, the Pharaoh. Now they wanted to serve a god of their own making, a golden calf. They said of the calf, "These are your gods, O Israel, who brought you up out of the land of Egypt!" (Exod 32:8).

The people rejected their deliverer and created a fake god. In conversation with Moses, God says that he should destroy the people. Moses suggests that this would be bad for his reputation, and God agrees. Instead, God decides to show his greater power by *not destroying* the rebellious people (Exod 34:6–7). Before he moved to renew the Covenant, however, the text reports an extended discussion concerning whether God will go with and remain present with them (Exod 33:16–17), and whether God will ultimately forgive them or not (Exod 34:5–7). God's forgiveness was not at all taken for granted.

Before coming to a resolution with Moses, God agreed to show Moses his glory as he hid in the cleft of the rock. That "glory" was more than a visual show. It was the revelation of the identity of God to his emerging, failed, and faithless people. In this dramatic event the LORD declared that he is "The LORD, the LORD, the compassionate and gracious God, slow to anger, abounding in love and faithfulness, maintaining love to thousands, and forgiving wickedness, rebellion and sin" (Exod 34:6–7). The LORD decided that he would *go among his people, forgiving them,* even when they rebelled against him.

88. Exodus 32:1–8.

God declared that he would *re-make the covenant*. This is a renewal of the initial Sinai Covenant, with an important difference. He made promises based on his own faithfulness to his own word: "I will perform marvels . . . It is an awesome thing I will do with you" (Exod 34:10). The (613) laws were placed on a new foundation: God's forgiveness, faithfulness, and promises would secure the future of his people. His word would not fail, even though hindered by human rebellion and sin. This was and is the foundation of the blessing and the health of God's people.[89]

---

89. Meyer notes that whatever healing practices are used, in biblical law they are begun with prayers of petition to the Lord and they are concluded with prayers of thanksgiving. "Restoration to well-being was inconceivable without what we would call a holistic approach." C. Meyer, "Wellness and Holiness," 132. Such practices and their contexts will be addressed again in chapter nine.

Chapter Three

What is Human Wholeness?

Descriptive Content from Deuteronomy

Shalom and Wholeness

A HEBREW CONCEPT USED in many health ministries is *shalom*,[1] a synonym for wholeness, well-being, or for the general thriving of a community. It is widely used as a name for retirement homes, (e.g., *Shalom Home*) shelters, and social service organizations where it can also be intended to mean "peace."[2]

Shalom includes many things in Scripture.[3] A first cluster of meanings is "to be complete" or "lack nothing" (material prosperity). A second meaning cluster includes "to be whole," "sound," as in the medical phrase, "a sound bone," or to be "OK." A third set of meanings refers to the safety and security of the weakest in a community, translated, "Be not afraid." It also has a component of justice. Without justice there is no *shalom* (Jer 6:14; 8:11). Finally, it can refer to fellowship and con-

---

1. The proposal is detailed below and in J. Bruckner, "Health" in *Dictionary of Scripture and Ethics*.

2. The word *shalom* is also used at the time of death. "Rest in Peace" (RIP) is very common. *Shalom* is also used in the famous *Kaddish* prayer, prayed in the Jewish community after the death of a loved one: "He who establishes *shalom* in his heights, may he establish *shalom* over us and over all Israel."

3. See L. Koehler and W. Baumgartner. *The Hebrew and Aramaic Lexicon of the Old Testament*; F. Brown, S.R. Driver, C.A. Briggs, *A Hebrew and English Lexicon of the Old Testament*, 1022. Cf. P. Yoder, *Shalom*, 10–19.

tentment, a meaning rooted in the sacrificial system's *shalom* offering.[4] The best general translation of this expansive biblical usage probably includes the encompassing words "well-being" or "health."[5]

The concept of *shalom* is a loose synonym for "wholeness" or "human health." When it is used today, however, the referent, content, and context are often broad, and unspecified. The word itself does not answer the question: what *is* human wholeness? The narratives of Genesis to Deuteronomy find the children of Israel often at odds with God on exactly this point (e.g.: worship of the calf at Sinai; the cry for meat in the desert; and participation in the ritual at Baal-Peor). Today the content of the terms "health," "wellness," and "well-being" is also contested and discussed.

The book of Deuteronomy, by contrast, is quite clear about what, specifically, is good for you (see "For Your Own Good," below). Here we find the concept that wholeness is relational and has a narrative, but also that the narrative is grounded in choosing to love the God who has demonstrated his love for a broken people.

Elements of Human Wholeness

Wholeness, like its opposite, brokenness, is relational, and always stands within someone's story. The book of Deuteronomy tells the story of people in relationship with God and each other. The biblical narrative witness always aligns human wholeness with human dependence

4. The *shalom* offering to the Lord included a meal of the sacrificed meat with family and friends.

5. John Wilkinson is one of the few recent biblical scholars to describe an Old Testament perspective on a whole and healthy person. See *The Bible and Healing*. Working from his expertise as a medical doctor and a biblical scholar, Wilkinson concludes that the Hebrew word *shalom* ("well-being") is the best umbrella term for human health and wholeness. Under this rubric he includes five subcategories: *justice* and *obedience* are conditions of attaining *shalom*; *strength*, *fertility*, and *longevity* are blessings of *shalom*. He offers these as general observations from the Old Testament narrative (Wilkinson, 11). For an overview of the history of the conversation in Old Testament studies on the meaning of the concept of *shalom*, see the following excellent anthology: P. Yoder and W. Sawatsky, editors. *The Meaning of Peace*. Some scholars argue for a much narrower definition of health within the broader context of God's purposes. See A. Verhey, "Health and Healing in Memory of Jesus.," 43, n. 18. The biblical perception of "health," however, is necessarily broad, in contrast to current medical and technological perceptions, though not as broad as the biblical concept of *salvation* or as general as the term *shalom*.

on God (Deut 5:6; 6:12, 21; Gen 2:7). The storied context (we all have back-stories) and relationality of communities are two key elements in describing human wholeness. The choices made in the actual story they recount is the third element.

Wholeness can be measured by relationship to others and to the One who creates. Wholeness has a narrative, and cannot be understood without understanding the story of how a community and the persons in it become whole. It is a story, like all good stories, with past, present, and future possibilities. The actual content of the story of Israel is rich with the wisdom of life-affirming living and the rejection of life-denying behaviors. *Shalom* sometimes describes *the result*. Deuteronomy, however, is about *the process of* love: being chosen by a loving God, and choosing to love God and each other in return.[6] "For your good" is a common refrain in the book. Wholeness is relational, has a narrative, and is grounded in choosing to love the God who has revealed his love for you.

Wholeness is Relational: Community

It may go without saying that reality is relational. Each of us is conceived in relationship, whether it is whole or not. Each of us is fed, nurtured, and taught how to be human in a community. Moreover, whether we are aware of it or not, our lives are given and sustained by the Creator of all that is. That relationship too, can be whole or broken. Human wholeness depends on the health of all of the relationships that constitute our being.

Recent research on the human brain is helpful for understanding the relationality of human wholeness.[7] Neither the body nor the brain is physically static. The body is constantly and often rapidly replacing its dying cells with others. The brain produces few new cells (it has many more than you will ever use), but it too changes at an amazing rate, especially when one is learning something new from someone or something outside of it. Learning and knowledge itself is essentially relational. The brain creates new pathways between the synapses as new thoughts and relationships are understood. Pathways that are no longer

6. This is typically called "a covenant" in deuteronomic language.

7. See Joel Green, *Body, Soul, and Human Life*, 122, 178–80.

used disappear (because of learned new ways of thinking). Your mind and your body are ever changing. The "you" of last year is a different "you" than now. What are constant are the *relational patterns* that the mind determines are ever true. That is the constant "you." One recognized scholar put it this way: "Our identity is formed and found in self-conscious relationality with its neural correlates."[8]

Deuteronomy does not speak in terms of neurobiology, but has a similar presupposition. Moses speaks to the people, reminding them: You are, because God has initiated a relationship with you. You are, because you have wandered these forty years in the desert together and have had a shared experience. You have learned what God has taught you through experience together. You are individuals within a community *in relation to* your Creator and sustainer.

The "you" in Moses' speeches is a fascinating feature in the book. It is not so noteworthy in English, but in Hebrew "you" can be singular or plural. The remarkable element is that both are used together, sometimes in the same sentence and regularly in the same paragraph. Moreover, similar verses mix them in different ways. For example,

> You (plural) recite them to your (singular) children and you (singular) talk about them when you (singular) are at home . . . (Deut 6:7)
>
> You (plural) teach them to your (plural) children, talking about them when you (singular) are at home . . . (Deut 11:19)

This is odd in any language. The random change between the singular and plural continually reminds the reader or listener that both individuals and the whole community are being addressed. The new learning and shared identity is for each person, but also for the whole community. It also highlights that individuals are not out of the picture, subsumed into a corporate identity. They remain individuals, not independent, but interdependent. This is a linguistic feature that embodies diversity within community. *A healthy relationality* is embedded in this rhetorical feature of the ancient text.

8. Ibid., 179.

Wholeness Has a Narrative: A Particular Community

Wholeness may be relational, but what keeps this relationality from remaining radically relative? Whole people and whole communities are not formed simply by moving from one random experience to another! Experience is vital, but without understanding, is essentially lost.

Wholeness and brokenness are formed by a person's story—more precisely by a series of stories with similar themes. A lifetime of stories shapes a person's identity. Something similar is true for the formation of the ethos of a community—a shared series of stories (or history) that are told and retold as the shaping stories of shared "memory." They form a portrait of community values and corporate identity.[9] Deuteronomy is such a story set within the overarching story of the many books of the Bible.

Deuteronomy in particular reflects the power of story for identity formation. Its most famous text begins with "Listen!" or "Hear, Israel!" (Deut 6:4) Deuteronomy itself is a retelling of the story of the Exodus and wilderness wanderings in a sermon by Moses just before they enter the promised land of Canaan. It is a story of the pursuing love of God that led and sustained the people in the midst of radical change, confusion, and multiple difficulties.

Stories become most important at times of life transition. They tell us where we have been, where we are, and where we are going— but not in a static way. Moses' retelling reshapes the community for that moment and for future moments. Remembering and retelling the story of wholeness and salvation is important for restoring wholeness in any community. Within that story is an older story, given as a further grounding of identity in past, present, and future. Moses reminds the people of a story set some five hundred years before the exodus, the story of Abraham, to whom God made promises.[10] He then ties that story to their story of exodus and deliverance in the wilderness. All this becomes the earliest creedal statement of Israel, recited at the festival of first fruits.[11] Every year, the ancient story is told, grounding the harvest in the providence of the Creator and redeemer.

9. Corporations and even restaurants sometimes tap into this phenomenon by writing the story of their origins for their employees and customers to read.

10. "My father was a wandering Aramean; he went down to Egypt and lived there as an alien." See Deut 26:1–10.

11. It is the earliest digest of Israel's faith; the core of their salvation history. G. von

Many people in contemporary society do not have identities shaped by the depth of any ancient story. They move from experience to experience without the wholeness and health that is possible within the meaning of relationships established in an overarching narrative like the Bible. When someone moves from the emptiness of "no story" to a community of faith in God grounded in Scripture and the relationship with God that it describes, wholeness is restored. Religious communities call this *conversion* or *transformation*.

Wholeness Requires Choices

Everyone has relationships that affect their wholeness, and everyone has a story (past, present, and future) within those relationships, for better or for worse. The future of those relationships, whole or broken, depends on the choices that are made. The patterns can be repeated or they can be changed. In the story recounted in Deuteronomy, wholeness means choosing between life-affirming living and the rejection of life-denying behaviors. It means *choosing one's primary patterns.*

The most important choice in the actual content of the story is between God and the god currently being served. It is a choice between the God who created all things, redeeming the Hebrew slaves from Egypt and other gods or another god made of a created power.[12] This God of life provided for them in the wilderness, gave them life-sustaining laws, and formed them into a vital people through four hundred years of monarchy, exile in Babylon, redemption and return to the land to rebuild the Temple.[13] Deuteronomy is about love, being chosen by a loving God, and choosing to love God and each other in return.

God Competes for Humanity in Deuteronomy

Against other forces that compete to define human health and vie for human allegiance, the ancient narrative claims to provide God's perspective on human vitality. During the course of Israel's history, the

---

Rad, "Israel's Earliest Creed," 43.

12. See Harrelson, *Ten Commandments and Human Rights*, 183.

13. Although the book of Deuteronomy is set in the plains of Moab forty years after the exodus, it has even the second temple in view. See Deut 30:1–10.

community and individuals within the community had opportunities to take on definitions of health and wholeness offered by other cultures. Not many were tempted to adopt an Egyptian view, given their historical sojourn there. They also had opportunity to take on the Canaanite and Mesopotamian (Babylonian and Assyrian) view of human relationships—to their gods and to other human beings.[14] Deuteronomy is quite aware of these options and addresses them directly. Deuteronomy recommends God's laws as the most excellent laws: "What great nation . . . has statues and ordinances as righteous as all this?" (Deut 4:8).

During the time of King Josiah (7th century B.C.E), the book of Deuteronomy played a most significant role.[15] While repairs were being done to the Temple, the book, which was not then known, was found in the archive. The young king and his advisors used it as a source for their sweeping reforms in Judah.[16] The first step was removing the false gods, especially the gods of harvest, sexuality, and fertility (the *baals* and the *asheroth*) which were being worshiped even in the Temple of the Lord. He also removed the practice of male prostitution from the Temple. He also put an end to parent's sacrifice of their children to Molech outside the walls of Jerusalem (done as a guarantee of their well-being). He ended the worship of the sun, moon, and stars. In their place he read the book of the covenant at Sinai in public.[17] They reinstituted the festival of Passover, which had fallen out of memory, again remembering God's deliverance from Egypt on their behalf.

The worship of false gods had led to many injustices in the society. Who your god is matters. We have similar contrasting possibilities today. One scholar of Deuteronomy notes that American values have shifted quite dramatically away from Christian values as other gods have gained allegiance. Coveting is a priority. Sexual license is expected to the extent that chastity is seen as an oddity. Extended family is commonly ignored and the God of Scripture is generally viewed as irrelevant. "The commands provide for God, family, faithful sexuality, and

14. There were many gods to choose from in the ancient east. Pharaoh, son on the Sun God Re; Canaanite fertility gods—the baals and asheroth; gods of safety and security like Molech; tamers of chaos, like Marduk of Babylonian order; gods of war and power like Asshur of Assyria; gods of personal destiny like the host of heaven.

15. Many scholars think that the final form of Deuteronomy was completed in the days of Josiah.

16. See the account of Josiah's thirty-one year reign in 2 Kings 22:1–23:25.

17. 2 Kings 23:1–3.

property protection in that order."[18] The book of Deuteronomy "knows" that the gods or God we have, matters for the health and wholeness of individuals and communities.

For Your Own Good

Deuteronomy repeatedly appeals to the common sense of the reader. Its motive clauses repeat creational arguments: "to do you good"[19] and "that you may live long in the land."[20] They echo the first chapter of Genesis and its seven repetitions that "God saw that it was good." God is source of this good life.

> And you shall rejoice in all the good which the LORD your God has given to you and to your house, you, and the Levite, and the sojourner who is among you. (Deut 26:11)

Turning to false gods has the opposite result.

> And as the LORD took delight in doing you *good* and multiplying you, so the LORD will take delight in bringing ruin upon you and destroying you. (Deut 28:63)

Yet, the invitation to return to God and the whole life is open.

> For the LORD will again take delight *in prospering you,* as he took delight in your fathers, if you obey the voice of the LORD your God, to keep his commandments and his statutes which are written in this book of the law, if you turn to the LORD your God with all your heart and with all your soul. (Deut 30:9b–10)

The goodness of life is a direct result of living according to what God has revealed in his covenant with the people.

> And the LORD commanded us to do all these statutes, to fear the LORD our God, for our *good* always, that he might preserve us alive, as at this day. (Deut 6:24; see 10:13)
>
> And you shall do what is right and *good* in the sight of the LORD, *that it may go well* with you, and that you may go in and

---

18. C. Wright, *Deuteronomy*, 66.

19. Deut 6:24; 8:16; 10:13; 12:28; 28:63; The Hebrew word for "good" (*tov*) in its verbal form is sometimes translated, "go well" or "prosper." The words in italics are all from the Hebrew word root *tov.*

20. Deut 5:33, 11:8, 22:7, 30:6, 32:47.

> take possession of the good land which the LORD swore to give
> to your fathers. (Deut 6:18)
>
> Be careful to heed all these words which I command you,
> *that it may go well* with you and with your children after you
> for ever, when you do what is *good* and right in the sight of the
> LORD your God. (Deut 12:28)

When a particular beneficial therapy is difficult for a patient we sometimes say, "It will be good for you." Deuteronomy uses the same kind of
motivation with a layer of rhetorical sophistication added.

> Then do not exalt yourself, forgetting the LORD your God, who
> brought you out of the land of Egypt, out of the house of slav-
> ery, who led you through the great and terrible wilderness, an
> arid wasteland with poisonous snakes and scorpions. He made
> water flow for you from flint rock, and fed you in the wilderness
> with manna that your ancestors did not know, to humble you
> and to test you, and in *the end to do you good.* Do not say to
> yourself, "My power and the might of my own hand have gotten
> me this wealth." But remember the LORD your God, for it is he
> who gives you power to get wealth, so that he may confirm his
> covenant that he swore to your ancestors, as he is doing today.
> (Deut 8:14–18)

The "great and terrible wilderness" sounds like a round of chemotherapy! The added layer is that this text has a future retrospective. That
means that Moses is describing a day in the future when they may forget the source of their newly found health and strength. He warns them
that it was their primary caregiver, God, who carried them through
their transformation through a very difficult healing and strengthening
process.

Choosing life, good, and loving a loving God is a necessary part of
the transformation in Deuteronomy.

> "See, I have set before you this day *life* and *good*, death and evil.
> If you obey the commandments of the LORD your God which
> I command you this day, by loving the LORD your God, by
> walking in his ways, and by keeping his commandments and
> his statutes and his ordinances, then *you shall live and multiply,*
> and the LORD your God will bless you in the land which you
> are entering to take possession of it. But if your heart turns away,
> and you will not hear, but are drawn away to worship other
> gods and serve them, I declare to you this day, that you shall

perish; *you shall not live long* in the land which you are going over the Jordan to enter and possess. I call heaven and earth to witness against you this day, that *I have set before you life and death*, blessing and curse; *therefore choose life,* that you and your descendants *may live, loving* the LORD your God, obeying his voice, and cleaving to him; for *that means life to you and length of days*." (Deut30:15–20a)

A Living Word

A simple yet comprehensive description of the aspects of the whole and healthy person is present in the most influential text in Deuteronomy, the *Shema* (lit. "Listen!").

Jews around the world recite it at least every morning and evening.[21]

> Hear (*shema'*), O Israel: The LORD is our God, the LORD is One.[22] You shall love the LORD your God with all your heart, and with all your soul, and with all your might. Keep these words that I am commanding you today in your heart. Recite them to your children and talk about them when you are at home and when you are away, when you lie down and when you rise. Bind them as a sign on your hand, fix them as an emblem on your forehead, and write them on the doorposts of your house and on your gates. (Deut 6:4–9)

Why would anyone today choose an ancient text like this as part of their back-story and community narrative? Jews must make this choice in every generation and not all do so. How did it come to be such a *living* word? The tradition provides at least three explanations.

First, the text itself claims that it is a living word. When Moses addresses the second and third generations of the people who exited Egypt through the Red Sea, he spoke to those who had been born in the wilderness and had no personal memory of the event. Yet, he claimed that God's promises were made directly to them: "Not with our ancestors did the LORD make this covenant, but with us, who are all

21. The *Shema* is recited with Deut 11:13–21 and Num 15:37–41 which restate and expand the *Shema*. It is and has been the most important single text in worldwide Judaism for more than two thousand years.

22. Observant Jews add this line in reverence for the Name of the LORD: "Blessed is the name of His Glorious Majesty forever and ever. God, King Forever."

of us here alive today" (Deut 5:3). The original language is even more emphatically redundant: "but with us, we, these, here, today, all of us, alive ones." The nearness of God and the direct address to the living generation accentuates this theme.[23]

> Surely this commandment that I am commanding *you today* is not too hard for you, *nor is it too far away*. It is not in heaven, that you should say, "Who will go up to heaven for us, and get it for us so that we may hear it and observe it?" Neither is it beyond the sea, that you should say, "Who will cross to the other side of the sea for us, and get it for us so that we may hear it and observe it?" No, *the word is very near to you*; it is in your mouth and in your heart for you to observe. See, *I have set before you today* life and good, death and evil. (Deut 30:11–15)

Struggling communities of faith within Scripture did embrace the *Shema* and Deuteronomy as a living word. Hundreds of years after the wilderness experience, the Israelites found wholeness and hope in this living word. One of its most powerful settings, as noted above, was during the days of Josiah's reform (seventh century BCE). They too heard the words as for themselves: "not with our ancestors . . . but with us, we, these, here, today, all of us, alive ones." Again, about two hundred years after Josiah, in the days of the second temple rebuilding, the story and covenant were embraced (fifth century BCE). The community struggled when they returned to Jerusalem following the exile in Babylon. Ezra and Nehemiah led the people in a renewal of the words of Moses.[24] Finally, we have the evidence from the Qumran caves. The library found there represents the most important texts for the community in Palestine (first century BCE). The book of Deuteronomy, with the prophet Isaiah, and the book of Psalms are the most represented there.

Jesus embraced Deuteronomy and the *Shema* in particular in his teaching about the kingdom of God (first century CE).[25] On three separate occasions he lifted it up as the most important and central text of the Scriptures. He taught that the *Shema* was a summary of all the law and the prophets (Matt 22:40), the greatest of all the commandments (Mark 12:31), and a path to eternal life (Luke 10:25, 28). To the *Shema* he added, "You shall love your neighbor as yourself" (Lev 19:18b). This

23. See also Deut 4:7–8.

24. Neh 8:1–8.

25. Deuteronomy is the most quoted book of the Torah in the New Testament.

summary of the Torah has been called the "Jesus creed"[26] given as a pathway given by Jesus to a living relationship with God.[27] The one who was called a living word pointed to the *Shema* as a living word.[28]

The second section of this book (chapters four through six) presents a close reading of the *Shema* through the lens of human health and wholeness. A simple yet comprehensive description of human health in Scripture is present in the vocabulary of the *Shema*, especially the phrases "with all your heart (*levav*), and with all your soul (*nephesh*), and with all your might (*me'od*)." The focus on this vocabulary, in context, will elucidate the assumed anthropology of the biblical text. What does it mean to choose to love God with all these aspects of ourselves? How does this make us and our communities whole?

The Context of the *Shema*

The *Shema* contains the three elements of deuteronomic wholeness: relationality, narrativity, and the choice to love the God who loves us, has made us, and can save us from slavery of all sorts. Relationally, it looks to the future, speaking of children and the promise of God for blessing.[29] Narratively, it remembers the past, set in the context of the story of the deliverance from Egypt.[30] It engages the present as a daily practice, focusing one's thoughts on love: God's love, our love for God, and for our families. The last letters of the first and last words of the Hebrew text are commonly written in larger letters to make a point. Taken together they form the word "witness" (*'ed*). This inclusion reflects the potential relational interaction of the reader, the writer, and the text itself. Contemporary readers are called to enter a living relationship with God through this ancient narrative witness.

---

26. See Scot McKnight, *The Jesus Creed*. McKnight calls this path to wholeness "spiritual formation."

27. Jesus said, "You are wrong. He is not God of the dead but of the living" (Mark 12:27). McKnight shows that Jesus also taught that one loves God by following Jesus.

28. John 1:14; This verse echoes the vocabulary of Exodus 34:6.

29. Deut 6:1–3; 6:7–25.

30. Deut 4:32–40; 5:1–33.

The Necessity of Dependence on God

Dependence comes in many forms, some better than others. The *Shema* defines this particular dependence as the dependence of mutual love between unequal partners. Our dependence on God is a real dependence, not a mutual dependence. The love is mutual, if we choose to love. The love sets the dependence of the created on the Creator in the best possible relational terms. It does not ignore the dependence, but bases it in trust.

Limitation and *disability* stand as the context of human health as represented in the *Shema*. It sets human health and flourishing solidly within an understanding of human dependence on God.[31]

> When your children ask you in time to come, "What is the meaning of the decrees and the statutes and the ordinances that the LORD our God has commanded you?" Then you shall say to your children, "We were Pharaoh's slaves in Egypt, but the LORD brought us out of Egypt with a mighty hand." (Deut 6:20–21)

Discovering one's limitation before God is part of one's healthy "heart" (*levav*), "soul" (*nephesh*), and "might" (*meʾod*), as we shall see in the following chapters. Neither the substance of limitation, nor the *Shema's* context of dependency, however, displace the *positive substance* of human health presented in the word-concepts of the *Shema*. The health of limitation is a substantive part of the positive concern for healthy living. This view affirms that life is a precious gift *from God*, requiring our attention and stewardship. It seeks to demonstrate a limited, dependent wholeness, firmly established in the love of God.

---

31. "Take care that you do not forget the LORD, who brought you out of Egypt, out of the house of slavery. The LORD your God you shall fear; him you shall serve, and by his name alone you shall swear." Deut 6:12–13; see Deut 5:6; cf. Josh 24:15–27; See also Genesis 2:17 and J.K. Bruckner, "Boundary and Freedom: Blessings in the Garden of Eden," 15–35. The enduring love of God is also contrasted with the limitation and finitude of human life in Ps 103:14–18. On the necessity of em in bracing our limitation/disability for human growth see Alasdair McIntyre, *Dependent Rational Animals*, 119–28.

Loving God[32]

The clear theological context of the *Shema* is the call to love the one and only true God: "The LORD our God, the LORD is one. You shall love the LORD your God with all your heart, with all your soul, and with all your might." This call precludes treating health itself as the ultimate good (*summum bonum*) or making a god of health and wholeness. The passage concludes with a strong warning against false gods, particularly tempting in the fatness of success.

> [When you have] houses filled with all sorts of goods that you did not fill, hewn cisterns that you did not hew, vineyards and olive groves that you did not plant—and when you have eaten your fill, take care that you do not forget the LORD, who brought you out of the land of Egypt, out of the house of slavery. The LORD your God you shall fear; him you shall serve, and by his name alone you shall swear. Do not follow other gods, any of the gods of the peoples who are all around you, because the LORD your God, who is present with you, is a jealous God. The anger of the LORD your God would be kindled against you and he would destroy you from the face of the earth. (Deut 6:11–15)

The health of the community or the nation is not the highest good (= God), nor is it the goal in Scripture.[33] The highest good is found in loving the creating and redeeming God. In this view of wholeness, we must take a step beyond our present culture's preoccupation with health in order to ask what positive pathways of health and wholeness are offered in Scripture.

This "wholeness" may include laying down one's privilege for the love of God in the world.[34] It could, but does not necessarily mean, relinquishing one's life or physical well-being for the love of God (Isa 53:4–12; Matt 5:10–12).[35] The love of the one God also means that a

32. A variation of what follows was previously published in Bruckner, James. "A Theological Description of Human Wholeness in Deuteronomy 6," *Ex Auditu* 21 (2005) 1–19.

33. Cf. Allen Verhey, "Health and Healing"; for a discussion of loving God in the health–conscious American context, see Brent Laytham, ed., *God Is Not*, 122–28.

34. See the section in chapter four on "Justice and Righteousness."

35. Jewish martyrs have always recited the *Shema* as they have died for their faith. Christian martyrs often recite the Apostles' or Nicene creeds, declaring their love of God above even their lives. Consider Jeremiah's suffering in his prophetic ministry and the suffering servant of Isaiah 53.

preoccupation with one's own "spirituality" or the so-called "soul" itself can be idolatrous.[36]

The Content of the *Shema*: All of Your "Everything"

After wandering for forty years in the wilderness, Moses stood before the people on the plains of Moab. As they prepared finally to enter the land of promise Moses reminded them of all that had transpired, from the crossing of the Sea to the Sinai encounter, to that very day. He challenged them to choose a particular kind of healthy life, given to them by God, so that it would go well with them.

> Hear (*shema'*), O Israel! The LORD is our God, the LORD is one! And you shall love the LORD your God with all your heart (*levav*) and with all your soul (*nephesh*) and with all your might (*me'od*). (Deut 6:4–5)

When Moses wanted to impress upon them that their love for God should proceed from absolutely *every part of their being*, he chose the words that are translated "heart, soul, and might." Centuries later this effort to describe the totality of a person's life was also emphasized by Jesus. When he recited the *Shema* on two separate occasions, he added the word that was necessary in the hellenistic world to describe an entire person: *dianoia* ("mind"). The Greek word *kardia* ("heart") was not sufficient to express the total meaning of the Hebrew word *levav* ("heart-mind").[37]

The effort to describe the totality of a person in the *Shema* is evidenced further in Jesus' conversation with the lawyer who asked him about the greatest commandment. The lawyer's expression of the *Shema* used the Greek words "heart and mind" to describe the Hebrew concept of *levav* (heart-mind). In each case, the linguistic effort was appropriate

36. See chapter five.

37. On three separate occasions Jesus lifted it up as the most important of the Scriptures. In each case, he added the word "mind," as was the tradition for Jews speaking in Greek, to be sure to fully describe the intent of the Hebrew *Shema*. He recited it in the middle of his ministry to the scribes and Pharisees (Mark 12:30) and at the end of his ministry to the gathered Pharisees and Sadducees in response to a lawyer who asked about the greatest commandment (Matt 22:40). On another occasion, Jesus responded to a lawyer who asked about inheriting eternal life by asking him what the law said. When the lawyer recited the *Shema* (including "mind") Jesus said, "You have given the right answer; do this, and you will live" (Luke 10:25–28).

to each socio-philosophical context. Each was attempting to describe a complete representation of a whole person.[38]

The *Shema* encapsulated the whole-life relationship of Israel before the Creator, and this whole-life was echoed by Jesus, as a description of all that we are. This commandment gives us a simple yet comprehensive summary of human wholeness in Scripture.[39] The Hebrew terms, translated in the Gospels, provide us with geography of human life in all of its complex relationships.

A Summary of Wholeness: All Your Heart, All Your Soul, All Your Might

The *Shema* provides biblical description of a thriving human being. The Hebrew words (*levav, nephesh, me'od*) behind the English translations (heart, soul, might) are multi-dimensional concepts.[40] They are windows into the vital and thriving life that God intended for humanity

38. The Greek word *kardia* is used to translate the Hebrew *levav*. In English, each is most often rendered "heart." Chapter four will describe the broad meaning of the Hebrew. The Greek *kardia* is also quite broad in meaning: "The causative source of a person's psychological life in its various aspects but with special emphasis on thoughts—heart, inner self, mind." For example, "the secret thoughts of his heart" (1 Cor 15:25). See Johannes Louw and Eugene Nida, eds. "kardia" in *Greek-English Lexicon of the New Testament Based on Semantic Domains*, 1:321. The specific motivation for including "mind" *nous* in this light is unclear, but the intention to describe "all of everything" is clear.

39. The *Shema* provides a contextualized vocabulary that elucidates the assumed anthropology of biblical texts.

40. The second section of this book focuses on the words of the *Shema* as a way of defining human wholeness. The method is not a historical description of the deuteronomist's anthropology. Rather, it is a theological construct of the whole person based on theological patterns and linguistic correlations within the Hebrew biblical text. This is properly described as a theological engagement of Scripture. A Danish study with similar linguistic interests was published in an earlier generation as if it were a historical description. See J. Pedersen, *Israel: Its Life and Culture*, vols. 1–2. Also see A.R. Johnson, *The Vitality of the Individual in the Thought of Ancient Israel*. Sharp criticism of the claim that the conclusions were historical descriptions was correctly made by James Barr in 1961. See J. Barr, *The Semantics of Biblical Language*. His insistence that scholars distinguish between words and concepts is also helpful. This does not, however, diminish the value of understanding the range of meaning of words in their context. Words have their meanings and ancient concepts may still be discerned. The caution taken is in the relationship between them. See M. Brown's discussion of J. Barr's concern regarding "root fallacy" and semantic ranges. Michael Brown, *Israel's Divine Healer*, 25–26; and J. Green, *Body, Soul, and Human Life*, 14–15.

from the beginning. "Heart," "soul," and "might" in this context describe a healthy, complete, created human being, turned toward loving God. These concepts provide a human geography of wellness, healthy communities, and human flourishing.

By contrast the words *body, mind,* and *soul* are the most common words used today to describe the aspects of a complete person, even among people who claim Scripture as a source of understanding the world. The World Health Organization constitution of 1948 described a person as *body, mind,* and *socially related.*[41] In 1984 the thirty-seventh assembly of the WHO concluded that *a spiritual dimension* should be included in the definition. This represents the functioning western world perspective: body, mind, socially related, with *spirituality* added on.

Although medical science deals primarily with seeking cures through diagnosing physical symptoms, researching physical causes of illness, and administering physiological and psychologically based treatments, increasingly health care takes the whole person into account. An understanding of the patient's heart-mind decisions, the relational and embodied dimensions of illness and health, and a broad range of resources for restoring or supplementing a patient's vitality can assist with the integrated care and treatment of the person as a whole.

If the ancient biblical text is taken as a guide for defining the well-being of the heart-mind (*levav*), the person in social relationship (*nephesh*), and all its sources for vitality (*me'od*), then the so-called spiritual dimension cannot simply be pasted on like a poultice to a person's chest. By definition and in every dimension of living, the God of Scripture is witnessed as the source and goal of our individual and communal health. God's acts of deliverance are the context given for living with and loving God. This is more than "spirituality." It is the source of wholeness and health.

Section two (chapters four through six) is centered on the words of the *Shema,* interpreted in the midst of their narrative and relational context.[42] In these chapters, it will become apparent that the Hebrew

41. This three-part division of the human person was offered in 1948 by the World Health Organization constitution. It describes a healthy person in terms of "physical, mental, and social well-being."

42. On the danger of having a "broad theological definition" of health, see Allen Verhey, "Health and Healing in Memory of Jesus." I agree that it is dangerous to misuse definitions of health, especially through abstraction from the biblical text. There is no

meanings of "heart," "soul," and "might" do not divide neatly along the lines of the typical "body, mind, soul, and social" distinctions. Neither do they, as it may first appear, ignore the physical body! Rather, they address the matrices of the human will (*levav*), the realm of embodied human relationships (*nephesh*), and the sources of human vitality (*meʾod*) as gifts of God. In the search for a broader description of health, we find that the *Shema* provides an anthropology grounded in a patient's heart-mind decisions, the relational dimensions of health and illness, and a broad range of resources for restoring or sustaining a person's vitality. Each of these concepts in turn will be investigated in chapters four, five, and six.

---

doubt that the ideas of suffering and salvation have been misused in the history of the church. Nonetheless, the way forward is not through avoidance of definition, but by interpreting biblical concepts within their biblical and theocentric contexts.

Part Two

Primary Word Concepts

Chapter Four

Levav: What is a Whole Heart?

"You shall love the LORD your God with all your heart . . ."

Deut 6:5a

"Blessed are the pure in heart, for they will see God."

Matt 5:8

Introduction

IN ENGLISH, "HEART" HAS a wide array of peculiar meanings. It is widely used in country songs ("Achy Breaky Heart"), by coaches (put some "heart" in it!), to describe certain movie stars ("heartthrob"), and literally, to describe our most crucial organ. The same word, appearing frequently in English translations of the Bible, is originally the Hebrew word *levav*, the meaning of which includes intelligence and decision-making as well as emotion.[1] It is also translated as other English words, including mind, will, and sense. The original meanings give us a window into the broad concept and the intention of the *Shema* when it says

---

1. The Hebrew word *levav* also appears as *lev*. Lexical studies have shown that these words are used interchangeably and have no difference in meaning.

to love God with "all your *levav*." The meaning shifts slightly in New Testament Greek texts.

The second part of this chapter, "Sick and Broken Hearts," looks at biblical texts and terms that describe a "heart" or "heart-mind," that is dis-integrated or "not whole." The psychological practice of cognitive therapy uses a similar understanding in its work on uniting the beliefs and decisions/actions of patients. This section will also survey terms used to describe hearts where the beliefs and actions are internally consistent, but are dead set against loving God and others.

The final section of this chapter identifies key biblical concepts associated with whole, healthy, and integrated hearts unified in loving God and others. A healthy, whole heart is active and is known by its decisions and practices. The narrative links a whole heart and a person's integrity, attention to God's revelation, worship, and justice. Finally, recent studies in neuroscience demonstrate that attention to God is a leading edge of human growth and health, and further the evidence for the congruent heart-mind as a necessary component of healthy human life.

What is "Your Whole Heart"?

THE ENGLISH USE OF the word "heart" reflects a dualism between the human heart and the mind. In English, the "heart" is the seat of the emotions and the mind is for thinking. This split is inherited from the European enlightenment, during which Pascal famously said (originally in French), "The heart has its reasons that Reason knows not of." Hebrew treats the dualistic split between head and heart (reason and emotion) as a sickness.

The Hebrew term *levav*, translated as "heart," is more accurately understood as the "heart-mind."[2] The "heart" (*levav*) is the seat of decision-making, the will, and understanding. It is the seat of mental-emotional well-being. It can be conceived as the *integration* of a person's intelligence and passions.[3] A whole and healthy *levav* is an integration

2. The ancient Hebrew was not substantially different in feeling and thinking. They just used a different set of words to describe and integrate them.

3. In his magisterial survey, J. Preuss said that in the Hebrew Bible, the heart is the seat of the psyche. See Preuss, *Biblical and Talmudic Medicine*, 104. Rabbinic Judaism later followed Platonic categories in assigning emotion to the heart and the logical

of your passions and your intellect in a unified will that becomes your identity in the community.

In the *Shema* the expression, "with all your heart" is better translated "with your whole heart." The *Shema* says, "Love God with that" and, as we shall see, it means to love others with that integration as well. It means that all your talents, abilities, and attention are focused on living a life that honors God and causes others to give thanks to God for you.

Various meanings of "heart" (levav)

When the *Shema* uses the word *levav* "heart," a broad range of meanings are included.[4] The whole concept, however, is not present every time the word appears in a sentence. The broad range illustrated below demonstrates the many specific meanings of *levav* in the Hebrew Bible. Together they form a composite view of the *concept of* wholeness of the "heart."

The word is used eight hundred and fifty three times in the Hebrew Bible. Each context emphasizes one or more of the aspects of the human heart (*levav*).[5] A survey of the contextual meaning of the word reveals a wide representation of each of the aspects named below.

Intelligence (the noetic center) is located in the human "heart-mind." *Levav* is translated "mind" or "understanding" thirty-eight times. Even when it is translated "heart" it often means intelligence.[6] Various aspects of intelligence are represented.[7]

---

control of emotion to the "soul." See *Midrash Rabbah* Eccl. 1:16 and Fred Rosner, *Medicine in the Bible and the Talmud*, 77–80.

4. The lexicographical meanings reflect the range: 1. the heart; 2. seat of vital force; 3. one's inner self; 4. inclination; 5. determination; 6. the will; 7. attention, reason; 8. the mind; 9. the conscience; 10. inside, middle. Kohler and Baumgartner, *The Hebrew and Aramaic Lexicon*, 13–15. The heart refers to "the center of the human physical and spiritual life [and] to the entire inner life of a person." Alex Luc, "lev," in *New International Dictionary of Old Testament Theology and Exegesis*, 2:749–54. See M. Brown's discussion of J. Barr's concern regarding "root fallacy" and semantic ranges. Michael Brown, *Israel's Divine Healer*, 25–26.

5. The categories and statistics that follow are from H. J. Fabry, "*leb, lebab*" in *Theological Dictionary of the Old Testament*, 7:399–437.

6. Ibid., 419–23. The *niphal* form the verb form of *levav* means "become intelligent."

7. Hebrew does distinguish the process of thinking using the word *da'at* (from *yadah*), but this too is a function of the *levav*. The *levav* is the center of consciousness.

- The *levav* "heart" is the seat of *wisdom and acuity*. "The wise of heart is called "perceptive" and "pleasant speech increases persuasiveness" (Prov 16:21). *Cognition* takes place in the *levav*: "Joab . . . perceived that the king's mind (*levav*) was on Absalom" (Deut 28:4) and "The minds (*levav*) of the rash will have good judgment, and the tongues of stammerers will speak readily and distinctly" (Isa 32:4). The *levav* "heart," does all the *remembering* in the Bible. "Remember this and consider, recall it to mind (*levav*)" (Isa 46:8a). Confusion and stupidity are also located in one's *levav* "heart." "Those who *did* not *regard* [make room in their heart for] the word of the LORD left their slaves and livestock in the open field" (Exod 9:21) and "I observed among the youths, a young man without *sense* [needing a heart]" (Prov 7:7b).

- The *"heart-mind" is also the seat of the passions (directed emotions or affective center)*. Often, when *levav* is used, the emotive side of one's will is primary.[8]

  - In *gladness, joy, and sadness*: "A glad heart makes a cheerful countenance, but by sorrow of heart the spirit is broken" (Prov 15:13) and "Your words were found, and I ate them, and your words became to me a joy and the delight of my heart; for I am called by your name, O LORD, God of hosts" (Jer 15:16). In *fear and despair*: "Our kindred have made our hearts melt by reporting, "The people are stronger and taller than we" (Deut 1:28). In *affection and trust*: "Now Joab son of Zeruiah perceived that the king's mind (*levav*) was on Absalom" (2 Sam 14:1).

  - *The word "heart" (levav) also is used to describe decision making* of the highest order. In these cases, the passions and intelligence are focused in acts of the human will (also known as the volitional or ethical center).[9]

    - This includes one's *internal driving force*. "If I say, 'I will not mention him, or speak any more in his name,' then

---

Modern Hebrew uses several words for "mind" using participles that mean literally, "the *that* that thinks" and "the *that* that remembers."

8. Fabry, *TDOT*, 414–19. Emotions themselves come from the kidney or bowel!

9. Ibid., 423–34

within me (lit. in my *levav*) there is something like a burning fire shut up in my bones" (Jer 20:9) and "So they came, both men and women; all who were of a willing heart" (Exod 35:22). The *conceiving and planning* done to attempt to accomplish one's will in the world, are done by one's *levav* "heart." "What do mortals get from all the toil and strain with which they toil under the sun? For all their days are full of pain, and their work is a vexation; even at night their minds (*levav*) do not rest. This also is vanity" (Eccl 2:22–23). It is also a synonym for *conscience.* "Afterward David was stricken to the heart because he had cut off a corner of Saul's cloak" (1 Sam 24:5).

- Finally, the *levav* "heart" is the location of virtues and vices that affect decision making: "Wait for the LORD; be strong, and let your heart take courage; wait for the LORD!" (Ps 27:14) and "You have not set your heart to honor me." (Mal 2:2)

- The concept of "your whole heart" (not divided)[10] and "all your heart" (all its aspects; not partitioned) in the *Shema* is an attempt to embrace the full spectrum of meaning of the heart-mind. The concept includes the will, thoughts, emotions, and decision-making. It is the locus of mental-emotional health, the integration of a person's passion and intelligence. When a person's intellect and passions are at odds the heart-mind is "sick" in some way. In contemporary terms we could say that the "heart" is the locus of human bio-psychological identity formation, growth, and personal transformation. It is the leading edge of a person's life.

Choices (bachar) of the Heart

Bachar ("choose" or "decide") is the primary action of the heart-mind (*levav*). The biblical tradition addresses this aspect of health in key

10. "Whole heart" is sometimes expressed with the combination of *shalom* and *levav* (see 1 Kgs 11:4; 15:3; 1 Chron 28:9; 29:19; 2 Kgs 20:3; Isa 38:3).

narrative traditions that require a person and a community to remember Israel's choices, thus forming a habit that shapes one's own life decisions.[11] It calls one to invest one's heart-mind in the tradition of good choice by remembering God's acts of deliverance and rehearsing the choices of the past.

Deuteronomy is famous for its thirtieth chapter, especially for Moses' admonition to the people to "choose" on the plains of Moab before they cross the Jordan to enter into the land promised to Abraham.

> See, I have set before you today life and prosperity, death and adversity . . . I call heaven and earth to witness against you today that I have set before you life and death, blessings and curses. Choose life, so that you and your descendants may live, loving the LORD your God, obeying him, holding fast to him; for that means life to you and length of days. (Deut 30:15, 19)

The choice seems simple but is not: choose between life and death; choose between life-preserving behaviors and life-destroying behaviors. Our experience is not substantively different than Israel's. Analogously, many of the most acute health care issues today seem simple, yet are not: tobacco and alcohol abuse, the spread of STDs, cardio-vascular disease, and physical fitness exercise. Nonetheless, the health of the heart-mind (*levav*) is related directly to choice. The choice for life is made possible in part through hearing and remembering the choices of the past. The Psalmist demonstrates this kind of investment in long-term choice in the midst of a call to worship.

> O that today you would hearken to his voice! Harden not your hearts, as at Meribah, as on the day at Massah in the wilderness, when your fathers tested me, and put me to the proof, though they had seen my work. (Ps 95:7b–11)

Moses' call to the people to "choose" was echoed by Joshua when all Israel gathered at Shechem (Josh 24:14–27). While calling for choice (*bachar*) based on the recitation of God's mighty acts (Josh 24:2–13), Joshua also declared to them the difficulty of simply choosing the LORD and a life of health. When the people declared their allegiance to the LORD, Joshua confronted them with their inability to make such a hasty decision (Josh 24:19–20). When they insisted on their choice and recited their memory of deliverance, Joshua insisted on an additional

---

11. E.g. Deut 30:15–19; Josh 24:2–14; Deut 8:1–20.

witness, a cleansing of idols, an "inclination of the heart," and a "great stone" as a physical reminder of the choice. It is possible that early Israel's tribes gathered yearly at Shechem to renew the covenant and confirm their choice.[12]

Sick and Broken Hearts

The biblical metaphor extends to the pathology of the *levav* "heart." A heart may be "sick" in a variety of ways. When the intellect and passions are united to one will or purpose, we can say a heart is "whole." When they are not, but are divided or dis-integrated, dis-ease is indicated. The heart-mind is "not whole." The holistic integration of one's intelligence and passions may be used for good or evil and for loving God or not, but its integration is the first element of a healthy heart-mind.

Dis-integrated Heart-Minds: Scripture

A series of words and metaphors are used with the Hebrew word "heart" to describe different kinds of human brokenness in relation to others and to God. Each of them, in contrast to "a whole heart," is a partial or a heart damaged in some way by a failure or inability to integrate one's intelligence and passions.

Lying and flattering for the purpose of exploiting others is described as a "double heart." "They utter lies to each other; with flattering lips and a double heart they speak. May the LORD cut off all flattering lips, the tongue that makes great boasts, those who say, "With our tongues we will prevail; our lips are our own—who is our master?" (Ps 12:2–4)

Solomon, generally known for wisdom, ironically at the end of his life lacked wholeness.

Solomon's heart was *"warped"* and *"not whole"* in his decision to invest in and pursue false gods (1 Kgs 11:4; also in 1 Kgs 15:3; 1 Chron 28:9; 29:19). By contrast, Hezekiah, whose reputation is greater than Solomon's in Scripture, followed God with a "whole heart" (2 Kgs 20:3;

12. A. Alt, M. Noth, G. E. Mendenhall, and others suggested that Israel gathered yearly, or alternately, every seven years, perhaps for the Feast of Booths, at Shechem for a covenant renewal ceremony. See G. E. Mendenhall, *Law and Covenant in Israel and the Ancient Near East.*

Isa 38:3). The nation became a divided kingdom because of Solomon's policies (1 Kings 11–12). Under Hezekiah's reform and leadership, it saw its finest hour (2 Kings 18–20).

Ezekiel proclaimed hope for the exiles when he used two "heart" metaphors for their brokenness. God said, "I will give them *one heart*" in contrast to their previous pursuit of many abominations. Secondly, he said, "I will remove the *heart of stone* from their flesh and give them *a heart of flesh*" indicating their lack of love for the Creator of their flesh.

A "*deficiency of*" or "*lacking*" *a heart* is an expression used for broken marital relationships. "He who commits adultery *has no sense* (lit. "has a deficiency of *levav*"); he who does it destroys himself" (Prov 6:32).

People with dis-integrated hearts have difficulty making decisions with integrity. They often demonstrate actions opposed to their stated values, as when someone says, "I acknowledge that stealing is wrong, but I need money to pay my debts" or "I acknowledge that in general adultery is destructive, but my case will be different." In Scripture this is a description of self-delusion and illness. The heart-mind is ill because it is not integrated.[13] This is also called commonly called hypocrisy.

Paul of Tarsus described a classic example of this illness in his autobiographical comments.

> I do not understand my own actions. For I do not do what I want, but I do the very thing I hate. Now if I do what I do not want, I agree that the law is good. But in fact it is no longer I that do it, but sin that dwells within me. For I know that nothing good dwells within me, that is, in my flesh. I can will what is right, but I cannot do it. For I do not do the good I want, but the evil I do not want is what I do. (Rom 7:15–19)[14]

Genesis 3:10 illustrates alienated selves (Adam and Eve) who had previously had an integrated identity. Eating from the tree while

---

13. A recent survey of adolescents indicates the common acceptance of such dis-integration. Intense feelings of abandonment by adults have led to the formation of a youth culture of isolation. Chap Clark, *Hurt: Inside the World of Today's Teenagers*, 42, 146–152.

14. For a discussion of the interpretations of Paul on conversion see S. J. Chester, *Conversion at Corinth*.

knowing it was wrong was a divided heart in action.[15] Before the "sin" that split them in two, they were not afraid, but walked with God in the garden "in the cool of the evening;" they were not self-conscious, but at home in their bodies; and they did not "hide" to avoid relationship with God.

After the sin, Adam made a variety of comments to God that demonstrated his newly found disintegration. God asked the therapeutic question, "Where are you?" Adam's rapid and alienated responses are telling: "I heard the sound of you; I was afraid; I knew I was vulnerable (naked); and I hid myself." (See Gen 2:9–10.)[16]

Adam's and Eve's hearts had been divided. A reintegration was possible, in spite of the enduring consequences of the "original sin." Their reconciliation with God is seen as God clothes them and remains present to them. God claims to be present and to "dwell with" those whose hearts are "broken."

> I dwell in the high and holy place, *and also with those who are broken* and humble in spirit, to revive the spirit of the humble, *and to revive the heart of the broken* . . . I have seen their ways, but I will heal them. (Is 57:15b, 18a)

Life-changing events always require re-integration of the heart, whether they are traumatically negative or dramatically positive. Post-traumatic symptoms may require community or professional help for the one who has difficulty in processing, making "sense" of, and integrating experiences of trauma. Turning to faith in God also requires a process of reintegrating the intelligence and passions in relation to the new experiential data found in loving God and being loved by God.

---

15. See chapter one, "Consequences of Self-Deception: Heavy Relational Losses."

16. More pedestrian examples of disintegration and reintegration of a divided heart are possible. The re-integration of a heart takes place and in many ways in human experience, but it always takes some time. A common experience is going on vacation and finding that you cannot relax because, for the first three days your "heart" is still integrating the events of the past weeks and months. People who practice religious disciplines of silent retreat for prayer and meditation often find that three or four days are required to begin to hear God speak.

Dis-integrated Heart-Minds: Insights from Cognitive Psychotherapy

Cognitive therapy provides examples of contemporary reflection on dis-integrated heart-minds. It is a treatment that helps a person identity the dysfunctional beliefs that lead to a variety of psychological and behavioral disorders.[17] The paradigm works at a similar intersection of thoughts, passions, will, and behaviors as that described by the Hebrew word-concept *levav*. It helps a patient identify and record the distortions in their information processing that lead to self-destructive behaviors.

Cognitive therapists treat a variety of disorders and illnesses including depression, panic disorder, agoraphobia, social phobia, obsessive-compulsive disorder, bulimia, personality disorders, and impulse control disorders (including family violence). These problems occur when "erroneous core beliefs distort information in a maladaptive fashion and generate inaccurate perceptions and inferences in specific situations."[18] The issues rise generally from "automatic thoughts" with specific negative interpretations that rise unbidden in the person's ongoing stream-of-consciousness. By identifying the consciously accessible negative thinking and maladaptive information processing, a patient may begin to generate alternative explanations for problematic events in his or her life. Dysfunctional beliefs and information distortions often have their root in dysfunctional core beliefs of the person's larger meaning systems.

The Lord God may have been the first cognitive therapist. When Cain was vexed, trying to figure out what to do about his brother Abel, God asked him, "Is it good for you, for you to be angry?" This attempt to help Cain process his anger through an examination of his thought process was ultimately unsuccessful, but it demonstrates the method.[19] God often makes claims in Scripture about functional and dysfunctional core beliefs by asking questions or pointing out erroneous thinking. For example:

---

17. A.T. Beck, "Cognitive Therapy" in *Encyclopedia of Psychology*, vol. 2, 169–72. See also J.P. Foreyt and G.K. Goodrick, "Cognitive Behavior Therapy" in *Encyclopedia of Psychology*, 2nd edition, ed., vol. 1, 245 –48.

18. Beck, "Cognitive Therapy," 169.

19. God may have been more successful with Jonah. See Jonah 4:3–11 where Jonah is depressed and wants to die.

"To whom then will you compare me, or who is my equal?" says the Holy One.

> Lift up your eyes on high and see: Who created these [stars]? Why do you say, O Jacob, and speak, O Israel, "My way is hidden from the LORD, and my right is disregarded by my God"? Have you not known? Have you not heard? The LORD is the everlasting God, the Creator of the ends of the earth. He does not faint or grow weary; his understanding is unsearchable. He gives power to the faint, and strengthens the powerless. (Isa 40:25, 27–29)

This questioning represents the dysfunctional core beliefs repeatedly addressed in Scripture: the denial of one's created status and denial of the network of relationships of God's provision. The language of the *levav* is again the focus.

> You said, "I shall be mistress forever," so that you did not lay these things to heart or remember their end. Now therefore hear this, you lover of pleasures, who sit securely, who say in your heart, "I am, and there is no one besides me." . . . You felt secure in your wickedness; you said, "No one sees me." Your wisdom and your knowledge led you astray, and you said in your heart, "I am, and there is no one besides me." (Isa 47:7–8, 10)

These basic distortions, that "I am self-made" and "I am self-sustaining" reflect and aggravate a dis-integration of the heart-mind. The claim is that this dis-integration has the potential to lead to both psychological and physiological consequences. For this reason, Scripture often focuses on human choices of allegiance and behavior as a primary factor of the healthy heart-mind.

A Grieving Heart

A person with a whole and integrated heart turned toward their neighbor and toward God may be sick, nonetheless, due to external circumstances. Nehemiah experienced a sickness of his whole heart while in Persia, thinking of the rubble that once was Jerusalem (Neh 2:2). Jeremiah experienced it while being faithful in the midst of a corrupt people (Jer 8:18).

A common external cause of grief of the heart and sickness is in relation to one's enemy. The expression "melted hearts" is used to describe the experience of fear of a stronger opposing force (Deut 1:28; 20:8; Josh 5:1; 14). In the Psalms, the "enemy" is abstracted and the trouble is unspecified in relation to one's enemies. For example,

> How long must I bear pain in my soul, and have sorrow in my heart all day long? How long shall my enemy be exalted over me? Consider and answer me, O LORD my God! Give light to my eyes, or I will sleep the sleep of death, and my enemy will say, "I have prevailed;" my foes will rejoice because I am shaken. (Ps 13:2–4)

Sickness may ensue when one is assailed by slanderers.

> But you, O LORD my Lord, act on my behalf for your name's sake; because your steadfast love is good, deliver me. For I am poor and needy, and *my heart is pierced within me*. I am gone like a shadow at evening; I am shaken off like a locust. My knees are weak through fasting; my body has become gaunt. I am an object of scorn to my accusers; when they see me, they shake their heads. Help me, O LORD my God! Save me according to your steadfast love. (Ps 109:21–26)

When the Psalmist describes physical attack, he says,

> I am poured out like water . . . my heart is like wax; it is melted in the midst of my bowels. (Ps 22:14 KJV)

Lament in the midst of grief is an opportunity for healing and the restoration of relationships, according to Scripture. Relief from the oppression is the healing that is sought by the lamenter, but healing begins within the lamenting. A person with a previously divided heart may find the new situation that causes grief to be an opportunity for a broader healing and the restoration of a whole heart, even in the midst of grief. The subject of healing through lament will be addressed in chapter eight.

Whole Heart-Minds Set Against God and Others

Human health in Scripture can be measured in part by whether or not a heart-mind is whole or not. Its integration is the first element of health from this etymological perspective. The second element of health, however, involves the *purpose* of that integration. The terminology of the ancient text uses a variety of expressions to describe whole and integrated hearts that are set against loving God and others.

The integration of one's intelligence and passions may be used, of course, for selfish or even evil purposes. The powerful dictators of the world use this integration quite effectively for their own ends. Scripture equates the abuse of the powerless with unfaithfulness to God. In this worldview, unfaithfulness to God through the worship of false gods always leads to the abuse of God's good creation. For example, when the Pharaoh refused to let the Hebrew slaves go, it was described as a refusal to let them worship God. In the prophets, the legal and economic abuse of the powerless is considered sin and rebellion against God. Their standards reflect standards of justice and mercy established in biblical law (*torah*). A failure to love God with a whole heart is also a refusal to love one's neighbor.[20]

Several expressions are used for this kind of whole hearted rebellion against God: haughty and arrogant hearts (Prov 16:5; 18:12; Obad 1:3); hearts turned away from God (Deut 30:17; Jer 17:15); hearts that desert God (Ps 40:13); hearts that go astray and go after idols (Isa 21:4; Ezek 20:16); hearts that are unfaithful (Prov 14:14) and false (Hos 10:2); hearts that are deluded and seduced into serving other gods (Deut 11:16); and "fat-hearted" meaning a lack of compassion in relation to others and arrogance in relation to God (Ps 119:70; 17:10; Isa 6:10). When one is actively resisting God, the person is described as being stubborn or "hard-hearted" in decision (Exod 7:13; Ps 95:8; Deut 29:19).[21]

The most extreme expression of the unified heart against God is from Genesis 6.

> The LORD saw that the wickedness of humankind was great
> in the earth, and that every inclination of the thoughts of their
> hearts was only evil continually. And the LORD was sorry that

20. So the *Shema* says, "love God" with your whole heart. In the last century, Stalin and Mao did not hesitate to create policies that led to the starvation of tens of millions of people, in the interest of "the people." Love of God and love of neighbor was not part of the calculation of their hearts.

21. For a fuller accounting of "hardened heart" in Exodus see J. Bruckner, *Exodus*, 95; Alex Luc, *New International Dictionary*, 750. A hardened heart is softened by prayer (a heart turned toward God) and an understanding heart-mind (perception and wisdom). See Exod 9:26–29; 10:16–19.

he had made humankind on the earth, and it grieved him to his heart. (Gen 6:5–6)

The "inclination" of the heart to evil (*yester ra'*) was manifest in corruption and violence (Gen 6:11–12). This integration of the human heart against God is measured in human terms. When people live as if there is no God, the whole society becomes sick. The prophet Jeremiah laments the slow demise and destruction of Israel in his day.

> My joy is gone, grief is upon me, my *heart is sick*. Hark, the cry of my poor people from far and wide in the land: "Is the LORD not in Zion? Is her King not in her?" Why have they provoked me to anger with their images, with their foreign idols? . . . For the hurt of my poor people I am hurt, I mourn, and dismay has taken hold of me. Is there no balm in Gilead? Is there no physician there? Why then has *the health* of my poor people not been restored? (Jer 8:18–22)

A related expression of opposition to God is "stiff-necked," used to describe a person whose heart is wholly set against loving God and neighbor.[22] The solution is the circumcision of the heart.

> Circumcise your *hearts*, therefore, and do not be *stiff-necked* any longer. For the LORD your God is God of gods and Lord of lords . . . He defends the cause of the fatherless and the widow, *and loves the alien*, giving him food and clothing. And you are to *love those who are aliens*, for you yourselves were aliens in Egypt. (Deut 10:16–19; see 30:6; Jer 4:4)

When a person with an integrated heart is turned against God, the text refers to it as evil since it results in a violent and abusive society. A "wicked heart" is one that plans to circumvent God's law of protection for the poor (Deut 15:9). So the *Shema* says to love God and to love one's neighbor with "all your heart." In the Bible both are generally measured by what one decides and does, not by good intentions.

---

22. "Stiff-necked": Exod 32:9; 33:3–5; 34:9; Deut 9:6, 13; 10:16; 31:27; 2 Kgs 17:14; 2 Chron 30:8; 36:13; Neh 9:16–17, 29; Prov 29:1; Jer 7:26; 17:23; 19:15.

An Integrated Whole Heart: Loving God[23]

The *Shema* declares that the purpose of the whole human heart-mind (intelligence-passion) is to love God. Scripture is rather specific about what "loving God" means. The basic elements of a healthy heart focused on loving God are integrity (*tamim*) of the heart itself, keeping (*shamar*) God's word, our work/worship (*'eved*) of the living God, and working for justice-righteousness (*tsedequah*) in the community by service and acts of mercy to the helpless and needy.

Psalm 119 includes each of these foci, providing a summary of whole, integrated heart of the psalmist seeking to love God.[24] The whole psalm is a prayer, attending to God in an act of praise, petition, and worship. The first stanza repeated declares the themes of integrity[25] and attention to keeping/observing God's word.[26]

> Blessed are those whose way *has integrity*, who walk in the instruction of the LORD! Blessed are those who *keep* his testimonies, who seek him with their *whole heart*, who also do no wrong, but walk in his ways! Thou hast commanded thy precepts *to be kept diligently*. O that my ways may be steadfast in *keeping thy statutes!* Then I shall not be put to shame, having my eyes fixed on all thy commandments. I will praise thee with *an upright heart*, when I learn thy *righteous* ordinances. I will *observe* thy statutes; O forsake me not utterly! (Ps 119:1–7)

These aspects of integrity and keeping occur throughout the Psalm with attention to the community, which is embedded in the "righteous" law. Justice-righteousness is measured by one's relationships in the community, which are guided by God's "testimonies," "statutes," "commandments," and "ordinances." The root for "righteous" occurs in thirteen verses and the other vocabulary over a hundred times.[27]

---

23. Portions of this section have been previously published in *Ex Auditu* 21 (2005) 1–19. A close reader will note that I have adjusted various ideas since 2005.

24. The "heart" is mentioned throughout Psalm 119 fifteen times.

25. "Integrity" (*tamim*) and its Hebrew synonym, "upright" (*yashar*), are found in Ps 119: 1, 7, 80, 128, and 137.

26. The vocabulary of "keeping" appears thirty-one times in Ps 119 (*shamar*, twenty-one times and its synonym *natsar* ten times).

27. "Righteous" and "righteousness" in Ps 119:7, 62, 75, 106, 121, 123, 138, 142, 144, 160,164, 172.

Characteristics of a Whole Heart: Integrity (tamim)

"Integrity of heart" is synonymous with "all of heart" and "a whole heart."[28] The psalmist prays, "May my heart have integrity (*tamim*; "be healthy;" NRSV: "be blameless") in thy statutes, that I may not be put to shame!"

The English meanings generated from the Hebrew root *tamam* include the following: complete, integrated, sound (of bones), whole, healthy, undivided, morally innocent, impeccable, honest, blameless, free of blemish, unscathed (of sheep for sacrifice).[29]

"Integrity" means having an undivided heart-mind in relation to God. "Noah was a righteous man, with integrity (*tamim*; or "blameless") among the people of his time, and he walked with God" (Gen 6:9). Noah was undivided in his heart-mind, i.e., he was a person whose intelligence and passions were integrated in relation to God. The psalmist declares, "Blessed are those whose way has integrity" (Ps 119:1a).

"Integrity" (*tamim*) also means undivided motivation in relationship to others. In the book of Genesis, Abraham and Sarah told King Abimelech of Gerar that Sarah was Abraham's sister. As a result, she was added to the king's harem. God came to Abimelech in a dream and told him he was about to die because Sarah, another man's wife, was in his tent. Abimelech's response, accepted by God, was "I am innocent. I acted in integrity" (Gen 20:5). This relational integrity meant that Abimelech acted in good conscience in accordance with the facts that he knew. God recognized this as integrity, even though those facts were in error.

The concept of integrity is rooted in the realm of sacrificial law. Here it means the coordination of one's intention and one's action. It means not cheating. The instructions for a peace (*shalom*) offering were to burn up the whole (*tamimah*) rump (the entire fat of the tail) of the sheep (Lev 3:9). The intention of the one bringing this kind of offering was to give thanks to the LORD. To have this intention, and hold back some of the fat for oneself would have been disingenuous. It would lack integrity (*tamim*).

28. A. Luc, *leb/lebab*, 751.

29. L. Kohler and W. Baumgartner, *The Hebrew and Aramaic Lexicon of the Old Testament*, II:1748–50.

*Characteristics of a Whole Heart: Keeping (*shamar*)*

The second aspect of loving God with a whole heart is "keeping" (*shamar*) God's revealed instruction. The word *shamar* is used repeatedly and specifically of the Sinaitic commands, especially by the deuteronomist. One cannot overestimate the centrality of the memory of the Exodus and the consolidation and formation of a new sociality created in Israel through the giving of the Torah (instruction).

Shamar is like a code-word in Scripture for keeping the instruction and commandments given at Sinai. Keep and be kept. "Keep in mind, watch, guard, preserve, take care of, treasure up, retain, observe, protect as property in trust."[30] It means attending to God's word by regularly hearing or reading to keep your understanding fresh and integrated with new levels of your understanding of the world.

In English a "keeper" may be an archivist who cares for inherited treasures or a soccer goal keeper. In each case, focused attention is necessary. Ongoing attention is necessary to make sure something vital to your health remains in your life, even if difficult to keep it there: tending the goal; daily interaction; protecting; and awareness of slippage.

One scholar explains the meaning as "an act of watchful protection" demonstrating that God engages in similar activity on our behalf: "Watch over (*shamar*) me God" (Ps 16:1); "Keep (*shamar*) me as the apple of your eye" (Ps 17:8); and "Preserve (*shamar*) my life" (Ps 86:2).[31]

The first indication that "keeping" God's instruction is vital to a healthy heart-mind is in Genesis 2:15. "The LORD God took the man and put him in the Garden of Eden to till it and *keep (*shamar*) it.*"[32] "Keeping" is the heart of the ideal partnership established by God for human thriving. The means of "diligently keeping" (*shamar*) the commands is very specific in the *Shema*. It means learning, teaching, talking, binding, and writing the words of God.

> And *these words*, that I am commanding you today, *shall be on your heart*; and *you shall teach them diligently* to your children and *shall talk of them* when you sit in your house and when you

30. Brown, Driver, Briggs, *A Hebrew Lexicon*, 1036. For a sampling of the admonition to keep God's instruction, see: Exod 19:5; 20:6; Lev 18:5, 26; 19:19, 37; 20:8, 22; 22:31; Num 15:22; Deut 4:2, 40; 5:10, 29; 6:17; 7:9; 8:2; 11:1; 13:4; 26:17, 18; 27:1; 28:9; 30:10, 16.

31. Ellen Davis, *Getting Involved with God*, 194.

32. See "What is Good Dominion?" in chapter one.

> walk by the way and when you lie down and when you rise up.
> *And you shall bind them* as a sign on your hand and they shall
> be as frontlets on your forehead. *And you shall write them* on
> the doorposts of your house and on your gates . . . *You should
> diligently keep* (*shamor tishmerun*) the commandments of the
> LORD your God, and His testimonies and His statutes that He
> has commanded you. (Deut 6:6–9, 17–18a)

Keeping and being kept is a primary theme of Psalm 119. The psalmist celebrates God's instruction in Scripture as such a treasure. He
expresses love for God's law because of the way it has expanded and
transformed and kept his life precious. The Psalm begins, as we saw
above, with the claim that those who learn God's word with a whole
heart will be blessed (v. 1) and will praise him for it (v. 7). The psalmist
memorizes the word: "I have laid up thy word in my heart" (v. 11); runs
(v. 32) and walks (v. 59) in the way by living according to the torah; and
asks the Lord to expand his heart (understanding of and desire for) for
the life-giving way of the Lord (vv. 32, 34, 36).

The New Testament celebrates God's word as enduring and powerful. Jesus asserted that no part of it will pass away as long as the earth
endures.[33] In the same sermon he intensified the commandments to
include the *thoughts of one's heart*. "You shall not kill" includes insulting
a sister or brother. "You shall not commit adultery" includes looking
with lust.[34] The epistle to the Hebrews carries a similar awe for the word
of God and its value for the integrity of the human heart:

> Indeed, the *word of God* is living and active, sharper than any
> two-edged sword, piercing until it divides soul from spirit, joints
> from marrow; it is able to judge the thoughts and *intentions of
> the heart*. (Heb 4:12)

Characteristics of a Whole Heart: Worship and Work ('Eved)

The third aspect of loving God with a whole heart is attending to God's
worship and one's work. This is reflected in the Hebrew word *'eved*,
which means both "worship" and "work," with the general meaning of

33. Matt 5:18.

34. Matt 5:17–37. See also the discussion on the Ten Commandments in chapter
two.

"serve." The concept of *'eved* relies heavily on its biblical context for its translation. Its first meaning is to "till" the ground or more generally to "work" or "labor." In relation to daily employment it is translated "to serve in order to acquire" or "to do business." In a cultic setting it is translated "to worship" or "to honor" God.

Sabbath keeping as worship is central in Scripture but "serving" the LORD in one's daily employment through ethical practices is also essential for a healthy individual and community. When the ethics of daily action and worship became separated in Israel, the prophets expressed God's outrage. "I hate, I despise your religious feasts, and I cannot stand your solemn assemblies" (Amos 5:21). Expression of God's "hate" is reserved for this kind of "sick" separation (a divided heart) as well as for the worship (*'eved*) and serving (*'eved*) of other gods (Jer 44:4). It is considered hypocrisy.

A primary biblical narrative for understanding idealized relationships between people, work, and God is in Adam's work with God in naming the animals. God plants a garden and places the human in it "to serve" (*'eved*) and "keep" (*shamar*) it.[35] God formed the animals and brought them to the human to see what he would name them. "And whatever the human called every living creature that was its name" (Gen 2:19b).

Adam "works" (*'eved*) with God.[36] Within the boundaries of God's creative action, Adam had freedom to participate in the ordering of the world and in the work of God. God also had placed a forbidden tree in the garden to provide the ideal possibility that each day the human would choose to trust God's word that it would be better not to eat from it. In this way, the human's restraint was an act of acknowledgement and worship (*'eved*) of God. Recognizing this boundary on a daily basis was also Adam's act of service (*'eved*). All the other trees of creation were within his freedom to experience and control.

This implied proposal at Eden is made more explicitly at Sinai. There the people are instructed to tell the truth about who God is through acts of worship. They repeatedly tell the story of deliverance,

35. Ellen Davis translates this "work and watch it" highlighting the fact that one always "works for" someone. She also notes that "watching" the soil means protecting its fertility according to "divinely established rules and constraints attached to our use of the soil." Davis, *Getting Involved*, 192–93.

36. See J. K. Bruckner, "Boundary and Freedom: Blessings in the Garden of Eden."

praising God for creating, rescuing, and sustaining life. A person with an integrated heart-mind in Scripture serves (`eved`) God in daily work (`'eved`) and worship (`'eved`).

Characteristics of a Whole Heart: Justice (tsedeqah)

The fourth aspect of loving God with a whole heart is the practice of *tsedeqah*, meaning both "justice" and "righteousness." *Tsedaqah* generally refers to external and observable actions in the community, not to one's motives or intentions. A *tsadiq* (righteous person) is simply a person whose good reputation is known in the community. The content of one's reputation especially includes acts of compassion and mercy to the poor.[37]

In the Wisdom Literature (esp. Job and Proverbs) a *tsadiq* has specific characteristics. This person cares for the poor, the fatherless, and widows, defends their causes in court, is a good steward of land and the non-human creation, lives at peace with neighbors, and is a joy to the family.[38] The actions of a *tsadiq* clearly contribute to the long term health and well-being of the community.

The law is clear about serving God with a whole heart by loving one's neighbor.[39] As was noted in chapter three, this became part of the Jesus' summary of the law: love God, love your neighbor (Deut 6:5; Lev 19:18). The law expresses that those with whole hearts will *love*. Loving is a means to a whole heart, especially in loving those who are difficult to love in any community. The law designates the people least likely to receive just care, much less love, and declares: "You shall love the immigrant as yourself, for you were immigrants in the land of Egypt: I am the LORD your God" (Lev 19:34b; also in Deut 10:19). Loving "those people," of course, requires intelligent action, not just warm feelings. Widows, orphans, and the very poor are also repeatedly named.[40]

---

37. See Mogensen's discussion of J. Pedersen's contribution concerning *justia salutifera*. Bent Mogensen, "*Sedaqa* in the Scandinavian and German Research Traditions," 67–80.

38. See J. R. Donahue, S.J., "Biblical Perspectives on Justice," in *The Faith that Does Justice*, 70.

39. In a famous story about a Samaritan, Jesus defined "neighbor" as the one who gives aid to the one in desperate need. See Luke 10:27–37.

40. See e.g., Deut 10:18; 24:19–21; 27:9.

The biblical concept of justice-righteousness is based in God's commitment to compassion toward those who are being bullied, cheated or abused. Justice and righteousness are turned toward the person in anguish, the person who cries out to God for help. Israel's early tradition provides us with unequivocal words of God to Moses at Sinai, where God says that if anyone of his newly delivered slaves becomes an oppressor of widow, orphans, immigrants, or any "neighbor," God will kill his own people (Exod 22:21–24, 27).

Biblical justice means starting with loving God and neighbor. A well-know Jewish scholar offers a biblical perspective of justice:

> Justice is an interpersonal relationship implying both a claim and a responsibility. Justice bespeaks a situation that transcends the individual, demanding of everyone a certain abnegation of self, defiance of self-interest, disregard of self-respect. The necessity of submitting to a law is derived from the necessity of identifying oneself with what concerns other individuals or the whole community.[41]

Justice-righteousness (*tsedaqah*) also has a creational dimension.[42] According to the prophets, when justice is not practiced, the fish, animals, water, and trees are adversely affected. An unjust people destroy the non-human creation. Animals, birds, and fish died because of unrighteousness (Hos 4:1–3). God makes a covenant with the animals, because the people had failed (Hos 2:18). God spoke to the earth, because the people were not listening (Jer 22:29). They were warned that if they did not keep the covenant (including Sabbath rest for the land) the land would vomit them out (Deut 20:19). God comforted the soil and animals concerning the invasion of the land because of the people's unrighteousness, saying "Do not fear O soil; Do not fear, animals of the earth" (Joel 2:21–22).

When Jeremiah and Ezekiel say, "You say peace, peace (health, health) but there is no peace (health)," it is because there is no justice-righteousness (*tsedaqah*).[43] These biblical witnesses declare the necessary connection made for us by God between the health of the

---

41. A. Heschel, *The Prophets: An Introduction*, vol. 1, 209.

42. On the use of the term "creational" in place of the political and clinical term "environmental" see U. Duchrow and G. Liedke, *Shalom: Biblical Perspectives on Creation, Justice, and Peace*, 48–49.

43. Jer 6:13–14; 8:11; Isa 57:19–21.

environment and human health. Isaiah and Jeremiah broadened Israel's concept of justice and shalom by insisting that the innocent who suffer must be given a voice in society, for this is redemptive for the society.[44]

In the New Testament, the links between justice, justification of the sinner, and the righteousness-justice of Christ are a central concept. Justification and justice are inextricably tied together, part of the transformation of the whole heart. They all come from the same linguistic root, in Greek and in Hebrew, though the English masks the connection.[45] Christian justification is made possible by Christ's righteousness-justice in the great interchange of the cross.[46] Acts of justice must be done by Christians, no longer as a works-righteousness but because Christians have been made "ambassadors" of Christ's righteousness, justice, and justification. This means that the gospel and justice, as in the best practices of Christianity, come together. The challenge to the church is to display this undeserved justification/justice as living sacrifices (Rom 12:1). This is done by not returning evil for evil but overcoming evil with good (Rom 12:21). Christians are admonished to give their enemies water when they are thirsty, as a surprising witness to a surprising gospel which calls sinners to be made right with God (Rom 12:20). In this way, Paul writes, Christians participate in the ministry of reconciliation, "since God is making his appeal through us" (2 Cor 5:20).[47] The interior and the exterior life act as one in a whole

44. H.C. White, *Shalom in the Old Testament*, 25.

45. The Hebrew *tsedeqah* is translated both "righteousness" and "justice" as are the Greek noun *dikaiosyne*, and verb *dikaioo*. All the English manifestations are present in Romans 3:24–26 (NRSV; English translations vary widely because the word associations are so close): They are now justified (*dikaioo*) by his grace as a gift, through the redemption that is in Christ Jesus, whom God put forward as a sacrifice of atonement by his blood, effective through faith. He did this to show his righteousness (*dikaiosyne*), because in his divine forbearance he had passed over the sins previously committed; it was to prove at the present time that he himself is righteous (*dikaios*) and that he justifies (*dikaioo*) the one who has faith in Jesus.

46. For our sake he [God] made him [Jesus] to be sin who knew no sin, so that in him we might become the righteousness/justice of God (2 Cor 5:21).

47. New Testament scholar Max Lee comments on 2 Corinthians 5:18–21: "Justice, like evangelism, is a means by which human beings can encounter the risen Lord. The Christian activist who fights for justice and the evangelist who preaches the gospel work together, hand in hand, to share the message of reconciliation to a dying world . . . At the same time, we are willing to suspend justice and vindication *for ourselves* so that the greater work of reconciling our enemies to Christ can become a reality. We are called to follow Jesus into those dark places where human dignity

heart, growing in acts of mercy, even as personal change is effected by the love of God.

Growth of the Heart-Mind: Neuroscience and Scripture

In Scripture, the heart-mind is the cutting edge of human formation in each person as they grow in understanding, relationship, and practice throughout their life. In contemporary terms we could say that it is the seat of human bio-psychological identity formation, growth, and personal transformation.

The heart-mind is the dynamic personal surface of change. It is constantly receiving information and understanding, processing experiences, rejecting and accepting truth claims, and integrating ideas and feelings in new combinations. The heart-mind is the place where a person's identity is shaped and can be transformed by new understanding. Growth happens in the *levav*.

Recent research by neuroscientists on the brain and religious experience offers insight into growth in the human heart-mind. Though many scientists agree that religious experiences and practices are generally life-affirming,[48] neuroscientists are interested in the growth of the capacity for *wonder* in the human brain.[49] Studies show that an experience of wonder initially creates disequilibrium in the brain, followed by a reassessment of reality through reintegration. This leads to the growth of the heart-mind (in biblical terms).

Experiences of wonder are described as follows.

> Wonder—a surprising encounter with something that strikes a person as uniquely real, true, and/or beautiful . . . Deeply rooted in the biological processes of the body, defying all externally imposed constrictions, continually decentering and recentering the self in its relation to the ever-changing world, the power to create new visionary worlds is what enables humans to grow and flourish . . . the clearest indication that this visionary power

stands in jeopardy, sin rules, and misery is rampant. Wherever there is suffering and despair, Jesus is waiting for the church to interfere . . . The love of Christ compels us to enter the fray as ambassadors of the just and reconciling God. He is on mission to save fallen humanity" (forthcoming).

48. See Kelly Bulkeley: *The Wondering Mind*, 35–43. See chapter six in this book, "All Your Might," for more on this basic idea of human growth.

49. Bulkeley builds on the work of Lee Irwin, *Visionary Worlds*.

is alive and well in peoples' lives is the frequency with which
they experience moments of wonder.[50]

Scripture has many verbs to describe the kind of growing experiences possible in relation to God and the world. The heart-mind may
"tremble" and "leap" in the midst of a powerful storm (Job 37:1).
It may ponder difficult questions and answers (Prov 15:28). It may
"overflow" with poetic verse, praising something wonderful (Ps 45:1)
or "grow hot" with the dissonance of a difficult experience and write
a song of distress (Ps 39:3). The hearts/minds of a whole community
may "overflow," being "stirred" to give far more than is needed in their
generosity (Exod 36:2–7).

Growth begins when a heart is "inclined" toward God, or one
asks for God to cause the inclination to "grow" or "widen" one's heart
(Ps 119:32, 36).[51] A psalmist reflects on the experience of being transformed from bitterness of heart to new unexplained confidence that
God will be the strength of his heart forever (Ps 73:21–22, 26). Affliction is sometimes the agent that leads to growth because it shocks
an unresponsive "fat heart" (Ps 119:70–71). Neuroscience notes that
experiences of wonder often leave a person overwhelmed, disoriented
and vulnerable until reintegration takes place.[52] Some growth comes
through the experience of the conviction of sin, repentance, and God's
forgiveness. The promise in Scripture is that God is capable and willing
to give people a new heart-mind through repentance.

> *A new heart I will give you*, and a new spirit I will put within you;
> and I will remove from your body the heart of stone and give
> you a heart of flesh. (Ezek 36:26)
>
> Repent and turn from all your transgressions; otherwise
> iniquity will be your ruin. Cast away from you all the transgres-
> sions that you have committed against me, *and get yourselves a
> new heart* and a new spirit! Why will you die, O house of Israel?
> For I have no pleasure in the death of anyone, says the Lord
> GOD. Turn, then, and live. (Ezek 18:30–32; see also Deut 4:29;
> Jer 24:6–7; 32:39–41)

50. Bulkeley, *The Wondering Mind*, 42.

51. For a summary of God's influence on the heart-mind see Fabry, *"leb/lebab,"*
425.

52. Bulkeley, 43.

The road to a healthy heart in David's psalm is through a contrite heart.[53]

> You desire truth in the inward being; therefore teach me wisdom in my secret heart. Purge me with hyssop, and I shall be clean; wash me, and I shall be whiter than snow . . . Create in me a clean heart, O God, and put a new and right spirit within me . . . Restore to me the joy of your salvation, and sustain in me a willing spirit . . . The sacrifice acceptable to God is a broken spirit; a broken and contrite heart, O God, you will not despise. (Ps 51:6, 7, 10, 12, 17)

Perhaps the most often named experience of the wonder of the heart-mind in Scripture is *joy*.[54] Joy is a gift from God (Ps 4:7; Eccl 5:20).[55] The psalmist faints in worship responding with "my heart and my flesh sing for joy to the living God (Ps 84:2). Joy strengthens trust in God (Ps 33:21). It is described as "the best medicine" for the heart (Prov 17:22). The Lord's presence causes a heart-felt joy and gives one an otherwise unexplained security (Ps 16:9).[56] Exulting in joy often takes place in corporate worship as people are called to experience the joy of the Lord (Ps 105:2–3).

The author of Psalm 119 draws his reflections to a close with rejoicing, even in the context of persecution. This joy is experienced not as a fleeting emotion of gladness, but as a rich experience of wonder and reflection on God's word in the midst of trouble. "Princes persecute me without cause, but my heart stands in awe of thy words. I rejoice at thy word like one who finds great spoil." (Ps 119:161–62). The visible expression of joy is described as a glowing countenance (Isa 60:5; Prov 15:13) and the presence of "radiant enlightened eyes" (Ps 19:8).

53. Reconciliation with God is requisite to a whole heart. See e.g., Deut 30:2; 1 Kgs 12:27; Ps 94:15; Jer 24:7; Joel 2:12. False repentance is possible: Jeremiah 3:10.

54. The Hebrew word is *sameakh*. It is variously translated in English.

55. For joy as an expression of the heart-mind, see Fabry, *"leb/lebab,"* 415.

56. Whole communities may be joyful and express joy in a collective experience of God's gifts: 1 Kgs 8:66; 2 Chron 7:10; Isa 30:29; 60:5; 66:14; Zech 10:7.

Chapter Five

Nefesh: What is a Soul?

"...with all your *soul*..."

Deut 6:5b

And Mary said, "My *soul* magnifies the Lord."

Luke 1:46

Introduction

THE SOUL IS OFTEN understood as a separate aspect of a person which is somehow distinct from their body. Numerous cultures believe that death constitutes a dead body and a soul which somehow, somewhere endures. Many, if not most religious people share this radically dualistic thinking. *Problematically, this is not the biblical witness or what is confessed in the creeds of the church.* The Scripture teaches that a soul exists, not *in* a body, but only *as a body.* The biblical Hebrew word-concept *nefesh*, (translated "soul") is integrated with both the relational and the physical, contrary to notions of a free-floating soul.

An incomplete or misguided understanding of the biblical view of the soul can lead to misconceptions about human life, death, and life beyond the grave.[1] If the life to come is viewed as "disembodied," it can directly influence how we value, respect and care for our living bodies. The original implications of the word that appears as *soul* in English Bibles have been lost in translation, aided by false hope of inherent human immortality. This chapter will show that the biblical words (Hebrew: *nefesh;* Greek: *psyche)* translated *soul* have a much wider and nuanced meaning than their English translation. Understanding the body-based and relational foundations of the original words provides a necessary and helpful shift in understanding ourselves, health in our communities, and the substance of our hope in the life to come.

This chapter will provide a history of the interpretation of the human soul, beginning with the Hebrew word *nefesh* in its various contexts, moving through the influence of Greek philosophy on Jewish and New Testament (in Greek, *psyche)* meanings of soul and concluding with the contemporary debate between monist (unified), dualist (body/soul split), and trichotomous (three-part) perspectives of the human being. The Bible and neuroscience agree that a monistic, integrated perspective balances the strictly dualistic thinking which posits the body/soul divide.

Throughout this chapter we will be maintaining and discussing three basic biblical theses:

- A person's "soul" exists, not *in* a body, but only *as a body.* The soul is physical.

- A soul-life is simple existence. Death is final; there is no inherently immortal soul.

- Eternal life is grounded in relationship with God and the body of believers in the resurrection of the body.[2] It is therefore physical and necessarily related to God.

---

1. This may be a difficult chapter for the reader, since the biblical data and contemporary discussion about it challenge long held assumptions and explanations about the human person and life after death.

2. This is sometimes called "conditional immortality" in the Judeo-Christian tradition.

Soul in the Hebrew Bible

The *Shema* includes the command to love God with "all your *soul.*" Yet *Webster's Dictionary* definition is almost the opposite of what is meant by the word "soul" (*nefesh*) in Scripture: *The vehicle of individual existence, separate in nature from the body, and usually held to be separate from the body in existence.*[3] The *Shema* certainly does not mean that you are to love God with your disembodied self! The English meaning of "soul" misses the necessary physicality, relationality, and unity of the original word *nefesh.*[4]

The Embodied, Relational Soul/Nefesh

A person's *life* (*nefesh*/soul) exists, not in a body, but only as a body. The human did not become a being (or creature) abstractly, or differentiated from its body, but physically and in relation to the One who breathed in the first breath (Gen 2:7).[5]

Translators use the word "soul" for *nefesh* in more than half of its occurrences. Though we may automatically import the English definition, and by default, the Greek philosophical concept of the psyche-soul (see below), this is a problem both in the Hebrew texts and in the Greek texts of the New Testament. Ironically, it is the older ways of thinking about the ancient narrative that concur with discoveries of contemporary neuroscience.

The word *nefesh* has a range of meanings that ground it as a physical concept.[6] It is most often translated "soul" but also frequently translated "life" or "person" or "self." Its body-based meaning is often noted by scholars in verses where it means "throat" (esophagus, in reference

3. W.A. Nielson, ed. *Webster's New International Dictionary of the English Language.*

4. A.R. Johnson summarizes the problem as follows: "In Israelite thought man is conceived not so much in dual fashion as 'body' and 'soul' but synthetically as a unit of vital power." A.R. Johnson, *The Vitality of the Individual in the Thought of Ancient Israel,* 88.

5. Genesis 2:7. Scholar Brevard Childs put it this way: "Man does not *have* a soul, but *is* a soul . . . a complete entity, not a composite of parts from body, soul, or spirit." B. Childs, *Old Testament Theology in a Canonical Context,* 199.

6. D.C. Fredericks, *"nepes" New International Dictionary of Old Testament Theology and Exegesis,* vol. 3, 133; Seebass, *"nepes"* in *Theological Dictionary of the Old Testament,* 9:497–519; *Theological Wordbook of the Old Testament,* 2:587–91. With these standard references see discussion in Green, *Body, Soul, and Human Life,* 54–60.

to the appetite; e.g., Hab 2:5; Prov 25:25; Ps 107:5, 9) or "neck" (e.g., Ps 105:18; 1 Sam 28:9) or "jugular" in reference to blood and pulse (e.g., Deut 12:23; Lev 17:11; Lam 2:12), or "breath" in reference to the trachea (e.g., Gen 1:20; 2:7; Jonah 2:5).[7]

This body-based meaning of "soul" (*nefesh*) is also present to denote the physical appetites of people (Micah 7:1; Eccl 6:7), animals (Jer 2:24), and even Sheol's appetite for the dead (Isa 5:14; Hab 2:5). The swallowing action of the esophagus is used both literally and metaphorically to speak of physical desires: "Yet whenever you *desire* (*nefesh*) you may slaughter and eat meat . . ." (Deut 12:15).

These body-based meanings represent a portion of the over seven hundred occurrences of the word *nefesh*. It is translated "life" or "person" about one hundred and fifty times. For example: "I will require the *life* of man . . . (Gen 9:5; with reference to life-blood) and "If a *person* sins" (Lev 4:2).

The use of nefesh is not limited to human life. It is used to describe the animals created by God and is translated "creature."

> So out of the ground the LORD God formed every beast of the field and every bird of the air, and brought them to Adam to see what he would call them and whatever Adam called every *living creature* (*nefesh khayah*), that was its name. (Gen 2:19)

If we translated *nefesh* as "soul" here, we would say that the beasts and birds were *living souls*. That is not intended in this text. They are, however, *living beings in relation to* God and Adam. They breathe. They are alive. They exchange glances. *Nefesh* means to be *physically alive* and to be *in relation*. "Living creature" (*nefesh khayah*) is the identical term used of the creation of the first human being.

> And the LORD breathed into his nostrils the breath of life and the human became a *living being* (*nefesh khayah*). (Gen 2:7)

The human did not become a *being* (or *creature*) abstractly, or differentiated from its body. Rather, its life was precisely *physical* and *in relation to* the One who breathed the first breath into the person. Adam became a *nefesh*; he was not supplied with one.[8]

---

7. On these concepts see especially H.W. Wolff, *Anthropology of the Old Testament*, 10–25.

8. Adam "became a *nefesh*, a soul. It is not said that man was supplied with a *nefesh* and so the relation between body and soul is quite different from what it is to us." J.

The nefesh "soul" always exists in relationship. Primary legal contexts in Leviticus stress God's concern for the life (*nefesh*) relationships. A life taken is tied to the life of the taker. Similarly, an effect on the life of the others in the community is tied to God's claim to all life. The relationship is clearly stated after the flood.

> For your own life blood (*nefesh*) I will surely require a reckoning: from every animal I will require it and from human beings, each one for the blood of another, I will require a reckoning for human life (*nefesh*). (Gen 9:5)

Every biblical context of *nefesh*, when it is translated "soul," is essentially relational and social.[9] We could translate the *Shema*, "You shall love the LORD your God with all your heart-mind and with all your personal and social life."

The source of life[10] (*nefesh*/soul) is God's breath or Spirit (*neshamah or ruakh*).[11] The essential meaning of "spirit" (*ruakh*) is "wind" or "breath."[12] A human being = dust + breath (*neshamah*) from God (Gen 2:7). God says, "My spirit (or breath/*ruakh*) shall not abide in mortals forever, for they are flesh; their days shall be one hundred twenty years." Here we see a shift in vocabulary, but the meaning is the same: human life = flesh + spirit from God.[13]

Job is the best biblical witness to the *source* of life/soul and breath: "In [God's] hand is the life (*nefesh*/soul) of every living thing and the

---

Pedersen, *Israel*, vol. 1, 99.

9. In case law *nefesh* is translated "life" and is an *ipso jure* reference to human *relationships* within a community. For example the law of retaliation (talion law) uses *nefesh* to refer to the person in relation, "Life for Life" (*nefesh tachat nefesh*; Ex 21:23; Lev 24:18; cf. Deut 19:21).

10. *Nefesh* ("soul") and *khayyah* ("life") are often used in parallel verses as synonyms. See Pss 7:5; 22:20; 30:3; 56:13; 74:19; 88:3; 3:22; Job 3:20; 10:1; 33:28.

11. See the excellent summary of God's spirit in Scripture by John Levison, *Filled with the Spirit*. His writing provides a background for this paragraph. See Levison, 14–23.

12. The word "spirit" in Scripture leads some readers to think of a ghost-like presence (like the English "soul" as an independently existing disembodied being). This is not the case in Hebrew or Greek, where it means wind, breath, human will, a demon, or God's Spirit. See Kohler-Baumgartner, *The Hebrew and Aramaic Lexicon*, 2:1197–1201; M. Van Pelt et al., *New International Dictionary of Old Testament Theology and Exegesis*, vol. 3, 1073–78.

13. See *ruakh* and *neshamah* used together in Gen 7:22, "breath of the spirit of life." See also the commentary by Levison, *Filled with the Spirit*, 17.

breath (spirit/*ruakh*) of every human being." Job is speaking particularly of the animals' life as a parallel with human life.[14] Job also shows
that "God's spirit" in human beings is their *breath*. He says, "As long
as my breath is in me and the spirit (breath/*ruakh*) of God is in my
nostrils" (Job 27:3). He affirms that he is made of God's breath (*ruakh*)
given as a gift and clay (Job 33:4, 6).[15] So, as Job corroborates, a human
being is *a living physical being in relation to others and to God.*

A person's life (nefesh/soul) is simply earthly existence. Human beings are not *inherently* immortal. In our natural state, death is final and
the soul is mortal. Without a body, a "soul" is truly dead because it does
not have a separate existence from the body. It is God's Spirit (*ruakh*)
that makes us alive, not our "soul." The psalmist repeats, "You remove
your Spirit (*ruakh*) and they go down to death (*sheol*)." This is true for
people and for animals (Ps 104:29–30).[16]

The ancient world in which Israel lived had hopeful illusions about
life beyond death. The biblical witness however, made a point of describing death as the end and enemy it was.[17] Isaiah mocks the oppress-
ing Babylonian king regarding his false hope in life beyond death:

> Maggots are the bed beneath you, and worms are your covering
> . . . You said in your heart, "I will ascend to heaven; I will raise
> my throne above the stars of God" . . . But you are brought down
> to Sheol, to the depths of the Pit. (Isa 14:1b, 13, 15)[18]

14. Both spirit and soul are used of the animals, denoting physical life. See Gen
6:17; 7:15, 22.

15. See also Job 34:14–15; Eccl 3:18–22; 12:6–7 and Levison, *Filled with the Spirit*,
18–23.

16. Biblical scholars are in agreement that the "soul" *nefesh* is not immortal in the
Hebrew Bible, but goes down to the grave in death (*sheol*). Only the dissenting James
Barr argues for the possibility of the meaning "immortal soul" in some texts. Yet even
he means "conditional immortality" in relation to and not independent from the life
that God gives and sustains by access to the Tree of Life (116). His key biblical warrants
are not convincing but based on an unusual reading of parallelisms oppositionally in
Isa 10:18; Job 14:22; Ps 63:1; and Ps 84:2. Even he states that this cannot be established
with certainty. See J. Barr, *The Garden of Eden and the Hope of Immortality*, 38–39;
compare W. Brueggemann, *Theology of the Old Testament*, 452–53.

17. H.W. Wolff outlines the opposing worldviews in *Anthropology of the Old Testament*, 102–117.

18. This ironic taunt uses the imagery of the Babylonian Gilgamesh Epic and its
kingdom of the dead (sheol) to show that the hope of ruling there is false. Maggots
and worms "are the true sovereigns." Wolff, *Anthropology of the Old Testament*, 103.

Egypt had a similar illusion with its cult of the dead: "He goes living to his rest," and "He enters into his horizon, departs to heaven, and is united with the sun through the mingling of his divine body with his maker."[19]

Scripture does not share these false hopes. *Sheol* is simply the grave; the place in the ground where a body is placed when life is over: the grave is like a pit or a swamp (Ps 40:3; Lam 3:43); a person returns to the dust (Job 10:9, 34:14; Sir 12:17); death is destruction (Pss 16:10; 55:24, Job 9:31); it swallows people (Ps 41:3, Hab 2:5, Isa 5:14); it is a place of no memory of God; no praise is sung (Pss 6:6, 38:18); it is a place of stillness, darkness and helplessness; and dead bodies lay row on row, with no power and no hope; nothing moves (Ezek 32:23–32).[20]

Isaiah warns the people of Jerusalem against putting false hope in the cult of the dead and its hoped-for immortality.[21]

> Now if people say to you, "Consult the ghosts and the familiar spirits that chirp and mutter; should not a people consult their gods, the dead on behalf of the living, for teaching and for instruction?" Surely, those who speak like this will have no dawn! . . . They will look to the earth, but will see only distress and darkness, the gloom of anguish; and they will be thrust into thick darkness. (Isa 8:19–20, 22)

Conjuring the dead (necromancy) was a charlatan's trick (as most acknowledge séances are). Necromancy was forbidden in Scripture because of its foolishness.[22] The dead are dead and cannot return when they are summoned. This is what makes the story of the Samuel's return, King Saul, and the witch at Endor so fascinating. Many Bible readers assume that these stories mean that séances actually "worked" and that Samuel's ghost was just waiting to be conjured in some spiritual holding ground. On the contrary, this account demonstrates that only the Lord God has the power to raise the deceased. Certainly the

19. Cited in Ibid., 103.

20. See also Gen 42:38; 44:29–31; Isa 38:10, 17; Pss 9:15–17; 16:10; 49:9, 15; 88:3–6, 11; Prov 1:12. The concept of *sheol* is also used metaphorically in some texts to denote state of extreme trauma or distress. For example, addiction is a living death. Addiction to wine or to wealth (LXX), like Sheol, is never satisfied (Hab 2:5). On interpretations of *sheol* see also McDannell, *Heaven: A History*, 1–18. See also Green, *Body, Soul, and Human Life*, 153–57.

21. See discussion in Wolff, *Anthropology of the Old Testament*, 104.

22. Lev 19:26, 31; 20:6, 27; Deut 18:9–13; Isa 8:19.

ancients believed in the claims of necromancy, as Saul does in the text. The narrative is in this text to demonstrate that Samuel did not appear as a "ghost" but in a raised physical state.[23] He appeared not as the "soul" or "spirit" of Samuel, but as Samuel, speaking the word of the Lord (1 Sam 28:19).

No one was more amazed by the appearance of the raised physical Samuel than the witch. She made her living at séances, but she is shocked and terrified, realized that something was wrong with her usual gig, and under questioning by Saul says she saw "a divine being" (*'elohim*; 1 Sam 28:12–13).[24] This was really Samuel. The socio-historical provenance of the text leaves no room for a disembodied soul or "ghost" expected by a believer in necromancy.[25]

1 Samuel 28 is a polemical narrative that contrasts the power of the Lord God with the illusion of ghosts.[26] Saul receives no help at all for all his trouble. Samuel just reconfirms the broader biblical witness. There is no hope from the realm of death. Only the Lord God has the power to resurrect the dead. Other ancient cultures worked from the quantitative dualism of body/soul. Scripture counters with the qualitative distinction of this unified bodily life and the next dimension of unified bodily life.[27]

Other brief encounters with the hope of re-embodiment and recreation of the dead are present in the Hebrew Bible. A brief verse in the apocalypse of Daniel suggests a recreation from the dust: "Many of those who sleep in the dust of the earth shall awake, some to everlasting life, and some to shame and everlasting contempt" (Dan 12:2). The dead dry bones of Ezekiel 37:1–14 have Israel's return from exile to rebuild

---

23. Samuel's appearance can be understood as similar to the appearance of Moses and Elijah on the Mount of Transfiguration with Jesus. No one considers that they are "ghosts." Peter offers to build them shelters! (Matt 17:4; Mk 9:4; Lk 9:33).

24. A long history of interpretation of this text is documented by Klaas Smelik, "The Witch of Endor: 1 Samuel 28 in Rabbinic and Christian Exegesis till 88 A.D." My interpretation follows a major stream of rabbinic and Christian close readings.

25. Bill Arnold, "Soul-Searching Questions about 1 Samuel 28" in *What about the Soul?*, 81.

26. See Smelik, "The Witch of Endor," 176. When a text contradicts the Torah (the practice of necromancy) Scripture must be understood in another way. The text itself provides this "other way" in the surprise, fear, and uncertainty of the woman.

27. See Bill Arnold, "Soul-Searching Questions about 1 Samuel 28," 75–83.

the temple as their primary historical referent, but point to the radical belief that the Lord God can recreate his human creation from *nothing*.

Scripture's witness is that a dead human is not equal to a corpse plus (+) disembodied ghost or "soul." A dead human being is a corpse minus (-) the living breath (*ruach*) of life given by God. The corpse is dead, but so is the person (*nefesh*/soul) in all their relationships. The person is dead, existing only as a memory that has no memory; and has potential only as *a memory of God* that God may re-embody as a new creation.[28]

Life (*nefesh*/soul) as a concept in New Testament Greek

The biblical view of a unified bodily life (*nefesh*/soul) encountered a second major challenge in the quantitative dualism of body/soul in classical thought. The Greek language and the corresponding Hellenistic philosophical concepts dominated the thought world of the Mediterranean and Judaism for several hundred years before the birth of Jesus and Christianity.

In Greek thought, body (*soma*) is distinct from the soul (*psyche*). The essence of a person is thought to be in the soul (*psyche*). In Plato, the body is a prison and the soul is liberated in death to a higher spiritual life.[29] This quantitative dualism affected every thinker. For example, Philo, a Jewish philosopher in the first century BCE adopted this Greek conception of body and soul.[30] In the inter-testamental book *Wisdom of Solomon*, the soul (*psyche*) is burdened by the body (*soma*) and lives on when the body dies (Wis 9:15; 3:1–9).[31] Dualistic thought pervades both Jewish and Christian thought today. Many assume that at death, either a disembodied soul goes to heaven or hell, or that the soul waits in an intermediate state to be united with a new body.[32]

28. The thief on cross said to Jesus, "Remember me when you come into your kingdom." In being remembered by God, the members of one's body may be re-created.

29. See the notation of sources in Plato in Eduard Schweizer, "Body," 767–72; see discussion of Greek philosophical categories concerning the body in Hans Schwarz, "The Content of Christian Hope," 555–574.

30. S. A. White, "Human Person" in *The Oxford Guide to Ideas and Issues of the Bible*, 207–8.

31. G. Bertram, A. Dihle, E. Jacob, E. Lohse, E. Schweizer, K. Troger, "*Psyche*," 608–66; and E. Schweizer and F. Baumgartel, "*Soma*," 1024–94.

32. S.A. White, "Afterlife and Immortality," 7–10.

The New Testament resists Greek philosophical dualism even as it uses Koine Greek vocabulary. When the New Testament uses the word human "soul" (Greek: *psyche*) it generally means human "life," not "soul," implying rather the Hebrew word *nefesh* (life).[33] For example: "Do not worry about your life (*psyche*), what you will eat or what you will drink." (Matt 6:25) or "Those who lose their life (*psyche*) for my sake will find it." (Mark 10:39).[34]

Studies of the meaning in each verse have determined that the New Testament writers generally had the Hebrew body-based unity of "life" (*nefesh*/soul) in mind, not meaning the Greek concept of an independent *psyche* or "soul." They did not adopt the dualistic concepts of the ruling Greek philosophical categories.[35] They use Greek words with Hebrew understanding.[36] This is possible because the basic etymology of *psyche* (from the verb *psuxo*), is "to breathe." It is the basic principle of animal life. The dictionary definitions include "breath," "life," "living being," and "person." The word "psyche" translated "soul" carries the monistic unified meaning of Hebrew "life" (*nefesh*/soul). In the New Testament "soul" (*psyche*) means is *a living physical being in relation to others and to God.* Like *nefesh*, the "soul" (*psyche*) in the New Testament means the life of a whole human person made of clay and the breath of God.[37]

New Testament Counteraction to Hellenistic Dualism

The Jewish writers of the New Testament actively resisted popular ancient notions of an inherent eternal disembodied soul. They counteracted this classical philosophy in two ways.

The First Countermove. The New Testament writers occasionally used the word "body" (*soma*) rather than "life" (*psyche*) to describe the

33. J. Chamblin, "Psychology," 766.

34. See also *psyche* as "life" in Jesus' words about laying down one's life (*psyche*) in John 10:11, 17; 15:13. See also Acts 20:24, 27:10, 22, 37; Rom 11:3; Phil 2:30.

35. For example see the discussion of 1 Peter 1:1–9 on the phrase "salvation of your souls (*psyche*)" with similar passages in N.T. Wright, *Surprised by Hope*, 151–52.

36. See an excellent summary of the history of NT scholarship on this issue in J. Chamblin, "Psychology," 765–67.

37. Certain texts are difficult to read in this monistic way. See discussion of these texts of Christian dualisms below.

essential being of a whole person. They did this especially in narratives where the Greek reader might expect a ghost or disembodied soul. For example, at Jesus' resurrection:

> The tombs also were opened, and many bodies (*somata*) of the saints who had fallen asleep were raised. After his resurrection they came out of the tombs and entered the holy city and appeared to many. (Matt 27:52)

Jesus used it to speak of his own essential being:

> "Destroy this temple, and in three days I will raise it up."

But he was speaking of the temple of his body (*soma*). (John 2:19, 21)

The apostle Paul speaks of the mortal bodies of Christians as the totality of their assets. Only God's Spirit (or breath/*pneumatos*) can give them life. There is no independent disembodied soul.

> He who raised Christ from the dead will give life to your mortal bodies (*somata*) also through his Spirit that dwells in you. (Rom 8:11)

The New Testament occasionally adopts a Hellenistic expression of life that reflects a dualistic tint; but even here the soul is described as perishable and not immortal.[38]

> Do not fear those who kill the body but cannot kill the soul; rather fear him who can destroy both soul and body in hell (*gehenna*). (Matt 10:28)

When Paul wants to make the point clearly, he uses the term "body" for the whole person in this life and in the next. The power to live in the next life is not humanly inherent, but is dependent on relationship to God. Simultaneously he puts the highest possible value on the human body as the temple of God's spirit.

---

38. Luke 12:4 omits the dualistic distinction altogether. Another text that appears to be, but is not a problem for monism, is 3 John 1:2. It looks like John is making a dualistic distinction between the body and the (eternal) soul: "Beloved, I pray that all may go well with you and that you may be in good health, just as it is well with your soul." Again, he is using Greek (*soma* and *psyche*) terms to speak of the two aspects of a person's life (*nefesh*). In a Hebrew first-century context it means clay and vivification in relation to God (God's breath). He is not implying an independent immortal soul, but the *psyche*, which we know is a body-based function, primarily of the brain.

> The body is meant . . . for the Lord, and the Lord for the body. And God raised the Lord and will also raise us by his power. Do you not know that your bodies are members of Christ? Or do you not know that your body is a temple of the Holy Spirit within you, which you have from God, and that you are not your own? (1 Cor 6:13b–15, 19)

Jesus counteracts Hellenism's dualism by using body/*psyche* in parallel as synonyms, *each one* as a reference to the unified bodily life (*nefesh/* soul) of a person!

> Jesus says, "Do not worry about your life, what you will eat or what you will drink, or about your body, what you will wear. Is not life more than food, and the body more than clothing? (Matt 6:25; Luke 12:23)

Finally, at the height of his polemical letter to the Romans, Paul uses language that would surprise a Greek philosopher and perhaps many Christians. "Spiritual worship" is not done with a "soul" or "spirit" but with what you are: a body of clay and the gift of God's breath. "Present your bodies as a living sacrifice, holy and acceptable to God, which is your spiritual worship." (Rom 12:1).[39]

The Second Countermove. The first countermove to the Hellenistic understanding of the independent and disembodied soul is the apostle Paul's writing about the "body" (*soma*) as the essential being of a person. The second countermove is the New Testament narrative of the *resurrection of Jesus' body.* The New Testament also opposes popular notions of an inherent eternal disembodied soul that persists beyond the grave. Not even Jesus' "soul" endured beyond the grave. The claim is that God raised Jesus in a new, but similar body. If life beyond the grave was to be possible, it would be an *embodied* existence.

The scriptural roots of human life (soul) are physical and relational (Hebrew: *nefesh* and Greek: *psyche/soma*) and demonstrate the God's commitment to embodiment and corporeality. In the New Testament it is ironic that Hellenistic thought and confusion about Greek vocabulary moved some Jewish and some Christian theologians to a more "spiritual" and dualistic conception of human life. *The central radical New Testament doctrines are the incarnation (God in the flesh) and resurrection of the body.*

---

39. See also 1 Cor 6:20.

The primary claim is presented in the Gospel of John 1:1–18. Jesus was the eternal Word made flesh. In his first letter John reminds his readers that they saw with their own eyes and touched him their hands and are thereby reliable witnesses (1 Jn 1:1–3).[40] After he is raised in a new body by God, he could move through doors and disappear (John 20:19, 26; Luke 24:31) and yet be recognized by his old wounds (Luke 24:39; John 20:27). The Hellenistic worldview was present in his disciples, who thought they were seeing a ghost (Luke 24:37–39).

To prove his bodily presence, Jesus walked seven miles and ate dinner (Luke 24:13–33), invited others to touch his hands and feet (Luke 24:39); invited Thomas to put his finger in the wound in his hand and his hand in his lance wound in his side (John 20:27); and cooked a breakfast of fish and bread over a charcoal fire for some of his disciples (John 21:7–13). He said, "Look at my hands and my feet; see that it is I myself. Touch me and see; for a ghost does not have flesh and bones as you see that I have" (Luke 24:39). Jesus even ascends to heaven in a *body* (Acts 1:1–2, 9–11).

Both Judaism and Christianity are, in their primary historical ancient texts, embodied and community-based faiths, not religions about independent immortal souls.

Contemporary Perspectives

Students and scholars of the Hebrew Bible have long recognized that human life (*nefesh*/soul) is *monistic*, i.e., that a soul-life is simple existence and that natural death is final. You are clay (or dust) vivified by the gift of the breath of God. Life beyond the grave will depend on God's re-creation of the heavens and the earth and creation of a new human body-life. This is the two-aspect version of monism: The only duality of human existence in Scripture is dust and breath (Gen 2:7).

This position has not necessarily been widely held in Judaism or in Christian churches, and may be a surprise to readers who have a theological background. Church teaching from the earliest church fathers discussed whether the apostle Paul was describing a two-part (body and soul) or a three-part (body-soul-spirit) human being.[41] The Greek

40. See also 1 Jn 5:6–8.

41. J. Chamblin, "Psychology," 765–75.

fathers preferred three parts but the Latin fathers, Augustine and the Protestant reformers of the sixteenth and seventeenth centuries often taught dualism. In the last decades, however, biblical and theological scholarship has begun a major sea-change concerning the understanding of humanity in Scripture.[42]

The ancient text (the Hebrew Bible and the New Testament) offers a monistic perspective of the human being that counter balances the negative effects of dominant dualistic thinking about the body-soul. The reasons the monistic perspective has begun to gain ground in the last thirty years are numerous: the medical community's dissatisfaction with the treatment of patients as simply bodies; a return to spirituality; a reassessment of the influence of Descartes and Western philosophy; neuroscience's advances in brain research;[43] and scholarship's reappraisal of the New Testament and its Hebraic roots.[44] In the last two decades dozens of issues of *Time* and *Newsweek* have carried articles on themes related to a person as a unified human document.

The reappraisal of *monism* (a person as a unified being) has led to a growing debate in biblical and theological studies between those who hold a trichotomous, dualist, or monist perspective of the human being. In the sections that follow, I will briefly summarize these perspectives, supporting a *monistic view of the person with two aspects*: common clay (or dust) vivified by the gift of the breath of life from God. *Common clay* means that we are by nature made for *community*.[45] The gift of the breath of *life* means that we are full alive only in relation to God. We are *living physical beings made in relation to others and to God.*

A Three-part Person: Three-aspect Monism.

The trichotomous view of humanity (three-aspect monism) is based on the vocabulary of "spirit-soul-body" (pneuma-psyche-soma). It is centered by Paul's first letter to the Thessalonians: "May the God of peace

42. For example see P. Hefner, "The Human Being," 333–35; A. Hoekema, *Created in God's Image*, 210.

43. See the extensive bibliography in J. Green, *Body, Soul, and Human Life*, 183–206.

44. See J. Chamblin, "Psychology," 765–68.

45. See chapter three: we are made for the love of our neighbor and the love of God, according to the ancient text.

himself sanctify you entirely; and may your *spirit and soul and body* be kept sound and blameless . . ." (1 Thess 5:23).[46] Contemporary adherents describe these as three aspects of a unified person in what may be called three-aspect monism.[47] As in two-aspect monism, the body *(soma)* represents the physical aspect and "soul" *(psyche)* the life force within it. This aspect is expanded to include the will, which is the location of the battle between good and evil forces for the person.[48] This soul has inherited iniquity, and experienced pain, and damage in living, and is in need of healing. The soul itself (conscious will + life force) is mortal, dying at death. Both people and animals have this kind of life (soul).

Three-aspect monism employs the language of "spirit"[49] to speak directly about a Christian's experience of the activity of God in the world through the Holy Spirit.[50] The "spirit" is the *potential for eternal life* present in all people. It is, however, dormant or dead in non-believers and must be enlivened or awakened by the creating Holy Spirit to enter that potential of eternal life through the Gospel.[51] Until that time a great emptiness and restlessness marks a person's life (soul).

The spirit of a person may be animated by the Holy Spirit through faith in Christ. In Christ, the awakened spirit of the believer shares already in the life of the Spirit. The human spirit becomes the house and stronghold of the Holy Spirit in one's life (body-soul). The Holy Spirit "dwells" in the person's spirit. Conversely, the human spirit that houses this Spirit is also "seated" already with Christ in "heavenly places" in

46. This is the only verse where body, soul, and spirit occur together. "Soul" and "spirit" occur together in Heb 4:12, Phil 1:22, 1 Cor 15:45; and Matt 12:18. Cf. Isa 42:1; see parallel use in Job 7:11 and Isa 26:9.

47. This is largely an oral tradition in the worldwide Pentecostal churches. I am grateful to Stephanie Stultz for her articulation of this teaching in this tradition. The trichotomous view has classical roots in the eastern Greek fathers. For a general summary, see P. Hefner, "The Human Being," 333.

48. The soul can be renewed and healed, but it is also the place where "iniquitous roots" of life-denying familial patterns are lodged. The ministry of God's word and power of the Holy Spirit may be brought to bear against these roots for the healing of the soul (person).

49. See discussion and citations above. In Hebrew or Greek, *ruakh* and *pneuma* mean wind, breath, good and bad human will, a demon, or God's Spirit, depending on the context.

50. "Do not quench the Spirit" (1 Thess 5:19).

51. Thus it is written, "The first man, Adam, became a living being" *(psyche)*; the last Adam became a life-giving spirit *(pneuma)*" 1 Cor 15:45.

anticipation of the new creation.[52] This place of identity and authority gives a person the power to minister healing to others in the Name of Jesus.[53]

A difference between a three-aspect monist and a two-aspect monist can be seen in the interpretation of Hebrews 4:12.

> For the word of God is living and active, sharper than any two-edged sword, piercing to the division of soul (*psyche*) and spirit (*pneuma*), of joints and marrow, discerning the thoughts and intentions of the heart.

In two-aspect monism, the division made is between a person's life (*psyche*/soul) and her breath (*pneuma*/spirit). The interpretive focus is on two physical metaphors in parallel (life-breath/joints-marrow) to show how the word of God discerns the heart. This is a very effective metaphor when you consider how to divide a person's life from their breath or their joints from marrow without killing them. By comparison, the word is living and *sharper* than that. In three-aspect monism, the division is between the "soul" (life and will) and "spirit" (life with the Holy Spirit). The word of God makes this fine division.

Radical and Wholistic Dualism

The caricature of all dualisms is that the body is a container for the soul or "a ghost in the machine."[54] No scholar in the current discussion, including those who argue for a body-soul dualism, expresses the relationship in such a radically dualistic way. Yet, this remains the common perception of dualism. *Radical dualism* does argue that the body holds the soul until the body dies; then the soul endures into the next life in (some kind of) spiritual state. Common human religious beliefs worldwide, including shamanistic and animistic religions, have some version

---

52. Eph 2:5–7; 1:20–23.

53. "Standing firm in one spirit, striving side by side with one mind for the faith of the gospel" (Phil 1:27b) indicates the corporate spirit of the Thessalonians which is the Holy Spirit providing a common spirit within each of them.

54. The expression "the ghost in the machine" is, accurately or not, the negative legacy of Descartes' mind-body dualism. It was coined by Gilbert Ryle, *The Concept of the Mind*. His critical description of Descartes was carried into popular profile by Arthur Koestler, *The Ghost in the Machine*. See also neuroscientist Steven Pinker, *How the Mind Works*.

of this dualism. In public dialogue, the soul is seen as a "ghostly user" and the brain a "pocket PC for the soul that manages information."[55]

Some argue for a distinction between the terms *dualistic* and *dichotomous*, the first representing a true Platonic and Gnostic body/soul split;[56] the second represents the tradition of Aristotle and Thomas Aquinas, who insisted on a unified human being, but argued that the soul has substance and is capable of independence from the body after death.[57] Dichotomous dualism is also called *wholistic dualism*, and represents the traditional views throughout most of Christian history.[58]

Radical Monism and Biblical Monisms[59]

Radical monism is often called reductive or *eliminative materialism* because it reduces a person to nothing more than a physical organism.

55. See S. Pinker, "How to Think about the Mind," 78.

56. Augustine follows a Platonic line holding a middle ground between the Manichean corporeal divinity of the soul and the Platonic ascendancy of the inherently immortal soul. The mature Augustine modified his view of the soul in relation to the body and in relation to God. Rather than the Manichean position that the soul was a corporeal particle of the divine, he asserted the soul's createdness (*Johannes evangelium tractatus* 39.8). Rather than the Neo-Platonist view that a divine soul was trapped in the body (imprisoned), he asserted the necessarily good mixture of body and soul as God had created it (*De Trinitate* 15.7.11). Although he believed that the rational soul was superior to the body, he was not dualistic. The body has radical significance in his anthropology. Because of the doctrines of incarnation and the resurrection of the body, his "ideal is not escape from the body and the world, but reestablishment of the inner equilibrium by unification of all one's levels of being." He anticipated in his resurrection "to be healed as whole, for I am one whole; not that my flesh be forever removed, as if it were alien to me, but that it be healed, on whole with me" (*Sermones* 30.3.4). Stephen J. Duffy, "Anthropology," 26; Roland J. Teske, S.J., "Soul," 808. Augustine also recognized that all bodily living beings have a "soul" (anima) that gives life and animates the body, providing abilities of perception and memory. According to Augustine, human beings are distinguished not by the "soul," but by reason (ratio) and the mind (mens). *De Trnitate* 12.1.1–12.3.3; 12.15.24; *Confessiones* 10.7.11. See Sheri Katz, "Person," 648.

57. Thomistic theology follows Aristotle, holding the essential unity of human beings but that that body and soul are distinguishable and separable parts. God created us to be body-soul unities, but the soul is separated from the body at death and waits to be reunified, made whole, at the resurrection. Aristotle revised Plato's dualism, asserting an indivisible human being. Aristotle's conception is called "hylomorphism."

58. Articulated especially by John Cooper, *Body, Soul, and Life Everlasting*.

59. See further concise summary of these positions in J. Green, *Body, Soul, Human Life*, 29–32; J. Chamblin, "Psychology," 765–68.

It eliminates the soul altogether as a function of the brain, and is thus incompatible with Scripture. Many neuroscientists claim this position, demonstrating that all religious experiences and emotions can be measured by MRIs.[60] In this view, the sense of "self" is simply "a vast assembly of nerve cells and their associated molecules."[61]

There are neuroscientists who have modified this view. In the last twenty years substantive literature has emerged as theologians and neuroscientists who take Scripture seriously have begun a dialogue. These scholars generally agree that close reading of biblical texts and the results of MR imaging are not necessarily incompatible.

The Bible and brain research both point to a basic truth about human existence, expressed as a biblical *monism*.[62] Its basic tenet from the neurological side is that religious experiences can be observed (by MRIs) as a particular form of brain activity, but that they are not fully explained by that activity. Brain activity does not exclude an external source (God), nor does it explain life transformations rooted in religious experience. It does mean that experiences of God are always embodied, primarily in the brain. From the biblical side, "life" is understood as a *nefesh* and not a traditional dualistic "soul" (half of a dualistic person) but is the essential aspect of the human self.[63] The "soul" is understood as a more integrated part of a unified, bodily, relational, and growing life with God and with others.

A significant opponent of biblical monism argues that Paul describes a wholistic body/soul duality.[64] The chief objection is that

60. See neurological studies published in the journals *Neuron* (2004), *Science* (2001), *Psychiatry Research* (2001); *JNMD* (1988), *Neuropsychiatry* (1997), *General Psychology* (1987), *and Clinical Psychology* (1993) as cited in Warren Brown, "Human Nature, Physicalism, Spirituality, and Healing," 114–16.

61. Francis Crick, quoted in J. Green, *Body, Soul, and Human Life*, 31.

62. The monist discussion has resulted in new terminology and distinctions: "emergent monism," Phillip Clayton, *Mind and Emergence: From Quantum to Consciousness*; "Nonreductive Physicalism," Nancy Murphy, *Bodies and Souls, or Spirited Bodies?*; "Open-system Emergence" and "Deep Physicalism," Gregory Peterson, *Minding God*; "two-aspect monism" Malcolm Jeeves, *Human Nature at the Millennium*.

63. J. Green, *Body, Soul, Human Life*, 31.

64. See philosopher J. Cooper, *Body, Soul, and Life Everlasting*; cited by J. Chamblin, "Psychology," 767–68. Chamblin supports "wholistic dualism" as Paul's position, against recent Pauline scholarship which he reviews (766–67). Cooper's crisp descriptions of "illicit dualisms" is helpful. See Cooper, 198–209. Cooper is cited widely as having established Paul's dualism. See James Moreland and Scott Rae, *Body and Soul*,

monism reduces the soul to "materialism" contrary to Paul. Yet this is not the necessary conclusion of body-based biblical monism. Rather, it defines the human "soul" (*nefesh/psyche*) as the *living physical human being that is created in relation to others and to God.* It is the *living relationship* (soul) to God that gives us the potential for eternal life.[65]

The chief concern in opposing this kind of monism is the logistics of eternal life. If our soul (life in relation) is not ontologically distinct and independent, we cannot be *guaranteed* that we will have personal existence after we die. That will remain in God's hands. God must raise us. It remains God's initiative. On the other hand, this is all a matter of faith in any case. There is, perhaps, somewhat more security in teaching and believing that your soul exists, regardless of God's future activity.

The apparent logistical need for an ontologically distinct disembodied soul after death is the so-called "intermediate" state. After death and before the resurrection of the body, where do people exist and in what "state"?[66] In Catholic teaching, for example, substantive souls are in purgatory.[67] The concept of paradise as a blissful waiting room for the resurrection has recently garnered much attention among scholars.[68] Yet Scripture is very elusive about this place and "state" so that there is no single teaching acknowledged across the Christian Church.

The "intermediate state" is not necessary for a biblical understanding of the afterlife. What is essential is the teaching of the bodily resurrection in the new creation of the heaven's and the earth.[69] What follows is a description of life after death from a two-aspect monist (common clay and God's breath) understanding of the biblical text.

17–47; Philip Johnston, "Humanity," 564–65.

65. The trichotomous view calls this potential "spirit."

66. See Green's clear summary of refutation of Cooper's views of souls existing in *sheol* after death. Green, *Body, Soul, and Human Life*, 152–57.

67. See John Paul II, *Crossing the Threshold of Hope*, 186; Peter Kreeft, *Everything You ever Wanted to Know about Heaven . . . But Never Dreamed of Asking*, 61–71; Kreeft follows the tradition of St. Catherine: "Purgatory is joyful, not gloomy—thus not detracting from the joy and triumph of Christian death . . . the pains of purgatory are incomparably more desirable than the most ecstatic pleasures on earth!" Kreeft, 62. See *St. Catherine of Genoa, Purgatory, the Spiritual Dialog*, 84.

68. See N.T. Wright, *Surprised by Hope*, 165–88.

69. Ibid., 147–64.

Resurrection Monism and the New Creation of Heaven and Earth

The third biblical thesis stated at the beginning of this chapter was:

- *Eternal life* (or the eternal "soul") is grounded in relationship with God (who does the raising) and the body of believers as the resurrection of the body. It is therefore *physical* and necessarily *relational.*[70]

The Resurrection is physical. N.T. Wright has reconvened biblical scholars around the physical nature of the new creation in Scripture.[71] No one "goes to heaven" when they die. They may "be with the Lord," or in "paradise," or enter eternity in the new heavens and the new earth, but the ultimate destination is a physical existence in God's new creation. The common biblical teaching is that, at the end of time, God will recreate the heavens (sky) and the earth, resurrect the dead *in bodies*, and bring in a reign of justice and peace that will never end.[72] "Heaven" is short-hand for the biblical "new heavens and new earth. It is a physical place. So is the resurrection of the dead a physically based existence, not a ghost-like designated experience. The New Testament opposes both ancient and current popular notions of an inherently eternal disembodied soul that persists beyond the grave.[73]

Resurrection is fundamentally relational because it is initiated by God. Even Jesus did not raise himself.[74] The ancient Apostles' Creed states: "dead and buried . . . the third day he was raised from the dead." Biblical teaching has always been that the faithful have a conditional immortality, dependent on God's promise of a new creation. For Jews,

---

70. Even many theological students are surprised to hear that Scripture and the tradition do not teach a doctrine of an inherently immortal soul or the persistence of a disembodied spirit beyond the grave. See Stendhal's elucidation of the New Testament teaching regarding the mortality and conditional immortality of the soul. Krister Stendahl, ed. *Immortality and Resurrection: Ingersoll Lectures*; and Benoit, P. and Murphy, R., eds. *Immortality and Resurrection.*

71. N.T. Wright is a British Anglican Bishop. The doctrine of the resurrection of the body in the new creation, however, can be found in Jewish and Christian teaching documents worldwide. Wright, *Surprised by Hope*, 147–64.

72. Isa 11:5–10; Isa 65:17–18; Rev 21:1–5; 22:1–15; Lk 24:37–43; Jn 20:27–28; 1 Cor 15:45–54; 2 Peter 3:13

73. For further reading on the subject of the history of Christian interpretations of the after-life see, J. B. Russell, *A History of Heaven*; and Colleen McDannell and Bernhard Lang *Heaven: A History.*

74. Acts 2:24.

this immortality is *conditional* on adherence to Torah, the word of Life. For Christians, this immortality is *conditional* on one's relationship to Christ, who does the raising up. Even Christ did not raise himself, but was raised by the Father. Jesus was truly and fully a mortal man as stated in the creeds. If Jesus, as God in the flesh, did not have an "immortal soul" and needed to be raised by the Father, then certainly we are not naturally immortal and require the same intervention. The key terminology of this relational resurrected transformation is "with Christ" and "in Christ."[75]

If the body is not naturally enlivened by an immortal soul, what is the source of the eternal life of the new body? It is the Spirit of God. In the book of Genesis, the Spirit (*ruakh*/ breath/wind) of God hovered over the waters and breathed into the clay to give the first human animation and life. In the New Testament, the breath (*pneuma*) of God is the Holy Spirit.[76] When Philip was transported *in body*, it is by this Spirit, as an anticipatory sign of what is possible in the new creation.[77]

In the new creation, we will be re-animated by God's Spirit. The continuity will be your body and its brain, renewed and revivified in a new amazing way. It will not be an inherently immortal, but a fundamentally physical soul/life. The soul you are is not something you possess. It exists only in relation to God and the rest of creation. When we think like Adam and Eve, that we can *possess* our own immortality simply by claiming we *have* a soul, we fall out of the essential, created, healthy relationship of daily dependence on God. The original sin is repeated in every generation that makes the claim that human beings are inherently immortal. We grasp the idea of immortality to avoid a relationship with the Creator and to deny our createdness. We are in denial about our lives and will, as a result, falter in decisions about our life (*nefesh*/soul) and death. This is a common and recurring theme in Jewish and Christian thought.

What happens at the time of death, before the new creation and the physical resurrection of the dead? What do the dying hope in and expect? Judeo-Christian dualisms offer differing slants, not on the

75. Phil 1:23; 2 Cor 5:8; 1 Thess 4:16. Green calls this "relational ontology" (180). See his discussion of this relational concept in the New Testament texts; Green, *Body, Soul, and Human Life*, 170–80.

76. 1 Cor 15:44; John 20:22; Acts 2:1–3; see E. Schweizer, "*soma*," 769.

77. Acts 8:39–40.

resurrection of the body, but on what happens between a person's death and the resurrection at the end of time.

The New Creation is Timeless. We now return to the question of the so-called "intermediate state." The question that dualists press on monists is, "What happens when a person dies, if they do not have a disembodied soul to carry them into the new creation?" The world-wide church does not have a unified teaching on what happens between death and the end of the world / new creation. This is, in part, because Scripture says so little about it. That should be our first clue. As N.T. Wright puts it, what is really important is the new creation, i.e., what happens *after life after life after death.*[78]

Still, the question persists. Two competing New Testament texts set up the uncertainty. Some theologians emphasis one in their speculations, others emphasis the other. Monism resolves the tension between them. In the first, from the cross of crucifixion Jesus says to the criminal next to him, "Truly I tell you, today you will be with me in Paradise" (Luke 23:43). This text implies that after death, he would be immediately with Jesus.

In the second text, Paul writes to the Thessalonians about the fate of those who have died. At the end of time, when Jesus returns, "God will bring with him [Jesus] those who are asleep (dead) . . . [those alive] will be caught up in the clouds together with them to meet the Lord in the air" (1Thess 5:14b, 17b). This verse is usually interpreted to mean that the dead are dead (asleep) until the resurrection. Paul is assuring the living that their deceased loved ones will be present when they that are living meet the Lord.

The usual question is, do those who die go immediately to "heaven" (or "paradise") or do they remain "asleep" until the end of time? Christian scholars have tended to answer with the compromise of an intermediate state (paradise/purgatory) where the dead wait until the end of time in the future, when the living and the dead will meet. In the last fifty years, however, with new understandings of time provided by quantum physics and string theory, another alternative seems more reasonable. This new possibility also removes the logical pressure to assume an independently existing immortal soul.

We arrive together, immediately when we die. If "eternity" is timeless, time is not a factor outside of our concept of a timeline. Every day

78. Wright, *Surprised by Hope*, 148–52.

is the "end of time" for those who die and cross into a timeless eternity. This means all the dead of all "time" arrive together. Many theologians have accepted this possibility as the best explanation of the textual data, describing it as another "dimension." The model of multiple dimensions helps to explain Jesus' post resurrection appearances as well as the confusion about "intermediate states."[79] Wright notes the recognized interpretive position, but presupposes that there is time in eternity.[80] If time as we know it ends when we die, we are immediately re-embodied in the resurrection and stand before God. To those who live on, we appear to be dead (asleep) until they enter the same reality and the new creation themselves. This concept is a particular comfort to parents whose infants die and seem to "precede" them into the new creation. We arrive together.

A New Monism in the Resurrection of the Body. Scripture declares a commitment to the unity of the whole and healthy person in this life, and the whole and healthy person in the life to come. This means that, in the new creation, we will also be two-aspect unified people. We will have a new body, with continuity from present body (including the brain) and the breath of God's Holy Spirit dwelling in us. This could be called "double monism":

- a monism of present human existence [A]: a earthly unified body (*soma*) with two aspects: clay and God's life/breath (*psyche/pneuma*)

- a monism promised in the new creation [B]: a "spiritual" unified body (*soma*) with two aspects: new material body + God's Spirit (*pneuma*)

Paul expresses this double monism in several texts.

> He will transform the body of our humiliation [A] that it may be conformed to the body of his glory [B], by the power that also enables him to make all things subject to himself (Phil 3:21).

79. Ernst Conradie, "Resurrection, Finitude, and Ecology"; L. van den Brom, *Divine Presence in the World*; Hans Schwarz, "The Content of Christian Hope, 568–570; Kreeft, "Is There Time in Heaven?" in *Everything You Ever Wanted to Know about Heaven*, 151–62.

80. Wright is in the unusual position of holding a monist viewpoint while maintaining an intermediate state (paradise) position. He allows, "except for those who believe eternity is timeless." Wright, 168; 162–63.

Paul's term "spiritual body" is not a body *made* of spirit, but *ventilated* by the Holy Spirit.[81]

> It is sown a physical body [A], it is raised a spiritual body [B].
> If there is a physical body [A], there is also a spiritual body [B].
> Thus it is written, "The first man, Adam, became a living be-
> ing [A]; the last Adam became a life-giving spirit [B]" (1 Cor
> 15:44–45).

Whether one thinks of a person's "soul" in terms of two-aspect monism, three-aspect monism, or as a wholistic dichotomy (substantive soul), a person's life/soul is relationally based, a gift of God, enlivened and sustained by God alone, and dead without God's breath of life.

The Health of Your Human Life (*nefesh*-soul)

We began the chapter by stating the problem that the common meaning of the English word "soul" misses the necessary relational and physical aspects that are present in Scripture. This deeply influences how we live our lives and think about our death and life beyond. Ludwig Feuerbach's infamous indictment, that *the world holds no interest for Christians since the Christian thinks only of the salvation of his soul*, serves also to push the question.[82] Are Christians simply candidates for heaven who do not want to be left behind? Feuerbach was working in the nineteenth century with a European Christianity that had become confused about its own biblical narrative. He rightly recognized that when a belief system is concerned only with its own spirituality and salvation, it has *lost its value* to God's good created world.[83]

Let me conclude with three upshots based on the three initial theses:[84]

- our embodied life is a primary value.

- our embodied life in relation to the community is a primary value.

---

81. E. Schweizer cited in J. Chamblin, 766.

82. L. Feuerbach, *The Essence of Christianity*, 287.

83. Matt 5:13.

84. The negative corollary is that an independent and separate spiritual soul is an illusion that is unhealthy for us as individuals, as communities, and as people of the Jewish and Christian faiths.

- our embodied life in relation to God is a primary value.

How does understanding the "soul" as embodied human life in relationship rather than a disembodied spirit affect our love for others and for God? We will conclude with two important ways: body-based reality and a relational measure of health.

Body-based Reality

Attention to human health is the measure of our love of others and of God. Health providers who attend to people's bodies are, whether they are aware of it or not, fulfilling God's purpose for them in the world. Those who care for the *bodies in a community* in public health, food preparation, elder care, hospice care, the nurture of children, etc. (the list could be very long) will be generally, by our definition, healthier people themselves because of their work. "Present your bodies . . . this is your spiritual service" (Rom 12:1).

A body-based reality also means that spiritual life is not separate from the body; that "spiritual" healing has a bodily effect; no longer do we consider the body the jurisdiction of biomedical cures, but the locus of healing in relation to the Creator and to others. The previous generation demonstrated the separation of the "spiritual" from the body in the medical isolation of hospital wards and the language of "healing" to religious contexts.

A body-based reality also serves as a critique of some "spiritualities." Radical asceticism in which one abuses their body cannot be accepted. When the ancient text says, "Your body is the temple of the holy spirit," this is the highest possible value placed on the human body (1Cor 3:16–18; 6:19). Those who work to help others overcome addictions are God's hands and feet on earth.

Finally, a body-based reality means that the body is healthy when one is reconciled to and in a covenanted relationship with the Creator of the body. For the Jew and the Christian, this means a wide variety of regular practices of faith, not least participating weekly in the worship of the Lord God. The practices of relationship to God will be addressed in chapter nine.

A Relational Measure of Health

If loving others and loving God is what one does with one's body-based soul, relationship is a primary measure of health. Individual isolation is a kind of sickness and alienation from one's community is a cause for intervening care. A relational measure of health means that individualistic spiritualities that neglect family life and the bodies of others are a kind of bodily illness. The human "body" and the Christian "body" are community-based. To neglect others or abuse them in pursuit of self-fulfillment is a spiritual sickness. Spirituality cannot be separated from the health of one's individual body or from one's community.

For the Jew and the Christian the body-based reality means regular covenanted relationship with one's local community of faith. For the Christian the language of the "body of Christ," referring to the church is instructive. A relational measure of health is reflected when the psalmist laments with the expression, "O my soul," (*nafshi*; Pss. 42:5, 11; 43:5; 103:1, 2, 22; 104:1, 35; 116:7; 146:1). This cry, made in the community and to God, indicates an alienated "soul" (*nefesh*; bodily life in relation with). The person has become sick through alienation from God, the community, and his or her own bodily self. This loss of well-being (*shalom*) is expressly relational. The biblical form of lament is a means for the person to find a way back to wholeness of relationship with God and others. This biblical and religious practice will be fully explored in chapter eight. The building of healthy "face to face" relationships as a healing practice will be pursued in chapter seven.

Conclusion

It is not likely that we will stop translating *nefesh* as "soul" in our Bibles or using the word in our discussions. Our culture has so imbibed at the fount of body-soul dualism that many cannot imagine our humanity another way. I do not expect that we will stop using the word "soul" and thinking of it in its English sense of "independent, disembodied, and immortal spirit." But that concept and definition are manifestly wrong and contradict both the claims revealed in Scripture and the discoveries of cognitive neuroscience. According to the ancient narrative, this sort of split is a sickness and the source of alienation and anxiety.

Practically, people will be slow to give up their belief in the true "self" as their immortal soul. They will no doubt struggle to think of their essential selves as complex living bodies in relationship to others and God. It remains, however, in an open reading of the ancient texts and now among neuroscientists, that your *psyche* (embodied life/ soul) is a function of your brain and your brain is an organ of your body. Emotions and spiritual experiences also originate in the brain of your body,[85] a brain created and redeemed by God. The majority of your brain, by far, goes unused. Could it be that the Creator has already staked out real estate in your brain for your growth in relationship to others and God's self? Whatever the case, the biblical witness is that until we focus on the care of the body and brain we have not done our "spiritual service to God" (Rom 12:1).

85. "New imaging techniques have tied every thought and emotion to neural activity. And any change to the brain—from strokes, drugs, electricity to surgery—will literally change your mind." S. Pinker is a neuroscientist at Harvard. Steven Pinker, "How to Think about the Mind," 78.

Chapter Six

Me'od: What Are the Elements of Strength?

"You shall love the LORD your God with all your *strength*."

Deut 6:5c

"Blessed are those whose *strength* is in You."

Ps 84:5a

THE *SHEMA* PROVIDES A biblical description of a thriving human being: "You shall love the LORD your God with all your heart, with all your soul, and with *all your strength*.[1] The third matrix of human health, translated here as strength (*me'od*) means more than is usually indicated by the English noun. The Hebrew word (*me'od*) behind the English translations "strength" or "might" is a multi-dimensional concept. It is a window into the vital and thriving life that God intended for humanity from the beginning.

If "strength" (*me'od*) was simply a category of physical strength, several other Hebrew words might have been used. The choice of the adverb *me'od* indicates a quality of strength such as energy, vigor, or vitality rather than physical, personal, or political power. "Strength" in this context portrays a complete, created human being, turned toward loving God. Generally, the phrase is interpreted to mean "love God

---

1. "All your *might*" in KJV, NAS, RSV, and NRSV.

with all the strength you have," or "Whatever your strengths are, love God with them." It fills out the human geography of wellness, thriving communities, and human flourishing.

Words Translated "Strength" or "Might"

In English versions of the Bible, the words "strength" and "might" are used in a variety of relational settings. In many cases strength refers to health. Hebrew has many words for "might" and "strength" as indicated in the italics.[2]

> When Jacob was told, "Your son Joseph has come to you," he summoned his strength (*khazaq*) and sat up in bed. (Gen 48:2)
>
> I am still as strong (*khazaq*) today as I was on the day that Moses sent me; my strength (*khazaq*) now is as my strength (*khazaq*) was then, for war, and for going and coming. (Josh 14:11)
>
> "Coax [Samson] and find out what makes his strength (*koakh*) so great." (Judg 16:5)
>
> There was no strength (*koakh*) in him, for he had eaten nothing all day and all night. (1 Sam 28:20b)
>
> You come and kill us [if you are able]; for as the man is, so is his strength (*gabor*). (Judg 8:21)
>
> - Reuben, you are my firstborn, my might (*koakh*) . . . excelling in power (*'oz*). (Gen 49:3)
>
> - David danced before the LORD with all his might (*'oz*). (2 Sam 6:14)
>
> - With him are strength (*'oz*) and wisdom; the deceived and the deceiver are his. (Job 12:16)
>
> - He delivered me from my strong (*'oz*) enemy, from those who hated me; for they were too mighty (*'amats*) for me. (2 Sam 22:18)

---

2. Commonly used synonyms are *'oz, khazaq, koakh*: *'oz* = "might" strength" adjectival form, "fortified" "powerful; *koakh* = "power" "ability" "mighty in battle"; *khazaq* = "strength" "force" adjective means "firm" "stout" "mighty" "forceful." See Brown, Driver, and Briggs, *A Hebrew and English Lexicon*, 304–6; 470–71; 738–39 and Kohler et al., *The Hebrew and Aramaic Lexicon*, 302–4; 468–69; 804–6. All these common forms of strength come from God. See Exod 13:14 (*khazaq*); Isa 40:31 (*koakh*(); Exod 15:2 (*'oz*); 2 Sam 22:18 (*'amats*).

- For thus said the Lord GOD, the Holy One of Israel: In returning and rest you shall be saved; in quietness and in trust shall be your strength (*khul*). (Isa 30:15)

The Unique Form in the *Shema*

The surprise in the *Shema* is that *none* of the above Hebrew words are used. The word for "strength" is a very unusual usage, unique in the whole Bible. The word *me'od* occurs over two hundred and fifty times and almost always is an *adverb* meaning "very."[3] Rather than indicating particular physical, personal, or political power, it implies a quality of strength such as energy or vitality. It would not make sense in English to say, "Love God with all your *very*" or all your "muchness," so English translators use "might" or "strength" for *me'od* only in this verse.[4]

Translators take their cue to translate *me'od* as "strength" from the third-century BCE Greek translation of the Bible from Hebrews,[5] which uses a Greek word for "strength" (*isxu*). They also reference the New Testament (first century CE), which uses yet another Greek word for "strength" (*dunam*) in its translation of the *Shema*.[6] These two Greek words are synonyms. Generally *dunam* means power, ability, capacity, or capability to act effectively and *isxu* means "strength," "power," or "might" of a person's or community's potential and capability.[7]

Inclusive and Expansive Strength

That *me'od* could not be easily or obviously translated precisely into Greek is to be expected, and the use of *me'od* in this verse remains

3. *Me'od* means "very," "much," "exceedingly," or "thoroughly." See R. Wakel, in Van Gemeren, *New International Dictionary of Old Testament Theology and Exegesis*, 824–27.

4. This peculiar use is repeated in 2 Kings 23:25. Usually the word *me'od* is used as an adverb and commonly translated "very" or "exceedingly." This is an odd word choice to communicate strength. One lexicon translates the nominal use of *me'od* as "muchness, life-force, abundance, increase" (see Brown, Driver, Briggs, *A Hebrew and English Lexicon*, 547).

5. Known as the Septuagint.

6. Mark 12:30, 33; Luke 10:27.

7. "*isxus*" in Louw-Nida, *Greek-English Lexicon*.

unusual and unique.[8] Why was *me'od*, normally meaning "very," used here? The first likely reason is that it is *inclusive* of all kinds of strength: physical muscle, financial, political, military power, etc. Whatever kind of strength you have, love God with that. The *Shema* is calling for the use of one's entire capacity and energy in the love of God. The second reason is perhaps more important for understanding the biblical concept of health and wholeness: the scope of *me'od* is *not limited* by these kinds of power. Those with recognized disabilities or chronic illness can also flourish (see section three in this chapter). Not everyone has physical power, fiscal strength, political or military power, *but everyone* has the possibility of *me'od*: vitality, flourishing, and thriving; Life with a capital "L." Everyone can choose to use the "might" of the vitality they have in loving God, whatever that strength happens to be.[9]

God as the Source of Added Strength

Another likely reason for using the adverb "very" (*me'od*) instead of any one of several nouns for "strength" is that "very" is not a *place or thing*. "Very" in this unique context is dynamism *between*. It is not a one-way street, but the locus of personal transformation. It can be pictured as a dynamic circle of energy where an interchange of energy between a person and the creating Holy Spirit may take place. In this interchange the person is changed, slightly or dramatically, into a new person. A person's ordinary created gifts and strengths are ordered according to the original creation. The Spirit converts and shapes the ordinary *very* into a *very that is turned toward loving, both God and one's neighbor.*

This experience is sometimes called conversion or transformation. It converts your created strength from serving your *self* and your own advancement in power in the world to serving the Creator of the world. When you love God with all your *very* (strength), the Holy Spirit can transform your *very* into a *very very* (a dynamic and relational *strong*

8. One scholar calls this unique use "a linguistically daring expansion of the use of the familiar emphatic particle." B. Kedar-Kopfstein, "*me'od*" in *Theological Dictionary of the Old Testament*, 8:41.

9. G. Von Rad interprets this inclusive strength as "intensity" or "utmost effort." Rabbinic interpreters suggest financial strength in relation to *mammon* (*Ber.* 16b). Cited in Kedar-Kopfstein, *Theological Dictionary of the Old Testament*, 8:41.

strength). An adverb is limited only by the verb or adjective to which it is related. In this case, it is the limitlessness of loving God.

This kind of *very very* is described in the super-charge of the Spirit (of the LORD) in Isaiah 40. Preaching to the community in exile, Isaiah proclaims this possibility as an extraordinary promise.

> He gives power (*koakh*) to the faint, and strengthens (*'atsam*) the powerless. Even youths will faint and be weary, and the young will fall exhausted; but those who wait for the LORD shall renew their strength (*koakh*), they shall mount up with wings like eagles, they shall run and not be weary, they shall walk and not faint. (Isa 40:29–31)

The potential for ordinary people to receive strength from God that transforms the community is attested in many places in the Hebrew Bible.[10]

> God is our refuge and strength, a very present help in trouble. Therefore we will not fear, though the earth should change, though the mountains shake in the heart of the sea (Ps 46:1–2).
> On the day I called, you answered me, you increased my strength of soul. (Ps 138:3)

In the New Testament, the community of faith is encouraged to recognize the increase in capacity for power that is possible from the LORD.[11]

> I pray that according to the riches of his glory He may grant that you may be strengthened (*kratos*) in your inner being with power (*dunam*) through his Spirit." (Eph 3:16)

This was Paul's personal experience.

> For this I toil and struggle with all the energy that he powerfully (*dunam*) inspires within me. (Col 1:29)
> I can do all things through him who strengthens (*dunam*) me. (Phil 4:13)

The weakest members of the community who "wait" on the LORD will experience amazing strength. Like Isaiah (40:29–31), Paul speaks of God's strength in those who are disabled in some way.

---

10. See Exod 15:2; 2 Samuel 22:33; Pss 28:7–9; 29:11; 46:1; 68:35; 84:5; 86:16; 92:10–14; 138:3; Isa 41:10; 45:24; Dan 10:10; Zech 10:6.

11. God's power (*dunam*) is given to humans also in Acts 6:8; 1 Cor 2:4; Eph 3:7; 2 Tim 1:7; 2 Pet 1:3.

> [God] said to me, "My grace is sufficient for you, for power (*dunam*) is made perfect in weakness." So, I will boast all the more gladly of my weaknesses, so that the power (*dunam*) of Christ may dwell in me. (2 Cor 12:9)

So he gives this blessing to the struggling Ephesian community.[12]

> Finally, be strong (*dunam*) in the Lord and in the strength (*kratos*) of his might (*isxus*) (Eph 6:10).
>
> Now to him who by the power (*dunam*) at work within us is able (*dunam*) to accomplish abundantly far more than all we can ask or imagine. (Eph 3:20)

The purpose of this power is so that those who receive this power might be a blessing to others:

> . . . who comforts us in all our affliction, so that we may be able (*dunam*) to comfort those who are in any affliction, with the comfort with which we ourselves are comforted by God (2 Cor 1:4).
>
> We might have (*dunam*) made demands as apostles of Christ, but we were gentle among you, like a nurse tenderly caring for her own children (1 Thess 2:7).
>
> . . . whoever renders service, as one who renders it by the strength (*isxus*) which God supplies; in order that in everything God may be glorified through Jesus Christ. (1 Pet 4:11b)

Paul describes access to this power as enlightenment given by God in Christ.[13]

> With the eyes of your heart enlightened, you may know . . . what is the immeasurable greatness of his power (*dunam*) in us who believe, according to the working of his great might (*isxus*). (Eph 1:18–19)
>
> God . . . has shone in our hearts to give the light of the knowledge of the glory of God in the face of Jesus Christ. But we have this treasure in clay jars, so that it may be made clear that this extraordinary power (*dunam*) belongs to God and does not come from us. (2 Cor 4:6–7)

The *Shema* in the Greek (Septuagint) opens the window to this kind of power when it says, "Love the Lord your God . . . with all your strength

---

12. See also Col 1:11.

13. The immeasurable strength (*dunam*) in God's people is the same power that raised Jesus from death (2 Cor 13:4) and will accomplish the resurrection (Phil 3:21).

(*dunam*)." So does the New Testament when it repeats it with "all your strength (*isxus*)." If Christians take the biblical text to heart, growing in the "light of the knowledge of the glory of God" with enlightened hearts, they will experience the dynamism of the *very very* strength; the "immeasurable greatness" and "extraordinary power" that comes from a relationship from God for the good of the community.

The Renewal of Strength: Change and Growth

In the same context that the apostle Paul counseled the Roman Christians to present their bodies to God as a "spiritual" worship, he directed them to continually "renew" their minds. The verb is the root of the English word "metamorphosis."

> Do not be conformed to this world, but be transformed (*metamorphousthe*) by the renewing of your minds, so that you may discern what is the will of God—what is good and acceptable and perfect. (Rom 12:2)

The direction of this metamorphosis in relation to loving God and others is amazing.

> Let love be genuine; hate what is evil, hold fast to what is good; love one another with mutual affection; outdo one another in showing honor. Do not lag in zeal, be ardent in spirit, serve the Lord. Rejoice in hope, be patient in suffering, persevere in prayer. Contribute to the needs of the saints; extend hospitality to strangers. Bless those who persecute you; bless and do not curse them. Rejoice with those who rejoice, weep with those who weep. Live in harmony with one another; do not be haughty, but associate with the lowly; do not claim to be wiser than you are. (Rom 12:9–16)

The renewal of strength of each individual is directed toward the good of the community. This is less obvious, but still the case in Isaiah's hopeful words, "those who wait for the LORD shall renew their strength" (Isa 40:30). He was speaking to a community in exile in Babylon who were about to be set free to return and rebuild Jerusalem. God gives "power (*koakh*) to the faint, and strengthens (*'atsam*) the powerless" for the purpose of this community building project.

Transformation and Strengthened Life in the Hebrew Bible

The experience of transformation that leads to increased strength of life for the community is a primary theme of Scripture. It can be typified by surveying two Hebrew words: "Life" from the verb root (*khayah*) and the verb "transformed" (*hapak*). They help expand the concept of "love God with all your *very*" through the stories of Scripture.

Life (*khayah*) *denotes vitality, vigor, and a quality of thriving.* At the beginning of physical life God "breathed into his nostrils the breath of life (*khayah*); and the man became a living (*khayah*) being" (Gen 2:7). This was the original source of the *very* life-strength. This same breath is still the source (see Spirit below). In Modern Hebrew the adjective from the root (*khayah*) is translated, "healthy," "vital," or "vigorous." It brings to mind the medical condition which persists in some children, called "failure to thrive." This odd designation denotes the absence of normal human growth and energy known as "thriving." For a child, "thriving" means incredible energy, curiosity, and increasing capacities for life.

The word is used to denote several important steps in the formation (health) and restoration (healing) of a whole person. It is used of the beginning of physical life and being. It describes the vigor of the Hebrew women who successfully resisted Pharaoh's attempted genocide (Exod 1:19) by giving birth quickly. The midwives Puah and Shiphrah, struggling for survival under oppression, succeeded in thwarting Pharaoh because, in childbirth, the Hebrew mothers were *khayeh* ("vigorous" or "lively"). Thriving life in this context involved the community of women who worked together under the most horrific circumstances. They had *very* (*me'od*). Their vigor demonstrated the *very* of their love for each other and for God.

Khayah also can mean "to heal" or "revive." When Israel camped at Gibeath-Haaraloth ("foreskin hill"), they waited for the men who submitted to circumcision until they were "healed" (*khayotam*; Josh 5:3). This act of loyalty to God was a radical expression of faithful love by those who had survived forty years of desert wandering.[14] God's command for this people, however, made this covenanting action a fundamental act of community health and life. The healing of the wounds was

14. Circumcision has demonstrated health benefits, but is generally judged to be elective surgery.

symbolic of the greater strength of identity in the Lord that was life and health to this wandering people (Deut 30:29; 32:47).

The third significant narrative use of "life" (*khayah*) is the unexpected flowing of life-giving water. Isaac moved with his flocks into a part of Canaan that his father Abraham had previously shared with Abimelech (Genesis 20; Genesis 26). His men began by re-digging the water wells that Abraham had used. At Esek they found *mayim khayyim* ("living water"), i.e., an artesian spring that flowed without drawing it (Gen 26:19). In the New Testament, Jesus compared himself to this kind of living water as the source of all vitality.[15] This is the source of the metaphor Jesus employs in his conversation with the Samaritan woman. "If you knew the gift of God and who it is that asks you for a drink, you would have asked him and he would have given you living water."[16] Later Jesus compares himself to the artesian's surprising source of water and thriving. "He who believes in me, as the Scripture said, 'From his innermost being shall flow rivers of living water.'"[17] The upshot is that the woman's life and that of her whole community are transformed.[18]

The experience of transformation (*hapak*) *leads to increased strength* for the community and for the love of God.[19] It is a means or agency of increasing human health and strength. Human might is dramatically augmented when person is transformed by God. Scripture has some notable examples of this kind of transformation.

Saul was changed (*hapak*) by the "Spirit of the Lord" early in his career from self-serving to serving the people and God. The text says that God "changed (*hapak*) Saul's heart" (1 Sam 10:6, 9 NIV). The shaman Balaam was hired to curse the wandering Hebrew people. The LORD turned the words in Balaam's mouth into a blessing (Numbers 22). "God . . . turned (*hapak*) the curse into a blessing for you, because the LORD your God loves you" (Deut 23:5).

When Israel fled slavery, the sea barrier to their liberation was transformed into a pathway of escape: "He turned (*hapak*) the sea into

15. John 4:10; 7:38; cf. Isa 12:3; Jer 17:13.

16. Cf. Jer 17:13

17. John 7:38. The Greek is *udatos zontos* just as in the LXX at Gen 26:19; cf. Isa 12:3.

18. John 4:39–42.

19. Various forms of *hapak* can mean "turn," "overthrow," "destroy," "change," See Kohler, et al., *Hebrew and Aramaic Lexicon*, 251–52.

dry land, they passed through the waters on foot—come, let us rejoice in him" (Ps 66:6). The flinty rock became a source of water: "Tremble, O earth, at the presence of the LORD, at the presence of the God of Jacob, who turns (*hapak*) the rock into a pool of water, the flint into a spring of water" (Ps 114:7–8). Jeremiah declared that mourning would be transformed (*hapak*) into gladness. "Then maidens will dance and be glad, young men and old as well. I will turn (*hapak*) their mourning into gladness; I will give them comfort and joy instead of sorrow" (Jer 31:11, 13).

The word *hapak* has two sides, like the sides of a coin. It can mean "destroyed" as well as "transformed." All transformation involves the end of something and the beginning of something new. Jonah's prophecy to Nineveh is succinctly delivered in eight words (only five in Hebrew!). "Forty more days and Nineveh will be overturned" (3:4b NIV 1984).[20] When the Ninevites heard the word "overturned" (*hapak*) they assumed that God meant "destruction." The word has a second possibility, however, as Jonah knows too well. When the Ninevites believed God and instituted major turning from their violent ways, they were "overturned" or "overthrown" (*hapak*) in the second way (Jonah 3:8–10). They were transformed in a way that "destroyed" a violent way of life.[21]

As with most increases in power and strength, the transformation of "overturning" in relation to God, the source of healthy strength, is not necessarily comfortable. Growth and healing have their associated healthy pains. Access to new sources of strength in relationship to God is not possible without repentance of lifestyles that destroy life. A person or a community that is transformed is de-centered and re-centered through an experience of wonder in relation the creating Spirit of God.

---

20. The NIV 1978 version and NLT have "Nineveh will be *destroyed*." KJV, RSV, NRSV, NASB all have "will be overthrown." The NIV 1984 version "overturned" is the best word for preserving both necessary possibilities of the Hebrew text. "Forty days" is the traditional length of time for reflection and purification. See Ex 24:18; Num 13:25; Mark 1:13.

21. The more difficult side of the word means "destroy." Sodom and Gomorrah are the main examples of this usage (Gen 19:21, 25, 29; See Gen 18:16–33). Being transformed (*hapak*) in the Hebrew Bible means "being overthrown by God." This may mean repentance and new life, or it may mean catastrophic destruction. See J. Bruckner, *Jonah, Nahum, Habakkuk, Zephaniah*, 90–96.

Brain Growth and Vitality: Experiences of Wonder and Transformation

Scientists as well as people of faith are interested in knowing what circumstances and practices lead to human health and strength. Neuroscientists have recently shown interest in the sources of human flourishing and vitality, particularly in the brain. The brain is the locus of control for all aspects of strength and growth.

A leading neuroscientist is working toward a new integration of cognitive neuroscience and religious studies through the investigation of human experiences of *wonder*.[22] Wonder is "the feeling excited by an encounter with something novel and unexpected, something that strikes a person as intensely real, true, and/or beautiful" (*Oxford New English Dictionary*). Powerful experiences of wonder may be encountered in prayer, recitation of texts, music, dreams, or visions. These encounters have the potential to be life-changing. Their physiological impact can quicken curiosity and create the impulse to explore new pathways.[23]

Tracing these experiences in the brain using MRI and EEG reading technology has yielded some valuable insights.[24] First, because very little of the brain can be assigned specific mental functions, vast portions are "available to play active roles in a variety of neural systems and psychological processes."[25] Therefore, the majority of its millions of neurons, axons, dendrites, and synapses are available for the "renewing of the mind."

Secondly, the recurring theme for neuroscientists' investigation of religious experiences is that they cannot be located in any one part of the brain.[26] An experience of wonder cannot be reduced to a spe-

22. Kelly Bulkeley, *The Wondering Brain*. Of particular interest are his discussion of dreams and visions (ch. 1) and contemplative practices (ch. 4).

23. Ibid., 16.

24. MRI is magnetic resonance imaging; EEG refers to electroencephalograph readings.

25. Bulkeley, *Wondering Brain*, 20. Babies and teenagers have two major bursts of neural production in frontal and parietal lobes which serve to integrate far-flung information. Unimpaired, they have the capability of learning with amazing speed. Bulkeley, *Wondering Brain*, 103.

26. There is no "phrenological trap of anatomical localization." Bulkeley, *Wondering Brain*, 18.

cific physiological function of one portion of the brain. Thirdly, certain kinds of meditative religious experiences have been observed as unique patterns that use a broad spectrum of the brain.[27] Other religious experiences of wonder have not yet been studied. Measured or not, they have a *decentering* impact that suspends the ordinary cognitive filtering processes of evaluation and categorization.

> Experiences of wonder by definition push the brain-mind system beyond its normal range of functioning, forcing it to make sense of extremely unusual input. Because experiences of wonder are encounters with the novel and unexpected, they defy conventional associative categories and transgress the normal boundaries of understanding. More that that, they stimulate an expanded development of those crucial metal processes that intervene between sensory input and motor output. Experiences of wonder quite literally stretch our minds.[28]

These experiences of growth are facilitated in communities of faith through many practices of worship and praise of God. (These experiences will be the subject of chapter nine.) Conversion and renewal are religious categories for talking about the recentering of one's life.

Not all encounters with wonder are "wonderful" in the happy sense. They can also be terrible. As in the discussion of *hapak* above, being decentered by a powerful experience can be painful. Much human growth and even flourishing can come through experiences of *painful wonder*.

> Every experience of wonder involves loss—the loss of one's previous center, the shedding of old ideas, the overthrow of one's previous sense of self and world. . . . To suddenly lose a loved one, a relationship, a home, a time of life, or a cherished ideal can be a genuine occasion for wonder in the sense of an unexpected revelation of a new truth or reality—the truth of human frailty, the reality of a hostile world. The old center is most definitely gone, but a new one is nowhere to be seen.[29]

27. Dozens of vetted studies in cognitive neuroscience have demonstrated a particular pattern of brain activity in the bilateral frontal brain coupled with reduced activity in the right parietal lobe that occurs only among people who meditate (both yogis and nuns). Many are cited by Warren Brown, "Human Nature, Physicalism, Spirituality, and Healing," 115–16; 126.

28. Bulkeley, *Wondering Brain*, 20–21; see p. 52.

29. Ibid., 24.

The experience of wonder is decentering and recentering of the self. With communities of faith, the experiences of suffering common to all people are both interpreted and embraced. Both painful and joyful wonder can be mediated by congregations who have a framework and a history of relationship with God for making sense of powerfully transforming experiences.[30]

In order to have vitality and growth, human health requires experiences of wonder. Encountering God in the variety of practices of the worshiping community prepares us for the expansion of our minds. Prayer, recitation of and meditation on the narrative and poetry of Scripture, lament, praise and offering music as direct communication with God, and visions of a new world: all these increase human vitality, are agents of flourishing, and the wonder of transformation in relation to God. The effects of these things may be measured by an MRI, but the source of their effectiveness is God's Holy Spirit. These experiences increase a person's capacity for encountering God.

The Source of Vitality and Growth: Strength and God's Spirit

God's Spirit is present and active in the ancient narrative whenever the community of Israel is significantly transformed. God's glory was *with* the people as they exited the slavery of Egypt, in pillars of cloud and fire that protected and guided them as they escaped. God's Spirit *fills* Bezalel with skill, intelligence, and knowledge for overseeing the community's building of the tabernacle (Exod 31:2–35; 30–31). God's dwelling presence descended *into the midst* of a worshiping people after the tabernacle is built in the wilderness (Exod 40:34–35). God put the Spirit that directed Moses upon the seventy elders so they could administrate Israel's justice system (Num 11:16–17; 25–29). God's Spirit causes Balaam to bless Israel, against Balaam's own will (Num 24:1–9).

It is in the worshiping life of the community that Scripture most regularly celebrates the transforming experience of God's presence. The expression of these experiences is celebrated by the psalmist.

> Awesome is God in his sanctuary, the God of Israel; he gives *power and strength* to his people. Blessed be God! (Ps 68:35)

---

30. See Jeff Levin, *God, Faith, and Health*, 177.

The experience of the wonder is described as blessedness. It leads to the restoration of a desolate place.

> Blessed are those who live in your house, ever singing your praise. Selah. Blessed are those whose *strength is in you*, in whose heart are the highways to Zion. As they go through the valley of Baca they make it a place of springs; the early rain also covers it with pools. (Ps 84:4–6)

A song of individual thanksgiving recognizes the transforming power of prayer.

> I bow down toward your holy temple and give thanks to your name for your steadfast love and your faithfulness; for you have exalted your name and your word above everything. On the day I called, you answered me; *you increased the strength of my life.* (Ps 138:2–3)

The biblical prophets regularly speak God's words directly in God's voice by means of God's Spirit. Isaiah, for example, speaks God's promise of his direct presence and help to strengthen the community of exiles in Babylon.

> Do not fear, for I am with you, do not be afraid, for I am your God; *I will strengthen you, I will help you,* I will uphold you with my victorious right hand. (Isa 41:10)

This ancient tradition of strength added to communities and individuals by God's Spirit has also become the subject of scientific inquiry. A study of prayer at the University of Louisville School of Medicine compared EEG patterns of Christians praying prayers of adoration and praise to God to previous studies of practitioners of yoga and Transcendental Meditation.[31] They expected the typical slower electrocordial rhythms in the alpha range but found the opposite. The pray-ers shifted toward the beta range of hyper-alertness. This potential vitality, according to this study (and the experience of many Jews and Christians) is available to any Christian adoring God in prayer by the power of God's Holy Spirit.

---

31. The study and its analysis are reported in Ibid., 167–68.

The Growth of Israel's Witness to the Spirit of God

We can trace the development of the phrase "spirit (*ruakh*) of God" which can also be translated "breath (*ruakh*) of God." This trajectory of growth demonstrates the many means that God has used to stimulate human growth and vitality.

In Genesis and Job "spirit of God" simply means the physical breath that God gives. This is the grounding of all human vitality and the "quintessence of creation."[32] Early in Genesis the "breath of life" becomes the "spirit (*ruakh*) of life," e.g., "in whose nostrils was the spirit of life."[33] God's "spirit" in humans simply refers to God's "breath" in these texts. Job uses the phrase "spirit of God" in a similar way: "as long as the spirit of God is in my nostrils."[34]

We begin to see a shift in understanding the "spirit of God" as the source of human vitality in the prayer of David after his responsibility for the death of Bathsheba's husband and son sinks in. David prays that God will give him a new spirit to transform him:

> Create in me a clean heart, O God, and put a *new and right spirit* within me. Do not cast me away from your presence, and do not take your *holy spirit* from me. Restore to me the joy of your salvation, and sustain in me a *willing spirit*. (Ps 51:10–12)

"Holy spirit" is usually understood by historical interpreters as a reference to physical breath of God (as in Genesis).[35] It is holy because it is from God. Nonetheless, this anticipates the transforming presence and indwelling of God's spirit in the prophets. David is asking for more than "new breath." He wants to be transformed and have his relationship with God revitalized. For him, the only means to this renewal is repentance, and forgiveness.

Ezekiel provides a fuller understanding of the power of God's spirit to renew, transform and resurrect a dead community. Ezekiel's vision report says that the Spirit of the LORD brought him out and set him in the middle of a valley full of dry bones (Ezek 37:1).

---

32. Levison, *Filled with the Spirit*, 15.
33. Gen 7:22; also in 6:17 and 7:15.
34. Job 27:2–4; 33:4; 34:14–15; see 104:30.
35. See Levison, *Filled with the Spirit*, 29–31.

> ... but there was no breath in them. Then he said to me, "Prophesy to the breath (*ruakh*) prophesy, mortal, and say to the breath (*ruakh*): 'Thus says the Lord GOD: Come from the four winds (*ruakh*), O breath (*ruakh*), and breathe upon these slain, that they may live.'" I prophesied as he commanded me, and the breath (*ruakh*) came into them, and they lived, and stood on their feet, a vast multitude. "Mortal, these bones are the whole house of Israel. They say, 'Our bones are dried up, and our hope is lost; we are cut off completely.' ... [Thus says the Lord GOD] ... I will put my spirit (*ruakh*) within you, and you shall live, and I will place you on your own soil; then you shall know that I, the LORD, have spoken and will act, says the LORD." (Ezek 37:8b–11, 14)

This text may be read simply to mean physical breath until the transition to the restoration of the community. The dry bones are a metaphor, but the restoration of the community is a real transformation for the people in exile, accomplished by God's spirit.

This double use of the *ruakh* of God (breath and spirit) is a transitional link to Ezekiel's fuller use of *ruakh* as "spirit" in declaring God's promises of a "new spirit" for the community 11:19–20; 18:30–32; 36:26–27. These promises are echoed by the prophet Joel.

> Then afterward I will pour out my spirit (*ruakh*) on all flesh; your sons and your daughters shall prophesy, your old men shall dream dreams, and your young men shall see visions. Even on the male and female slaves, in those days, I will pour out my spirit (*ruakh*). (Joel 2:28–29)

In the New Testament, the outpouring of the Spirit on the apostles marked the inauguration of Christian preaching with the transformation of the common Jewish men who had followed their rabbi Jesus.

> And suddenly from heaven there came a sound like the rush of a violent wind, and it filled the entire house where they were sitting. Divided tongues, as of fire, appeared among them, and a tongue rested on each of them. All of them were filled with the Holy Spirit and began to speak in other languages, as the Spirit gave them ability. (Acts 2:2–4)

This unique inauguration of the preaching of the gospel in many languages is followed in the New Testament by a more daily transforming activity of the Holy Spirit. While the presence of the Spirit gave some people ability that they did not previously have,[36] it was generally for everyone in the community, a source of communication, power, and joy.

> May the God of hope fill you with all joy and peace in believing, so that you may abound in hope by the power of the Holy Spirit. (Rom 15:13)

Even in midst of persecution, this joy is possible.

> And you became imitators of us and of the Lord, for in spite of persecution you received the word with joy inspired by the Holy Spirit. (1 Thess 1:6)

In spite of human failings, the renewal of the Spirit is offered.

> But when the goodness and loving kindness of God our Savior appeared, he saved us, not because of any works of righteousness that we had done, but according to his mercy, through the water of rebirth and renewal by the Holy Spirit. This Spirit he poured out on us richly through Jesus Christ our Savior. (Titus 3:4–6)

The measure of the transforming work of the Spirit is a human measure of health, and strength of character.

> By contrast, the fruit of the Spirit is love, joy, peace, patience, kindness, generosity, faithfulness, gentleness, and self-control. There is no law against such things. And those who belong to Christ Jesus have crucified the flesh with its passions and desires. If we live by the Spirit, let us also be guided by the Spirit. (Gal 5:22–25)

Many volumes of systematic theology have been written about the Holy Spirit and its work, from the early eastern and western church, medieval monasticism, the Reformation traditions, and Vatican II. Recently the work of Asian Christian theologians has offered significant insights for understanding the relationship between the concept of *Chi/ki/gi* (energy) and the Holy Spirit.[37] The tradition of Catholic, Orthodox, and Protestant faiths can be summed up in the ancient creed that

36. See John 20:22–23 where Jesus breathes on his disciples and gives them the audacious ability to forgive sins. See also, for example, Acts 8:39; Acts 9:40.

37. See especially Jong Chun Park, "The Paradigm of Korean Theology of the Spirit" in *Crawl with God, Dance in the Spirit*, 34–46; For an Asian Feminist reading see Grace Ji-Sun Kim, "In Search of a Pneumatology: Chi and Spirit."

describes the transforming work of the Spirit within the community: "I believe in the Holy Spirit: the holy catholic church, the communion of saints, the forgiveness of sins, the resurrection of the body, and the life everlasting."[38]

The *very* "might" and "strength" of the Spirit is measured by corporate and not simply individual standards. Perhaps the best measure of the "*very*" (*me'od*) of a community is how it understands the strength of persons with disabilities.

The Strength of Disability

Everyone has the possibility of *me'od*: vitality, flourishing, and thriving. The World Council of Churches has written a study document on the nature of human life that offers a biblical perspective on the world of disability, beginning with the premise that all people are created in the image of God and therefore are of infinite worth, "whatever their physical or mental condition."[39] As scholars with disabilities and others have shown, the body is our primary source of knowledge. For the person with a disability, what happens to one's body happens to one's world.

We find this concept sustained in the theology of the broken body of Christ. Christian identity and knowledge is established primarily by Christ's body, broken for our sake. This shift in identity away from normal cultural standards of "perfection" is in itself an experience of wonder and transformation. For this reason the Eucharist is a regular practice of Christian worship. In a similar way, Judaism's regular reference to deliverance from the slavery of Egypt recognizes that truth and wholeness come through brokenness and the grace of God's presence.[40]

Brokenness lies at the heart of this new definition of perfection.[41] Vitality of life comes through death: Jesus' death and the death and rebirth of human identity in Christ.[42] The strength of the *very* is made

38. Apostle's Creed, third article.

39. *Christian Perspectives on Theological Anthropology: A Faith and Order Study Document*, 24. See also my discussion of the image of God in chapter one.

40. For a history of the various views toward disability in the Hebrew Bible, see Saul Olyan, *Disability in the Hebrew Bible*. For the problem of stigmatization of the disabled see 125–28.

41. *Christian Perspectives on Theological Anthropology*, 26.

42. Rom 6:3–5; Col 2:12; In 1Cor 15:30 Paul can say, "I die every day."

possible through human weakness. "The perfection of God is a perfection of vulnerability and of openness to pain."[43]

The Apostle Paul suffered an unknown disability. He used this as an occasion to teach the central perspective of the better strength that is possible for those who are aware of their disability as a source of strength. This revelation came to him in the words of God in an experience of wonder: "My grace is sufficient for you, for power is made perfect in weakness." His insight for the Corinthian community was an embodiment of the gospel.

> So, I will boast all the more gladly of my weaknesses, so that the power of Christ may dwell in me. Therefore I am content with weaknesses, insults, hardships . . . for whenever I am weak, then I am strong. (2 Cor 12:9–10; see Rom 8:26; 2 Cor 11:30)

The World Council document concludes, from the perspective of people with disabilities, that the "mission of disabled people is to become apostles of inclusion, witnesses of vulnerability and partners in pain." They are in good company with the apostle Paul.[44]

Vulnerable and Dependent

A similar insight is offered by ethical philosophy. Human beings are fundamentally vulnerable and dependent for their survival on each other. This dependence and vulnerability must be acknowledged if we are to thrive and flourish. Our culture often teaches the opposite values: that I may flourish if I am independent and secured from any vulnerability.[45] Persons with disabilities know and can teach us that we are not yet fully aware of our radical dependence on others, aware of ourselves as vulnerable, and therefore, not yet rational people.[46] How we respond to persons who suffer with a chronic illness, debilitating disease, physiological disorder or are blind, deaf, or crippled reflects whether or not

43. *Christian Perspectives on Theological Anthropology*, 26.

44. Ibid.

45. A. MacIntyre, *Dependent Rational Animals*.

46. Ibid., 136–38. MacIntyre finds the most compelling evidence in irrational responses of revulsion that people have to a person with facial disfigurement. They are made in the image of God but we are repulsed, even knowing better. He argues that we can gain both self-awareness and a new vitality from what they have to teach us by their presence and experience.

we have been enlightened about our own condition. It is a projection of our own disability, one that is all too obvious to those who know their own vulnerability.[47]

We are all always somewhere on a continuum of disability, in need of a community of help for our vitality and growth. "There is no such thing as a dichotomy between 'disabled' and 'nondisabled' . . . Throughout our lives, from infancy to old age, we move back and forth along this scale."[48] Flourishing communities acknowledge this dependence and provide for those who are in seasons or conditions of more extreme dependence.

The exclusion of the severely disabled as "a fact of nature" obscures the actual fact that "the obstacles presented by those afflictions can be overcome . . . What disability amounts to . . . depends not just on the disabled individual, but on the groups of which that individual is a member."[49] Flourishing depends on the self-awareness and imagination of community. One community that did not fail to imagine the limitless value of disabled person was the pre-World War II German Bodelshwingh institutions.

A True Story of Vitality in Disability

In pre-World War II Germany, a young boy named Gunther was kept by his grandmother, who earned a meager living scrubbing other people's floors. He had suffered vitamin deficiencies resulting in severe bone deformities,[50] and was locked alone and sedated in a back bedroom during her long absences. His malnourishment and neglect continued until he was seven. When she decided she could no longer keep him, he was sent to Bethel, a small institution, primarily for epileptics, in Bielefeld, Germany. This was the beginning of hope for Gunther.[51]

47. T. E. Reynolds, *Vulnerable Communion*.

48. See discussion of MacIntyre in W. Brown, "Human Nature, Physicalism, Spirituality, and Healing," 121–22.

49. A. MacIntyre, *Dependent Rational Animals*, 75; cited also in Brown, "Human Nature, Physicalism, Spirituality, and Healing," 22.

50. Gunther suffered severe skeletal deformities from calcium and vitamin D deprivation as an infant and toddler. His soft warped bones and joints hardened into uselessness.

51. The whole story from Gunther's perspective, narrated near the end of his life in 1974, is told masterfully in Edna Hong, *Bright Valley of Love*. Edna Hong and her

Bethel was an institution rooted in Christian theology of the praise of God. Every day the value of every resident as an image-bearer of God was taught and practiced. Everyone had the capacity for hope through the language of praise. Gunther recalled that "even the deaf and dumb and very mentally retarded Dora, who could only squeal," understood the language of praise. "One had only to look in her eyes to know that her squeals spelled sheer delight. 'I love you,' her eyes said, 'and I am the happiest of all people.'"[52] He delighted and grew in the fact that a relationship to God was possible, no matter who you are, because you can offer your praise and thanks. He embraced this sense of fundamental vocation, thrilled that he had the potential to share in the transcendent life of God and God's community of love and respect.

Gunther memorized the following text, which remained significant to him until the end of his long life.

> I will bless the Lord at all times; his praise shall continually be in my mouth. My life makes its boast in the Lord; let the afflicted hear and be glad. O magnify the Lord with me, and let us exalt His Name together. (Ps 34:1–3)

It reflects the joyful experience of wonder and glory in the midst of his weakness and suffering. It describes the ultimate vocation of all those created in God's image, to be in communication with the Creator; to be empowered and transformed, no matter the circumstance. It is a call to the community from one severely disabled, to "exalt His Name together." Gunther's praise was made possible by a community that had been transformed from an ideology of independence, autonomy, and false securities to an ethos of love, respect, and the praise of God.

Thriving in the Midst of Adversity

Three terms are used in health research and practice to describe modes of human vitality: *resilience, hardiness,* and a *sense of coherence.* Research in these areas is helpful for understanding why some patients flourish in a crisis and others falter. Each is related to the biblical concept of (*me'od*) *very* or thriving. These concepts point to the reality that

husband Howard were renowned scholars, translating the complete works of Soren Kierkegaard into English.

52. Ibid., 51.

the health of the patient cannot be separated from their relational community or their narrative history.

Resilience

Resilience[53] in fabric refers to material that may be stretched and suffer friction and still maintain its integrity. In health care it "denotes a combination of abilities and characteristics that interact dynamically to allow an individual to bounce back, cope successfully, and function above the norm in spite of significant stress or adversity."[54]

Resilience can be measured when a person thrives *in spite of* adversity. As we will see in chapter eight, on the subject of *lament*, the ancient text provides a demonstration of extraordinary stress (catastrophic violence, dislocation, and the decimation of a country) and a people that not only survives, but lives to thrive. The Jewish community in Babylon is a case study *par excellence* of resilience (see chapter eight). One health ministry practitioner describes this as *hope* which sets aside fear and is willing to face great dangers because of that hope.[55]

Hardiness

Hardiness is described as 1) *control*: the ability to make good decisions: to appraise, interpret, and respond to health stressors (no powerlessness); 2) *commitment*: involvement with behavioral change (no alienation); and 3) *challenge*: perceives and receives change in personal

---

53. For the history of research on resilience see Kathleen Tusaie and Janyce Dyer, "Resilience: A Historical Review of the Construct." This history is marked by coping as a conscious process (1960s), brain plasticity (1970s), protective-risk factors (1980s), and resilience studies (1990s). Coping refers to taught approaches to adversity: creativity, social skills, humor, education, social support, and a belief system that provides identity and purpose. Plasticity studies refers to the brain's potential to change strategies or "bounce back" in the midst of adversity (i.e., to be transformed in the midst of *painful wonder*). Protective-risk refers to a community's ability to protect those most at risk from the effects of adversity (e.g., children). Resilience studies have focused on the successful re-integration of the self and personal growth following a disruption caused by adversity.

54. M. Rutter, "Resilience: Some Conceptual Considerations" in *Journal of Adolescent Health* 14 (1993) 598–611.

55. Gary Gunderson with Larry Pray, *Leading Causes of Life*, 133–46.

behavior as beneficial (no need for static security).[56] Each of these aspects is evidence of the relational aspect present in the ancient narrative. God continually calls upon his people to decide and choose life, to be involved with their own behavioral change as people made in God's image, and to recognize the challenge of trusting in God as a means to beneficial growth (no false idols of security). Hardiness is also generally described as *agency:* the capacity and power to continue in a changing world and to imagine new paths and a different world.[57] The concept of *hardiness* will be further addressed in chapter seven, "Face to Face."

A Sense of Coherence

Sense of coherence refers to the ability to find meaning in suffering. The primary sense of meaning is established when we confess that we belong to a larger story and believe the claim of the ancient narrative that God's purpose and order can bring order to chaos. How you tell the story of your illness matters.[58] A sense of coherence is enhanced and vitality increased when *connection* and *blessing* are also present. Connection means faith in the fact that we were created for relationship and community with others. Theses connections offer sustenance for life.[59] Blessing recognizes the necessary link between generations. In the giving and receiving blessing is the power to change lives and believe promises.[60] These concepts will be addressed in chapter nine. They are fundamental values inherent in the *Shema* and its counsel to teach our children the ways of God. With them, the gift of our *very* strength may grow and be turned to the love of God and of others in the world.

56. S.C. Kobasa, "Stressful Life Events, Personality and Health. See discussion and background on the concept of hardiness in Susan E. Pollock, "The Hardiness Characteristic."

57. Gunderson, *Leading Causes of Life,* 105–22.

58. See chapter eight and Arthur W. Frank, *The Wounded Storyteller.* Gunderson draws on the work of Anton Antovsky, who first developed the term "sense of coherence."

59. Gunderson, *Leading Causes of Life,* 63–86.

60. Ibid., 123–32.

Part Three

Primary Traditions of Restoration

Chapter Seven

Face to Face

WHENEVER TWO PEOPLE ARE face to face, an environment is created between them. That environment may be an environment of healing, hostility, or somewhere in between. It may contribute to the restoration of health, or to its destruction. It is possible for those in the healing arts to create environments of healing whenever they are face to face with another person. The biblical witnesses offer us several paradigms of healing and presence that are instructive for creating healing contexts.

The ancient stories and texts tell the whole truth about the ways that people suffer. Whether the suffering is from illness, fear, estrangement, or another kind of pain, telling the truth is an essential starting point for healing. Denial only reroutes, redistributes, or perpetuates the suffering. The full restoration of health is enhanced by a caregiver's ability to create a caring, healing environment where it is safe to tell the truth.

Though many people are restored to basic health with no conscious knowledge of God, Scripture claims that they are not without relationship to God. Every person is God's creature and all benefit from the goodness of creation, including the incredible restorative powers of the human mind and body. Day after day, God's providential provision is delivered. The intervention may be through medical expertise, community support, or prayer for healing, but healing comes from the LORD. It often comes through the healing hands of nurses, doctors, pharmacists, or therapists who may or may not know they are doing God's work.

God's provision through human intervention for the sick is an essential paradigm. Why help the ill or the sick? Why care for the corresponding health of our environment? The biblical response is that God has made it and declared it "good" (see chapter one). In the ancient narrative, when sickness (called "sin") and death interrupted that goodness (Genesis 3–11), God intervened to bring about restoration, including the restoration of health. He did this by blessing the creation with incredible resiliency and fecundity and by calling others, beginning with Abraham, to be a blessing to the world (e.g., Genesis 12, 15, 17, 22, 26, 32). This "calling" (vocation) was based on friendship and partnership with God, described most fully in the story of Moses and the Exodus from Egypt. On the basis of his friendship with Moses, God restored the former slaves of Pharaoh to safety and health.

Friendship with God, face to face, is a primary facet of the biblical perspective on the restoration of health. The word for "face of" (*pene*) and the word for "in the presence of" (*lipne*; literally, "to the face of") are from the same fundamental word "face" in Hebrew (*pamin*). Scripture shows the importance of the "presence" of God the healer by its use of the term "face/presence of God." Human face/presence is also essential to the restoration of another person's health.

Facing Sickness, Suffering and Death[1]

Hebrew narratives commonly use two words to communicate a *lack of wellness*.[2] The first word, *khalah*, usually translated "sickness," refers to living things that are weakened, wounded, grieved, diseased, in travail,

---

1. Our definitions of "sickness" and "illness" are deeply conditioned socially and culturally. "Emic" definitions are made from within a culture. Quite often, however, an outsider imports an "etic" definition. For example, some commonly present bacteria in the stomach is considered normal in many countries, but is defined as a sickness by visitors who are not psychologically or physically adapted to this norm. Epilepsy in the ancient world was considered demon possession and treated as such by Jesus. On the importance of the concepts "emic" and "etic" in medical anthropology, see John Pilch, *Healing in the New Testament*, 59–60. For literature and definitions of the terms "sickness," "disease," "illness," "cure," and "healing" see Pilch, 24–25.

2. A variety of other words are occasionally used in the Hebrew Bible for various kinds of infirmity: *dawah* for mental anxiety; *makkah* for wounds; *naggepah* for contagious disease; *deber* probably for bubonic plague. See H.W. Wolff, *Anthropology of the Old Testament*, 143–44. Cf. K. Seybold, "khalah," *Theological Dictionary of the Old Testament*, 4:399–409.

or infirm. The second word, from *ra'* is usually translated "evil" (as an experience of catastrophe) or "affliction," but sometimes (about 15 percent) means "ill" or "illness." In these instances, it is translated: "affliction," "adversity," "distress," "harmed," or "trouble," indicating that some illness and injury has external causes.[3]

Causes of Suffering

It is perhaps obvious that people are sick or suffer for many reasons. Scripture presents a wide spectrum of relationships that result in health or the loss of health. In Deuteronomy the whole people were warned about suffering the "diseases of Egypt" (boils, ulcers, scurvy, and "the itch") if they did not follow God's instructions for a healthy and obedient life (Deut 28:14–68), connecting diseases to their disobedience (sin). The general and specific purpose for the instructions was to assure an ongoing relationship to God and to protect them from unhealthy or unsafe practices (see chapter 2).

Commentators on the New Testament point to this deuteronomic worldview (i.e., sin causes illness) in the first-century disciples' question, "Who sinned, this man or his parents, that he was born blind?" (John 9) This is an important text for disavowing the easy connection between sin and illness. Jesus refutes a one-to-one correspondence between sin and disability by saying "neither this man nor his parents sinned" (John 9:1–3, 34). Similarly, when the tower of Siloam fell and killed eighteen victims, Jesus insisted that the victims were not greater sinners than those who escaped (Luke 13:1–5).

On the other hand, when Jesus healed a man who had been ill for thirty-eight years he said, "Do not sin anymore, so that nothing worse happens to you" (John 5:14).[4] Jesus sometimes forgave sins in his acts of healing.[5] The New Testament recognizes that ailments are sometimes caused or worsened by a person's sin and sometimes they are not. In the

3. Someone else's "badness" may cause "affliction" or "illness." See discussion below.

4. This post-cure word about his sin made the man so angry that he reported Jesus to the authorities for breaking the Sabbath. Sin is also forgiven with healing in Luke 5:17–26 (Mark 2:1–12; Matt 9:1–8).

5. See the treatment of the varied relationships between sin and sickness in Keith Warrington, *Healing and Suffering*, 57–60; see also Daniel Simundson, *Where is God in My Suffering?*, 9–18; 61–70.

same way, the most innocent people may suffer calamity and illness in the Hebrew Bible, as in the case of Job (see below). We must take care not to oversimplify the biblical witness on the causes of illness, sickness, and calamity. Both the Hebrew and New Testament texts offer a variety of explanations that do not follow a simple formula.[6]

The Innocent also Suffer. In Scripture, suffering may be the result of someone's sin, but it often has natural causes (2 Sam 4:4; 2 Kgs 4:18–20).[7] When Elijah was about to be transported to heaven by chariot, the text simply says, "He had fallen sick with the illness of which he was to die" (2 Kgs 13:14).

In the midst of his suffering, Job's friends tried to get him to repent of his hidden sins. God considered their theology itself to be wrong and a sin (Job 42:7–9). Satan was certain Job would curse God *to his face* for his innocent suffering, since God was breaking the falsely assumed rule that goodness equaled the blessing of health (Job 1:11; 2:5). Job's wife made a similar assumption (Job 2:9). One of his so-called friends tells him that he should stop insisting on his innocence before God, since both he and his (dead) children must be sinners.

> "How long will you say such things? Your words are a bluster-ing wind. Does God pervert justice? Does the Almighty pervert what is right? When your children sinned against him, he gave them over to the penalty of their sin." (Job 8:2–4)

This confrontation is theological malpractice. As with all invasive pro-cedures, a confrontation of sin can be done ignorantly. Job is the classic example of the suffering of the innocent, whose wisdom is vindicated by God at the end of a long period of suffering. God rebukes Job's friends twice saying, "*For you have not spoken of me what is right, as my servant Job has done*" (Job 42:7, 8).

An Enemy Has Done It. The cause of suffering does not always originate with the one who is sick. Sometimes the innocent suffer or die because of someone else's sin (Gen 20:3–9, 18; 2 Sam 12:14–23). The whole community may also suffer for the sins of its leaders (Isa 5:26–30; Hab 1:5–11). Children and grandchildren suffer many consequences of

---

6. For more on the subject of causes of sickness in the Bible, see Daniel Simundson, "Health and Healing in the Bible."

7. See chapter two for the prevention of sickness through keeping God's instruc-tion. For example see Lev 11:1–40; Deut 23:12–13.

their parents' and grandparents' sins, in alcoholism, substance abuse, and inherited, preventable diseases (see Exod 34:6–7).

Some unknown person's sin may cause suffering and sickness. Innocent people die in sin-bound wars of greed and expansion, both ancient and modern. The suffering of innocents in war zones is a result of the sin of individuals or of governments. In a fallen world, the consequences of others' sin abound. When someone is killed by a drunk driver, or gets cancer from environmental negligence, an unknown person has done it.

He Brought It on Himself. Sometimes injury or sickness of an individual or of the community is clearly a result of their own human malfeasance.[8] In the history of Israel, suffering is often blamed on rebellion against God.[9] In the books of Judges and Kings, the ailments of Israel are a result of doing "what is right in their own eyes" rather than walking in the instruction given by God at Sinai. The prophets Isaiah and Amos point to the same source of suffering, saying that even the attacks of the Assyrians and Babylonians were a result of the community's sins of greed, injustice, and violence.

When suffering is a result of human sin, the relationship between the sin and the suffering is obvious. When the delivered Hebrew slaves engage in the ritual prostitution at Baal-Peor, a plague breaks out. When Miriam brought a public accusation against her brother Moses for marrying an Ethiopian woman, God turned her skin very white (Num 12:9–16).

Healing and Forgiveness of Sin. When sickness is obviously related to a fault ("sin"), the Bible often connects words of forgiveness of sins with the healing of the physical illness. Some measure of health may be returned by confession of sin, forgiveness, and reconciliation.[10]

> Some became fools through their rebellious ways and suffered affliction because of their iniquities. They loathed all food and drew near the gates of death. Then they cried to the LORD in their trouble, and he saved them from their distress. He sent forth his word and healed them; he rescued them from the grave. Let them give thanks to the LORD for his unfailing love

8. e.g., Num 12:9–16; 1 Cor 11:29–30; Jas 5:16.

9. Gen 3; Exod 32:35; Lev 10:1–2.

10. See Pss 32:3–5; 107:17–20; 38:4; 39:8, 11; 41:4; Mk 2:5–12.

> and his wonderful deeds for men. Let them sacrifice thank of-
> ferings and tell of his works with songs of joy. (Ps 107:17–22)

When sin is confessed by the one who is suffering its consequences, the healing pastoral response is to offer the friendship and forgiveness of God.

> Bless the LORD who forgives all your iniquity, who heals all
> your diseases. (Ps 103.3; "Who forgives" and "who heals" are
> written in poetic parallel.)

Even when God administrates justice, it is clear that God does not enjoy anyone's suffering. God prefers to bring life and health.

> Cast away from you all the transgressions that you have com-
> mitted against me, and get yourselves a new heart (*levav*) and
> a new spirit (*ruach*). Why will you die, O house of Israel? For
> I have no pleasure in the death of anyone, says the LORD God.
> Turn, then and live. (Ezek 18.31–32)

The upshot is that sickness and illness have a variety of causes and solutions. They all potentially bring us face to face with God, either in lament or confession.[11] Determining the source of injury, if there is a source, may be important to treating the whole person. Sometimes this necessitates conversation about confession and forgiveness with the patient.[12] It may involve another perpetrator, or the confession of self-infliction. In other cases, discernment may determine that no one "sinned" is at fault. Ignoring the diagnosis of behavioral causes of illness opens the door for the recurrence of the malady or injury.

---

11. See chapter eight on lament and chapter nine on words of healing.

12. In healing ministries, the line between *true* guilt and *false* guilt is not easy to determine. In addition, the line between the *guilt of others and our guilt* is also entwined. The complicated relationships between mental, spiritual, emotional and physical health are not easy to untangle. As a result, it is important to ask for and pronounce the gospel of the full forgiveness of sin. Even if the guilt is "false guilt" (tak-ing responsibility for unintentional actions and accidental consequences) it needs to be lifted through words of compassion and forgiveness. In that case, saying, "It wasn't your fault" doesn't go as far as, "You are forgiven." This may be the tipping point of healing for those wallowing in guilt, true or false.

Facing Death

Everyone eventually faces death, which is understood in Scripture as the absence of God's spirit/breath. This profound absence is also expressed as the "hiding of God's face." The thought of facing our own death can be terrifying, and this fear may cause us to ignore or deny the reality of death. Yet the witness of Scripture is that this life will end.

> When you hide your face, they are dismayed; when you take away their breath, they die and return to their dust. When you send forth your spirit, they are created; and you renew the face of the ground. (Ps 104:29–30)

All people, whatever their merits or faults, suffer illness or trauma and eventually die. Sometimes the wicked prosper until their death and the more righteous suffer greatly for no apparent reason (Jer 12:1). Death is the natural end of all human life. There is a time to live and a time to die (Eccl 3:2).

Americans generally avoid the dead and dying, nursing homes, persons with dementia, severe disability, facial deformity, auto-immune deficiency syndrome, etc. and not just from the fear of contagion. In the Hebrew Bible a dead body was stigmatized in the levitical system of clean and unclean[13] and although this had benefits for managing the spread of bacterial infection, it contributed to the general problem of stigmatization of those with chronic illness, disabilities, or contagious skin diseases. Contemporary forms of stigmatization are quite evident, as aversion created and creates distance and isolation.[14]

If revulsion concerning the dead can be overcome, perhaps progress can also be made in facing (and transforming our care of) those with severe illness and disability. Rabbinic interpretation worked to overcome the problems of stigmatization through a ritual to purify (*taharah*) the dead corpse. The Jewish practice was formalized in the Middle Ages through a "holy fellowship" (*chevra kaddisha*) of those

---

13. Num 19:11–22; Num 5:2; Num 6:6–7.

14. Nedairm 64b. See Rachel Adler, "Those Who Turn Away Their Faces: Tzaraat and Stigma" in R. William Cutter, ed. *Healing and the Jewish Imagination*. Adler has an excellent summary of the meaning of "leprosy" (*tzaraat*) which is not Hansen's disease in the Bible but a general term for contagious skin diseases and molds, mildew, and house fungi.

who of prepared the dead for burial.[15] The body was washed in "living water" (spring fed source). In this flow of water "impurity is unblocked by immersion . . . it dissolves old forms and creates them anew." The final pouring litany declares, "She is pure! She is pure!"[16] The dead are then clothed in plain linen garments, corresponding to those worn by the levitical priests.[17] As the linen miter is set in place, Zechariah 3:5 is recited: "So they put a clean turban on his head and clothed him with the apparel; and the angel of the LORD was standing by."

Jesus' Face of Death. Christian theologians have also faced the natural human revulsion to the dead and to suffering.[18] The New Testament presents a reversal of human categories in claiming that the death of Jesus revealed the glory of God. This paradoxical claim is that in Jesus' facing death, God entered the experience of human suffering and death.

It was about 900 CE before Christian art portrayed Jesus as dead on the cross. Before that time, he was portrayed with open eyes. The occasion for the change was a century of unprecedented suffering and death in Europe. We may be tempted to treat Jesus' death as a mere pause before his power reasserts itself in the resurrection,[19] but Jesus' death, symbolized by his "dead face" is significant in its own right, as a subject for facing death and dying.

The dead face of Jesus is an expression of utter powerlessness: disappointment to his followers, a cause of grief to those who loved him; a sign of the victory of lies and violence. It is a literal physical face that has undergone bodily death. To have this as the face of our "primary other" is to have an unrepressed sense of death. It all allows us to be face to face with death, with less fear, because God himself has experienced death.[20]

Resurrection is no simple reversal or pat ending. Jesus' Lordship has always had suffering and powerlessness at its heart. As the apostle says, "For the message about the cross is foolishness to those who are

15. See Sylvie-Anne Goldberg, *Crossing the Jabbok*, cited in Adler, "Those Who Turn Away Their Faces," 157.

16. Samuel Heilman, *When a Jew Dies*, cited in Adler, "Those Who Turn Away Their Faces," 157.

17. Exod 28:39–42.

18. See especially Cambridge theologian David Ford, *Self and Salvation*, 202–6, 215.

19. Ibid., 202–6

20. Ibid.

perishing, but to us who are being saved it is the power of God" (1 Cor 1:18). The dead face of Jesus portrays a way of love whose normal fate in the world (as it is) is suffering and misunderstanding.[21]

The domination of death is challenged by Jesus' death even before it is overcome in the resurrection. He lived for God and others and trusted God in the valley of death. He faced everything: betrayal, violence, and abandonment; he faced sin, suffering, and evil; he faced dying and death. Michelangelo's *Pieta* depicts the dead Jesus' in his mother's arms and illustrates the power of the purity of this particular death. The Christian promise of sharing in the resurrection is tied to sharing in this death. In the Lord's Supper we share in the de-stigmatizing of death by sharing in this particular dying for our sake for the forgiveness of sins (1 Cor 11:23–26).

Face to Face with God the Healer

God's presence with a person creates a healing environment.[22] The "presence" is referred to as the "face" of God (same word in Hebrew) and is an expression of God's friendship and intended blessing of his creation. In the section that follows, we will discuss God's healing activity in the Hebrew Bible, the importance of God's face/presence in healing, and how the face of Jesus in the New Testament continues and expands the biblical perspective on the restoration of health.

God's Healing Activity

In Scripture, two key words are used to communicate the restoration of health: *rapha,*' meaning "heal" and *'arukah,* meaning "be restored to live longer."

---

21. Paul describes this humility in 2 Cor 4:7–11: "Wherever we go we carry with us in our body the death that Jesus died, so that in this body also the life that Jesus lived might be revealed. For Jesus sake we are all our life being handed over to death, so that the life of Jesus may be revealed in this mortal body of ours." See also 2 Cor 13:4.

22. In Scripture, healing is essentially relational rather than biological. For this medical anthropological definition of healing see Pilch, *Healing in the New Testament,* 60.

Rapha' is the verb root from which the word "healer" or "physician" comes.[23] The name "Raphael" means "God is a healer."[24] God is almost always the subject of the active form of the verb *rapha'* (32 times) as in "God heals," and "God healed." In the Pentateuch, the deuteronomic history, and the Psalms healing refers to physical healing. For example:

- Gen 20:17 God healed Abimelech and the women of his household.

- Num 12:13 "O God, please heal her" (Moses, concerning Miriam, after his marriage to the Ethiopian woman)

- Ps 6:2 O LORD heal me, for my bones are shaking in terror.

- Ps 30:2 I cried to you and you healed me.

- Ps 103:3 Bless the LORD who forgives all your iniquity, who heals all your diseases.

In the Prophets, the healing is usually metaphorical, for a sick society:

- Ps 147:3 He heals the broken in heart, and binds up their wounds.

- Jer 3:22 Return, faithless children, and I will heal your faithlessness.

- Jer 30:17 I will heal you of your wounds, says the LORD.

- Hos 7:1 When I would have healed Israel, the corruption of Ephraim was revealed. (God, like a surgeon, uncovering infection.)

- Hos 6:1 He has torn and will heal us.

- Hos 11:3 They did not know that I had healed them.

- Hos 14:4 I will heal their faithlessness.

The verb root *rapha'* is also used in a passive form.[25] The healing is physical and God's work is implied. For example:

- Lev 13:18 when a boil is healed

- Lev 13:27 when the itch is healed

- Lev 14:3 when the scaly skin is healed

23. For an additional discussion of *rapha'* see Brown, *Israel's Divine Healer*, 25–30.

24. Its homonym is *raphah*, meaning "relax."

25. Seventeen times in the *niphal* form, meaning "it is healed."

In the Prophets the passive form usually is used in the context of God's active healing.

- Isa 53:5 He was wounded for our transgressions, crushed for our guilt, upon him was the punishment that made us whole; by his stripes (bruises) we are healed.

- Jer 17:4 Heal me and I shall be healed.

- Ezek 47:8 . . . the stagnant water will be healed (become fresh).

- 2 Chron 7:14 (God's response to Solomon's dedicatory prayer) If my people who are called by my name humble themselves, pray, seek my face, and turn from their wicked ways, then I will hear from heaven and will forgive their sin and their land will be healed.

Whether the healing is physical or a metaphor of some kind, God is the source.

> If you will listen carefully to the voice of the LORD your God and do what is right in his sight . . . I will not bring upon you any of the diseases that I brought upon the Egyptians, for I am the LORD who heals you. (Exod 15:26: This becomes one of God's titles: *yahweh-rephuka*.)

Immediately after these words, the text reports that they came, in the wilderness, to Elim with twelve springs and seventy palms, which was a place of restoration for the whole community. At the end of the wilderness wandering, God writes the last line of Moses' poem of "The Rock" (another of God's titles; Deut 32:4–39). "I am He; there is no God besides me. *I kill and I make alive, I wound and I heal*" (Deut 32:39).[26]

The second vital word of healing in the Hebrew Bible is *'arukah*, meaning "be restored to live longer" or, in older English, "tarry longer."[27]

---

26. The biblical claim is that God is not battling for life against another god who controls death. Satan would like to have that control and destroy the world, but cannot. The LORD is God of the living and the dead; of life and death. God removes Adam and Eve from the garden so that they will die, without access to the tree of Life. God also provides access to that tree of life again, as described in Revelation 22. For discussion of "the LORD of Sickness" in contrast to Greek cosmology, see H.W. Wolff, *Anthropology of the Old Testament*, 147–48. In contrast to the ancient east see M. Brown, *Israel's Divine Healer*, 67–78.

27. It is from *'arak*, which means, "a long time." See discussion in J. Wilkinson, *The Bible and Healing*, 54.

'Arukah can refer to new flesh growing (*being lengthened*) in a wound (Jer 33:6). The most well-known text using this word is from Isaiah.[28]

> Is this not the fast I choose, to loose the bonds of injustice . . . to share your bread with the hungry, to bring the homeless poor into your house, to cover the naked? Then shall your light break forth like the dawn and your healing (*'arukah*) shall spring up quickly; your vindicator will go before you and the glory of the LORD shall be your rear guard. Then you shall call and the LORD will answer, you shall cry for help and he will say, "Here I am." (Isa 58:6–9)

As we see from this brief survey of the contexts of the vocabulary of healing it is deeply set in the context of relationship to God. That relationship is made more specific in the concept of the presence of God's "face."

Face to Face with God

The primary relational environment of healing in Scripture is the "face" or "presence" (*panim*). It is the essential element in biblical healing and health. To be "face to face" is an image of health and salvation. It connotes being accepted, included, whole, protected, cared for, comforted, or saved. We also are known by our faces. Faces are the location of much of who we are: of expressing the emotions of crying, covering our mouths, hiding, smiling; of speaking, eating, drinking (utilizing four of five senses); of recognition by others, family resemblance, identity; of intimacy (touching face, kissing); of acceptance or rejection.

"Face" (*panim*) is a way of expressing the contrast between sin/disease and *shalom*/well-being/health from the beginning of Scripture.[29] It is found in every strand of the Hebrew Bible.[30] Adam and Eve hid from the face of the LORD God among the trees of the garden because of

28. See also Jer 8:22; 30:17; Neh 4:1; and 2 Chron 24:13. 'Arukah also has a homonym in the word *'arakh*, which means "dinner" or "food." In modern Hebrew, it is the basis for "hospitality" (*'orkhim*).

29. The connection between *shalom* (the biblical notion of health/wellness) and salvation, has been noted by many, but recently best developed by D. Ford. His definition of biblical salvation/*shalom*/well-being is rooted in the "full hospitality" of facing one another, including facing/being faced by God. Ford, *Self and Salvation*, 192.

30. *Panim* is translated "face" (365x), "presence" (75x), "countenance" (30x), and "person" (20x) in the KJV.

their broken relationship.[31] Cain protests that he will be hidden from God's face but is given the mark of protection on his face.[32] Hagar flees from the face of Sarai, but God meets her, talks with her, and makes promises of blessing. She is amazed and says, "God sees me" (*El-roi*) and "Have I seen God?"[33]

Many Hebrew expressions ("Hebraisms") use the word "face" as the primary environment of relationships:

- "before," or "in front of" = lit. "before the face of" or "in the presence of"
- "he hid his face from" = alienated from, cut off from
- "to lift up the face" = not ashamed; guilt-free relationship/ forgiven[34]
- "to seek the face" = to seek friendship[35]
- "face to face" = as a friend[36]

The "Face of God" (obviously) implies God's Presence. "Facing God" means standing in or seeking right relationship with God. God "hides" when humans set other "gods" or intentional sins between themselves and God, i.e., a refusal to seek God.[37]

> [If] I hide my face from them they will become easy prey, and many terrible troubles will come upon them." In that day they will say, "Have not these troubles come upon us because our God is not in our midst. On that day I will surely hide my face on account of all the evil they have done by turning to other gods. (Deut 31:17–18)

In the Psalms, salvation/health/well-being concepts are also linked to expressions of the face of God.[38] This is most evident in the expression

---

31. Gen 3:8.

32. Gen 4:14–16.

33. Gen 16:7–13; 21:17–20. The narrative oscillates between the presence of the LORD and the presence of the LORD's messenger.

34. See Ezra 9:6, Job 11:15; 22:26

35. See Ps 105:4; 2 Chron 7:14, Prov 7:15.

36. See Gen 32:30; Exod 33:11; Num 14:14; Ezek 20:35; 1 Cor 13:12.

37. Isa 59:1–4; see also Isa 1:15–18; 8:17–19; 45:15–16; 52:3.

38. Pss 31:16, 67:1–2, Ps 80:3, 7, 19.

"seeking the face" of the LORD in worship.[39] The majority of the occurrences are found in lament psalms, seeking the "hidden" face.[40]

In the prophets the theme of "face" has several aspects. People can hide their faces from God, as in the Servant Songs of Isaiah.[41] When God's face is hidden, it is because other gods have been placed "before his face." This causes a barrier between a person and God, so that "your sins have hidden his face."[42] When God's face is "hidden," it is not a permanent condition (Isa 54:8). The hope of the laments is based in this revealed faith.

The Aaronic Blessing. The face of the LORD is the agency of God's blessing. Very early in Israel's tradition, the LORD gave his Name[43] most explicitly to Moses at the burning bush (Exodus 3). Aaron was commanded to "put" this Name upon the people in what has come to be known as the *Aaronic Blessing* (Num 6:24–26). It was to be given from the door of the Tent of Meeting in the Tabernacle. "You shall bless" (Num 6:23) and "They shall put my Name on the Israelites, and I will bless them" (Num 6:27). The power for *shalom* ("peace," "health," or "wellness") is transmitted in the blessing.[44]

The ancient blessing speaks of God's face with a poetic structure. Six verbs are used in three parallel lines:

- The LORD *bless you* . . . . and *keep* you;

- The LORD *make his face shine* upon you . . . . and *be gracious* to you;

- The LORD *lift his face toward* you . . . . and *give* you *peace.*

The agency of God's blessing is the lifted and shining face of the LORD.[45]

---

39. Pss 24:3–6, 105:4, 27:8.

40. e.g., Pss 44:24, 88:14, 13:1.

41. Isa 53:1–3; 50:5–8.

42. Isa 59:1–2; 8:17; 54:8; Ezek 39:23–29; Jer 33:5; Micah 3:4.

43. Represented by the tetragrammaton *YHWH; usually rendered LORD, Adonai, or ha-Shem.*

44. "Blessing" ranges from a greeting, e.g., "the LORD bless you" (Ruth 2:4) to almost a magical, or at least an irrevocable action, e.g., Isaac's blessing of Jacob rather than Esau was irrevocable, even after the deception was discovered (Gen 27:30–38).

45. It is used liturgically in the Psalms: e.g., "We bless you in the Name of the LORD" (Pss 129:8, 128:5, 133:3, 134:3). The Aaronic Blessing has been found by archeologists, written on amulets and jars from the monarchial period (eighth century BCE).

Moses and Jacob: Face to Face with God. Two key narratives demonstrate being face to face with God as friend and the restoration of health.[46] The stories of God's friendship with Moses at Sinai and with Jacob crossing the Jabbok River are paradigmatic stories of friendships that cut in order to heal. The discovery of the friendship of God is the first step in the restoration of holistic health. These two face-to-face encounters demonstrate individual and community "healings" through both comfort and confrontation.

> So Jacob called the place *Peniel* ("face of God") saying, "For I have seen God face to face, and yet my life is preserved." (Gen 32:30)
>
> Thus the LORD used to speak to Moses face to face, as one speaks to a friend. (Exod 33:11)

The friendship between Moses and God saved a community from permanently turning their face away from God. It is a narrative of a comforting friendship in the midst of a crisis. The golden calf incident (Exodus 32–34) is a narrative about the first commandment: "You shall have no other gods before me" (lit. "before my face;" Exod 20:3). In its aftermath, God makes three progressive decisions about whether his "face" (presence) will remain with the people.

46. Concern about seeing God *face to face* is critical in Exodus 33:11a "The LORD would speak to Moses face to face, as a man speaks with his friend." A few verses later, a paradox is created by the clear warning given by God, "You cannot see my face, for no one may see me and live" (Exod 33:20; see Gen 32:31; Exod 19:21; Judges 6:22–23; 13:22; Isa 6:5). In this well-known encounter, the LORD showed Moses his back as he passed by. Yet the deep friendship of God in face to face encounter is corroborated in Numbers 12:7–8: "My servant Moses . . . with him I speak *face to face* (lit. "mouth to mouth") clearly and not in riddles; he sees the form of the LORD." The major tradition in Scripture is that one cannot see a manifestation of God and live, but that God *can* be seen. He was seen by Abraham and Sarah when he spoke through "three men" (Gen 18:2) who became "two messengers" (19:1) and spoke as the LORD (Gen 18:10, 13). Fretheim calls this and other theophanies (appearances of God) an "oscillation" because the LORD is present and speaking, represented as a human-looking messenger (*mal'ak*, sometimes translated "angel"). Hagar has a similar experience and says, "Have I really *seen* God and remained alive after seeing him?" (Gen 16:13). The seventy elders also *saw* the God of Israel (Exod 24:10), yet "God did not raise his hand against these leaders" (Exod 24:11). The same concern over seeing *someone* and speaking to the LORD is witnessed in Judges 6:22–23 and 13:22. God remained free to make exceptions to the rule, and allowed these people to live (Exod 24:10–11; see Num 12:8; Deut 34:10; Ezek 1:26–28). See discussion in T. Fretheim, *Suffering of God*, 91–93; 105 and in J. Bruckner, *Exodus*, 294–95.

a) No face, and no presence (32:7–14): At this point in the narrative God has only decided not to destroy the people. He has not decided to forgive their rebellion or to continue his project with them.

b) No face, but an angel of protection (33:1–6): *"I will not go up among you . . . you are a stiff-necked (obstinate) people. Only an angel will go before your face."*

At this point the narrative makes its essential turn. It reminds us that God had regularly been meeting with Moses in *the tent of meeting, face to face as with a friend* (33:11).[47] On the basis of this friendship, the LORD decided that he would, in fact, remain with the people in the wilderness.

c) Yes face 33:14–17 *"My presence (panim) will go and I will give you rest.* Moses' response was, "If your "face" (*panim*) does not go with us, do not carry us up from here."

As difficult as it was for them to live in the presence of a holy God, Moses could not imagine health or salvation for his people without this primary environment of relationship. His personal friendship with God saved an entire community.

Jacob crossed the Jabbok River, returning to meet his brother and his militia. The inward sickness of alienation from his brother Esau, from whom he had stolen the birthright, ran deep. His alienation from God had also been constant in the fourteen years he had been abroad. Jacob sent a generous present ahead of his now prosperous family. He said, "I may *cover his face* (appease Esau's anger) with the present that goes *before my face*, and when I *see his face* perhaps he will *lift up my face* (accept me)." After wrestling all night with a messenger from God, he was given a limp and a blessing. The messenger changed his name from "he grabs" (Jacob) to "God rules" (Israel).

When Esau and Jacob met, they embraced and wept in reconciliation. What happened *between faces* (Jacob/Esau/God) determined the outcome: confrontation, covering, meeting, speaking, prostrating, embracing, kissing, and weeping for joy. When it was over, Jacob realized that he had encountered the presence and restoring friendship of God's

47. See also Num 12:8 and Deut 34:10. In Deut 5:4 and Num 14:14 Moses indicates the God was "face to face" with all the people by means of his presence in the pillars of cloud and fire.

own self. The text concludes, "Jacob called the name of the place, *Peniel* (face of God) saying, "Because I have seen God *face to face*, and my life is preserved." (Gen 32:30).

Jacob was transformed to Israel-with-a-limp. God's persistent presence with Jacob helped him to tell the truth about God and be reconciled with his brother.[48] In the wrestling at Jabbok, God's messenger touched his hip and healed him. Afterward Jacob always walked with a limp. The inward sickness of alienation from his brother and God was healed. The outward limp became the sign of the healing between Jacob, God, and Esau.

The Resurrection and the Face of Jesus

The face of Christ shining "in our hearts" is a fundamental factor in Christian identity and strength. The biblical witness is that the *face of God* is shown in the *face of Jesus Christ*. It is this that communicates the healing work of God to the many cultures (nations) of the world.

> For we do not preach ourselves, but Jesus Christ as LORD, and ourselves as your servants for Jesus' sake. For God, who said, "Let light shine out of darkness," *made his light shine in our hearts* to give us the light of the knowledge of the glory of God *in the face of Christ*. But we have this treasure in jars of clay to show that this all-surpassing power is from God and not from us. (2 Cor 4:5–7)

Since Christ is the image of God in the flesh, the presence of God in the face of Jesus Christ is a source of identity and power for all who will allow him to dwell in their hearts.[49] The light of this face shining in believers' hearts is the New Testament interpretation of health and well-being (*shalom*). It is the Aaronic blessing, internalized in Christ.[50]

48. See the back story in Genesis 27–28. Note the conditional vow in 28:20. Jacob does not put away household gods until Genesis 35:1–4.

49. "So that times of refreshing may come from the *face of the LORD*, and that he may send the Messiah appointed for you, that is, Jesus." (Acts 3:20). See commentary by Ford, *Self and Salvation*, 193–202.

50. While Moses had to cover the shining of the glory of the LORD with a veil after meeting with him as a friend (not to frighten the people), Christ has removed the veil from the face: "And all of us, with unveiled faces, seeing the glory of the LORD as though reflected in a mirror, are being transformed into the same image from one degree of glory to another; for this comes from the LORD, the Spirit" (1 Cor 3:18).

Paul is only able to claim this source of strength because of the bodily resurrection of Jesus by his Father. Belief in the resurrection is primary for creating environments of health and healing as Christians. It removes the sting and fear of death. So Paul can write about strength: "I can do (am empowered to do) all things through Christ who strengthens me (Phil 4:13) and "Be strong in the strength of his might." (a triple strength blessing; Eph 6:10).

Face to Face in Caregiving

People are given the power to create healing environments, or to choose not to create them. This final section explores a variety of medical face-to-face relationships that have the potential to be healing environments: chaplain-patient; doctor-patient; patient-pharmacist-doctor; nurse-patient; congregation-patient; patient-God. Each of the outcomes depends on how presence is used with another.

Being face to face with other people is a common daily occurrence, and creating environments of healing requires intentionality.[51] Henri Nouwen tells of his discovery of the importance of human presence in a conversation with a hopeless and fearful man preparing to undergo surgery. When asked if he had anyone waiting for him when came out of surgery, the patient said, "Nothing and nobody."[52] What kind of response could possibly create hope? Hope could be created if Mr. Harrison "were to meet a man with a clear face who called him by his name and become his brother . . . whose real presence could in no way be denied."[53] Being "face to face" with each other means a meeting of two persons, both created by God, and in his image.

Not all cases are quite so desperate. My father was a vibrant human being; a face-to-face kind of person. After his quadruple bypass surgery, his excellent surgeon spoke to him about recovery protocols, but with the tone of one speaking to a small child. My father didn't respond, and stared out the window so that the doctor asked, "Can he hear me? Does he understand?" My wife, who was present replied, "Oh, he hears you." What she could not say was, "He is waiting for you to speak to him as a

51. See chapter nine on "healing words."

52. Henri Nouwen, *The Wounded Healer*, 54.

53. Ibid., 64.

person, not as a patient." They each played their roles as passive patient and knowledgeable doctor. Each was responsible for the fact that they never met as people. They were physically in the same room, but never met face to face. Martin Buber describes the same possibility: that when two people face each other and look each other in the eye, they become real to each other, rather than people objectively fulfilling their roles.[54]

Patients Face Their Physicians and Pharmacists

The wisdom of Ecclesiasticus (Ben Sirach) in the second century BCE speaks to a patient's regard for the image of God in the doctors who treat him.

> Honor physicians for their services, for the LORD created them . . . give the physician his place, for the LORD created him . . . they too pray to the LORD that he grant them success in diagnosis and in healing, for the sake of preserving life. (Sir 38:1, 12, 14)

Likewise, pharmacists are doing the work of God when they bring healing.

> The LORD created medicines out of the earth, and the sensible will not despise them . . . And he gave skill to human beings that he might be glorified in his marvelous works. The pharmacist makes a mixture from them . . . and from him health spreads over all the earth. (Sir 38:4, 6, 8)

Ben Sirach counsels the patient to view the medical staff as people whom God has gifted for their healing, while recognizing that the healing is from God. Prayer for healing, with confession of sin is, recommended.

> Their gift of healing comes from the Most High . . . My child, when you are ill, do not delay, but pray to the LORD, and he will heal you. Give up your faults and direct your hands rightly, and cleanse your heart from all sin. (Sir 38:2, 9, 10)

The wisdom of the ancient tradition recognizes that both ordinary and extraordinary gifts of healing are gifts from God. In any case, human beings are called to act in accordance with their gifts to create environments of healing for those who are sick.

---

54. Buber, *I and Thou*, 8.

Children Who Face Death

There is no "cure" for a child with kidney disease. Even if they receive a transplant, they will need another and another as their body grows. Two researchers, a pediatric nephrologist and a pastoral theologian, began asking some of these children about their sources of hope.[55] The children's responses corroborate the biblical witness. They say that hope and healing in the midst of chronic illness is made possible by the empowerment of being face to face with caregivers, friendship with God, and conversation with God.

Caregivers who take time to be present and listen to these children provide them with an opportunity to "claim power" over their illness in a variety of ways. The researchers report that when this happens, hardiness increases.

> Claiming power allows children with end-stage renal disease to take an active role in treatment by setting goals, advocating for themselves and monitoring and maintaining their own health. This facet of hopefulness is primarily agential; it focuses on children's abilities to influence outcome, access resources and participate meaningfully as a member of the interdisciplinary team . . . For some children claiming power includes identifying and enacting strategies to control anxiety as a means of resisting the intra-psychic suffering that can accompany the illness.[56]

A key to *hardiness* among the chronically ill is removing powerlessness. Being face to face/present with a helpless patient can provide them with control: the ability to make good decisions: to appraise, interpret and respond to health stressors.[57]

Children also report that hope and empowerment come from the presence of God. When caregivers allow patients to articulate and practice their relationship with God, they thrive within the confines of their illness. This thriving is possible because God's presence creates *coherence* and meaning. It gives them a place, with others in a larger story. They are not alone, nor is their story the whole story.

---

55. Duane Bidwell and Donald Batisky, "Identity and Wisdom as Elements of a Spirituality of Hope among Children with End-stage Renal Disease."

56. Ibid., 11.

57. See chapter six.

The experience of chronic illness and the intensity of suffering are often accompanied by feelings of isolation, abandonment, and aloneness.

> Attending to God provides spiritual consolation to children . . . by assuring them that God is present in their suffering and participates in the treatment process. This facet of hope is primarily relational and sapiential; it is activated through religious and spiritual practices such as prayer, worship, visitation, blessing, and the reading of scripture.[58]

The wider community of support is quite important to this caregiving. Among many Christians, the practice of the Lord's Supper is a practice of the real presence (face) of Christ. Some children invoke a family wisdom figure, such as a grandparent to help them attend to God. Cards and emails from people "who know God" and "thought about me" even if they "didn't know me" reflect the value of congregational members praying for the child at a distance.

Finally, researchers report that end-stage patients tend toward prayer to relieve anxiety during dialysis and speak intimately and personally of God's availability and *kinesthetic* presence with them in the midst of illness. They feel a real presence of real person. God listens to them and God speaks to them.[59]

Face-to-Face Nursing Practices

A shift toward more relational medical practice is well underway. Hospitals used to severely restrict visitors by space and policy as a matter of good healing practice. New hospitals are built with the potential healing presence of the family and community in mind. Rooms are larger and sometimes daybeds are provided.

Nursing instruction and textbooks have also undergone significant changes. The nursing care plans now: 1) *diagnose* the psychosocial ailment: e.g., anxiety, fear, ineffective coping, powerlessness, spiritual distress, and risk for dysfunctional grieving; 2) describe the nurse's *interventions*: e.g., validate, listen, encourage, acknowledge, provide,

---

58. D. Bidwell and D. Batisky, "Identity and Wisdom," 11.

59. Ibid., 11–12.

discuss, explore, consult;[60] 3) offer *rationales* for each intervention; and 4) describe the *desired outcome.*[61]

Nursing pedagogy includes instruction in the vitality of being face to face with a patient. It includes awareness of 1) one's presence as a person who is a nurse; 2) the value of a patient's community (family and others) in healing; and 3) the chaplain as a resource in the full spectrum of healing. Nurses are prepared to make "spiritual distress calls" to family or chaplains, PRN.[62]

Face-to-Face Care in Christian Communities

Local congregations often function as witnesses to and agents of the presence of God.[63] Many congregations have programs of lay ministry or parish nursing that care in the name of Christ for the holistic health of the congregation and surrounding community.[64] James writes that the sick "should call for the elders of the church and have them pray over them, anointing them with oil in the name of the LORD" (Jas 5:14). He is drawing on the theology of presence and Christian community as the Body of Christ that is affected by each individual in it. By anointing those who are ill, Christians show courage under the threat of disease[65] and do not exacerbate the natural alienation of the "sick."

When the community gathers in a collective act as the Body of Christ it "counters the cultural effects of isolation and marginalization." It becomes a witness against hiding the sick from the engaged presence of the community and of God. This kind of empowerment of the ill and of the community is the further subject of chapter nine.

60. Listening is "therapeutic communication." As a first step, the validation of a patient's experience of pain or anxiety is necessary. This comforting presence includes a willingness to let a patient "vent out" their pain, even when the content of their communication is erroneous or misdirected. This is akin to the biblical tradition of lament. See chapter eight.

61. Barbara Powe, contributor to care plans for "Psychosocial Support."

62. "per Registered Nurse." On the cooperation of medical and religious caregivers see, Karen Lawson, "Spirituality in Medicine: What is its Role, Today and Tomorrow?"

63. 2 Cor 5:18–19; See also 1 Cor 12:12–27.

64. Parish nursing and Stephen's Ministries are perhaps the most well known.

65. M. T. Lysaught, "Vulnerability within the Body of Christ: Anointing of the Sick and Theological Anthropology."

The future face to face meeting of bodily resurrection is the primary fact that undergirds all New Testament themes of health and healing (1 Cor 15:2–23). The reversal of the domination of death establishes transforming hope (Rev 21:3–7). In this hope, death is not removed, but muted by the possibility of peace in the midst of dying through the presence of the risen one. The hope and peace of the presence of Christ in the midst of devastation provides strength, hardiness, and resilience.

Being "face to face" with God is also the hope of the resurrection to come:

> Now we see but a poor reflection as in a mirror; then we shall
> see face to face. Now I know in part; then I shall know fully, even
> as I am fully known" (1 Cor 13:12).

The themes of light, the tree of life, water of life, Name of the LORD, and the healing of the cultures of the world are all carried in John's vision of the face of the Lamb on the throne in the new creation.

> Then the angel showed me the river of the *water of life*, bright
> as crystal, flowing from the throne of God and of the Lamb
> through the middle of the street of the city. On either side of the
> river is the *tree of life* with its twelve kinds of fruit, producing its
> fruit each month; and the leaves of the tree are for the *healing of
> the cultures*. Nothing accursed will be found there any more. But
> the throne of God and of the Lamb will be in it, and his servants
> will worship him; they will *see his face, and his Name* will be on
> their foreheads. And there will be no more night; they need no
> light of lamp or sun, for the *LORD God will be their light*, and
> they will reign forever and ever. (Rev 22:1–5)

Chapter Eight

Telling the Truth in Suffering

SUFFERING CAN TAKE MANY forms including illness, injury, grief, or depression. If one suffers in silence or isolation, the experience is compounded and may eventually lead to despair. On the other hand, many aspects of healing can begin when one who suffers begins telling the story of sickness or pain to someone they trust. The practice of biblical lament, which allows the truth to be told, forms a seedbed for hope and healing in the midst of grave illness or profound loss. Those in healing vocations can use biblical lament as a resource for restoring souls, and thus cultivate the possibility of hope and healing in the hopeless.

Hope and Therapeutic Lament

When a person suffers illness or injury, it is normal to ask "why?" or "how long will this go on?" Sometimes the questions are intensified in God's direction, in frustration, anger, or even rejection of a God who could allow suffering. This leads to further isolation of the one who suffers, and can lead to despair. In contrast, the tradition of biblical lament provides a road to healing for the one who suffers by helping create relational connections: by speaking to God; by speaking the details of suffering in the presence of others; and by connection to a long tradition of other people who have suffered and found hope in these relationships.

Hope and Despair

Everyone who suffers laments, but not all lament leads to hope. Honest complaint can also lead to despair. Many factors make the difference. If a lament falls on deaf ears, or is silenced by the community, or if the one who suffers is further isolated, the lament may only worsen the suffering.

Biblical lament differs from common complaint. The common meaning of "lament" is to cry out in grief, sorrow, mourning, or regret.[1] Most often this is a response to someone's death and is an undirected demonstration of loss. While Scripture does have a lament or two for the dead,[2] biblical lament is centered in *laments of the afflicted directed toward God within the community of faith.*

The laments of affliction found in Scripture are also more than complaining. Complaining is often seen as a lack of character or a sign of weakness. Biblical lament is a complaint that is a desperate cry for help and relief. Ironically, it requires a strong character to turn toward God and the community in hope rather than retreating into isolation and despair.

The term "lament" as it is used in this chapter means *a therapeutic monologue of complaint toward God.* It is a complaint because it expresses in detail the situation of suffering that is being endured. It is a monologue because it is not challenged or silenced by the listeners (God and the community), but allowed to stand as the expression of the sufferer's suffering. It is therapeutic because it allows the one suffering a voice with God and others that opens the possibility for the isolated person to re-enter relationships that have been cut off or never known. The sufferer becomes a witness to their continued relationship with God in the midst of their suffering.

Biblical lament changes things for the one who suffers and for those around them: it gives an isolated person a voice within a community (even if that community is only one other person); it helps the one who suffers communicate with God, his or her maker; and it begins the imaginative process of community and individual to find solutions

1. See *Webster's Third New International Dictionary Unabridged.*

2. See 2 Sam 1:17–27. See discussion of the difference between laments of affliction and the lament of the dead in Claus Westermann, *Praise and Lament in the Psalms,* 262.

to isolation. A person who can verbalize their suffering may find hope and healing rather than despair.[3]

Faith and Trust

Hope and despair are born in the same soil, in the same seedbed. That seedbed is the soil of suffering. The seeds of true hope grow in it as well or better than the seeds of despair, but the seeds must be planted. The biblical laments provide a resource for planting seeds of hope in the midst of suffering. They also provide a pattern for lamenting in a way that does not lead to despair.

When a person encounters real and enduring suffering that God does not remove, biblical laments offer hope in part because they are based in faith and trust of God. Lamenting to God in prayer provides the person of faith the possibility of hope with integrity. This is more than weak-kneed optimism. Laments tell the hard truth of situations and emotions to someone they trust. God already knows a person's thoughts and emotions. When the suffering one speaks of it in prayer, she tells the truth about her suffering and pain. In doing so, she enters into an honest conversation with her Creator and Redeemer. The deep faith that lament requires is a strong witness to hope in God.

It takes some faith to bring a complaint to the LORD. Yet the biblical tradition is strong. Abraham, Moses, Isaiah, Job, and Habakkuk questioned God and God welcomed and engaged their questions. People without much faith have trouble with this and ask, "Will God hear me if I complain? Will God turn away from me? Will he reject me if I bring my trouble to him?" It takes a significant faith not to be afraid of being unfaithful.

Scripture is an important resource because it has already provided many graphic complaints that can be used as they are by those who suffer. They give words to those who cannot form their own. Even Jesus used the lament of Psalm 22 from the cross: "My God, my God,

3. The psalms of lament are a resource for those who cannot articulate words of their own to speak to God about their suffering, e.g., those who suffer from clinical depression. There they may find a historical community of suffering that has given voice for more than three thousand years to people isolated by their suffering. The signs of clinical depression are evident in Pss 31:9–13 and 102:1–9. I am grateful to psychiatrist Randall Christianson for drawing these to my attention.

why have you forsaken me?" If Jesus can lament to his Father in heaven about something he does obediently and without sin, can we not also bring our deepest feelings to the one who already knows them?

An early church hymn writer observed that suffering ("shaking") can lead in two directions: "The same shaking that makes fetid water stink makes perfume [offer] a more pleasant odor."[4] Lament is praise of a high order. About one third of the one hundred and fifty Psalms are laments, making it the most common type of Psalm in the book.[5]

Psalm 13 and the Structural Integrity of Biblical Lament

The form and relational elements of the "individual's lament" can be seen in Psalm 13.[6] Combined, these elements demonstrate the struggle of an afflicted person in all their relationships. Their illness or situation has been exacerbated by intra-psychic suffering: fear, alienation, anxiety, and distress. The structure of the lament itself works to ameliorate this suffering in several specific relational ways.

The healing environment of the lament Psalms often begins with the *superscription*. In Psalm 13 it is, "For the director of music. A Psalm of David." Immediately we are aware that our experience of suffering is not the first. Also, we see that it is for public use, since the director of music has been given some direction. We have been ushered into an historic community of sufferers.

4. Hilary of Poitiers. This bishop died in 368 CE.

5. Scripture contains both individual and community laments. Individual lament psalms include Psalms 3–7, 13, 17, 22, 25–28, 31, 32, 35, 38–43, 51, 69–71, 77, 86, 88, 102, 109, 120, 130, and 139–143. The "penitential psalm" is a sub-category of lament and includes Psalms 6, 32, 38, 51, 102, 130, and 143. The community lament was used in public worship for brokenness of community and community crises. Like the individual lament, this community lament contains a petition and an invocation but instead of simply a description, it has a contrast and a double request. For an example of the structure of a psalm of community lament, see Psalm 80. It has the following structure: 1) Address to the LORD (vss. 1–3; Verse three is a petition that will be a refrain, repeating twice more in vss. 7 and 19); 2) Description of distress (v. 4–6; v. 12–13); 3) Contrast of present experience to the past memory of God's past blessing (vss. 8–11); 4) Petition (vss. 14–15); 5) Double request: let the evil perish/strengthen the good (vss. 16–17); 6) Vow to praise (vs. 18). Community laments include Psalms 12, 14, 44, 53, 58, 60, 74, 79, 80, 83, 85, 89, 90, 94, 106, 123, and 137. For further reading see Westermann, *Praise and Lament in the Psalms.*

6. Some individual laments also contain confession of sin or an assertion of innocence.

The distress of these first verses shows the distress of isolation in relation to God, to others, and within the suffering one's self.

The first formal element of biblical lament is an *address and petition to the LORD*.

> How long, O LORD? Will you forget me forever? How long will you hide your face from me? How long must I wrestle with my thoughts and every day have sorrow in my heart? How long will my enemy triumph over me? Look on me and answer, O LORD my God. (Ps 13:1–3a)

These verses call on God as "LORD" indicating some knowledge of God. A person who would use lament must be acquainted or introduced to God by a trusted counselor or friend.[7]

The second formal element is a *complaint describing the distress and request for help*.

> Give light to my eyes, or I will sleep in death; my enemy will say, "I have overcome him," and my foes will rejoice when I fall. (Ps 13:3b–4)

Often the lamenter is on the far edge of despair, imagining his own death. The "foes" are often mentioned, demonstrating the real and imagined alienation of the one who is suffering.

The third element is an *expression of trust in God*.

> But I trust in your unfailing love; my heart rejoices in your salvation.[8] (Ps 13:5)

The basis for hope is God's unfailing love and past provision are the bases for the hope that God will see and help the one who cries out for help.

The fourth formal element in biblical lament is a *vow to praise God*.[9]

---

7. Biblical laments always invoke the Name of the LORD, which is viewed as hope in itself. The Name of the LORD and his various titles (e.g., Our Healer) invokes God's presence. God's presence in the midst of lament creates a healing environment.

8. "Salvation" is understood in a very broad sense in the Hebrew Bible, generally including a blessed life and good health. See Terence Fretheim, "Salvation in the Bible versus Salvation in the Church."

9. The expression of trust and vow to praise are variable elements in the lament psalms. Perhaps the darkest lament in Scripture is Psalm 88. It is well-known for omitting the elements of trust and praise. They are variable elements, but most of the

I will sing to the LORD, for he has been good to me. (Ps 13:6)

The lamenter is able to imagine a better time of rejoicing and singing. This anticipatory use of the imagination is a vital element in finding relief in the midst of suffering. It creates an environment of hope through the use of a proleptic voice. For another example of the structure and content of a psalm of individual lament, read Psalm 102:1–28 which has the superscription, "A prayer of the afflicted, when he is overwhelmed, and pours out his complaint before the LORD."[10]

Lament, coming honestly before God, is biblical praise in a minor key. Lament is not the opposite of praise, because it turns toward God. The opposite of praising God is turning in on oneself: isolated, away from God and community. Lament turns toward God and as such becomes the seed of hope.

The laments have been prayed by individual readers of the biblical text since it became generally available after the protestant Reformation (sixteenth century BCE). Previous to that time they were read out loud and memorized in Jewish and Christian worship. The *relational* aspect of these laments has largely been lost in this shift, except in isolated communities that read or sing the whole Psalter.

The individual laments may serve as a means to hope for suffering people when they are read in communities of faith, with a rabbi, pastor, priest, mentor, or counselor. The lament form may also be useful for helping the afflicted write new laments. The critical movement to hope in the midst of suffering, fear, alienation, anxiety, and distress requires people who will act as witnesses to hope in the midst of suffering; those people who have moved from the edge of despair, described in the laments, to hope; and people who are wounded witnesses to suffering and hope through lament.

One such healer and scholar who has survived and grown through experiences of cancer and heart disease, describes the outcomes of his experience of illness.[11] In every case, suffering begins with alienation and isolation. What happens to one's body happens to one's self

---

lament psalms have them. Psalm 88 is nonetheless hope-producing, because the author is still talking to God and given voice in the community of faith.

10. The elements in Psalm 102 are: 1) address to the LORD, vss. 1–2; 2) complaint, 3–11; 3) trust, 12–17, 25–28; 4) praise, 18–22; 5) petition, 23–24.

11. Arthur W. Frank, *The Wounded Storyteller*.

(body-self).[12] Hearing of cancer, enduring surgery, undergoing chemotherapy all alter the self by disintegrating one's former experience of "self" in relation to others. Things will never be "the same" again.

A variety of possible personal narratives emerge in the wake of a person's disintegration: a person can enter the chaos of illness and treatment and never emerge from it until they die. It is also possible that a person will be "cured" and restored to their former way of being in the world, without learning very much. The best imagined result of suffering, however, embodied in the laments and Scripture, is that a person will be transformed. A positive life-transforming experience may emerge in the midst of the struggle with illness.[13]

The life that is transformed through illness and its suffering experiences a basic three-fold movement of growth: 1) the initial experience of the isolation and distress of illness; 2) a decision to turn toward life, light, and God 3) re-engaging one's life of relationship as a reintegrated person who is a witness to the wonder and vulnerability of life.[14] This movement generally mirrors what we have seen in the form of lament in Psalm 13 (distress, trust, testimony).[15] It forms the focus of the next three sections of this chapter: *1) the suffering of isolation; 2) leap toward the light; and 3) testimony.*

The Suffering of Isolation

Suffering begins when "a state of severe distress . . . threatens the intactness of a person . . . when an impending destruction of the person is perceived; it continues until the threat of disintegration has passed."[16]

12. Frank cites Eric Cassell and Arthur Kleinman who define suffering from a clinical perspective. They reject body-mind dualism; whole people suffer monadically.

13. Frank calls this the "quest" or "journey" narrative. Frank, *Wounded Storyteller*, 178.

14. "The ill person who turns illness into story transforms fate into experience; the disease that sets the body apart from others becomes, in the story, the common body of suffering that joins bodies in their shared vulnerability." Frank, *Wounded Storyteller*, xi.

15. It may not be a coincidence that A.W. Frank was formerly a Catholic priest. He is now a professor of sociology.

16. Eric Cassell, *The Nature of Suffering and the Goals of Medicine*, 31. Cited in Frank, *The Wounded Storyteller*, 169–70. See also Arthur Kleinman, *The Illness Narratives*.

Illness, injury, and the trauma of difficult experiences are only the beginning of suffering. Complex fears accompany illness and injury. An illness is like the exposed tip of the iceberg; the accompanying fear is like the larger iceberg below the water surface. This accompanying fear-disease often leads to an "embodied paranoia . . . not knowing what to fear most and then feeling guilty about this very uncertainty."[17] This is the experience of isolation, alienation from others and from God that traumatic experience often causes.

Unfortunately, many in the Christian community have found it difficult to express negative feelings, fears, and thoughts. Sometimes when a suffering person says, "I am beginning to doubt the existence of God," or, "If God does exist, he must not care much about people to let them suffer like this" they are "hushed" or advised against such sentiments. Most worship books and lectionary texts leave out the Psalms containing lament. When Bible readers encounter them, they wonder what such negative, uninspiring stuff is doing in the Bible. One scholar has noted a variety of reasons that Christians stifle laments.[18]

- We stifle laments because we want to help lamenters out of negativity, not to help them express it (Ps 22:14–15a). I am poured out like water, and all my bones are out of joint; my heart is like wax, it is melted within my breast; my strength is dried up like a piece of broken pottery.) We want to cheer them up.

- We stifle laments because laments often describe God as absent, cruel, unforgiving, indifferent, or powerless. They express a mistaken understanding of God. We stifle them because they are bad theology. So we argue theology with them. We end up stifling the sufferer as well as the biblical lament.

- We stifle laments because they are sometimes hostile toward other people. We are confused by the venting of hostility, even toward enemies who Jesus said to love. This is difficult for us to reconcile.

- We stifle laments because they make exaggerated claims of innocence for the sufferer and outrageous boasting of goodness. It sounds like bad theology again, though it is not.

17. Frank, *The Wounded Storyteller*, 174.
18. Daniel Simundson, *Where is God in My Suffering?*, 19–29.

The practice of biblical lamentation directly addresses this common human experience. It offers wisdom and a practical means for focusing and naming one's fears. It reorders emotions that have become disordered. It turns one, in a truthful way, away from isolation and back to God and the community. The truthfulness of the laments begins with vocalizing the hidden part of the iceberg. The lamenter describes his experience of alienation from God and others.

Psalm 22: Distress

Like other lament psalms, Psalm 22 begins by addressing the problem of alienation from God, directly to God.

> A Psalm of David. My God, my God, why have you forsaken me? Why are you so far from helping me, from the words of my groaning? O my God, I cry by day, but you do not answer; and by night, but find no rest. (Ps 22:1–2)

In these verses, we see the paradoxical juxtaposition of trusting God enough to address God in the midst of the experience of being isolated from God. This is the experience that can only be understood by those who suffer greatly and have the wisdom to begin to put their fears in order by speaking first to God. This is the Psalm used by Jesus from the cross.[19]

Throughout the experience of isolation, the lamenter speaks directly to God as his only hope. Continual direct address is made to God (four times), the LORD (seven times), "you" (twenty-one times). Third person address of "he," "his," and "him" are made an additional twenty-one times (in thirty one verses). For example:

> Yet it was *you* who took me from the womb; *you* kept me safe on my mother's breast. On *you* I was cast from my birth, and since my mother bore me *you* have been my *God*. Do not be far from me, for trouble is near and there is no one to help. (Ps 22:9–11)

Isolation from others is also dramatically expressed. In the laments this is often presented as public mocking which is often interpreted metaphorically. Whether or not it is actual mocking in the original context, for example in this psalm of David, it has been reapplied in

---

19. Matt 27:46; Mark 15:34.

the practice of those who read it as representative of the alienation of chronic or extreme illness.

> But I am a worm, and not human; scorned by others, and despised by the people. All who see me mock at me; they make mouths at me, they shake their heads; "Commit your cause to the LORD; let him deliver—let him rescue the one in whom he delights!" (Ps 22:6–8)

Even the "embodied paranoia" of disordered and disintegrating fears that accompany illness is seen in the lamenter's anguish over his taunting and deriding enemies (Ps 22:12–18). His suffering is exponentially increased by the "encircling evildoers." The suffering is real and embodied.

> Many bulls encircle me, strong bulls of Bashan surround me; they open wide their mouths at me, like a ravening and roaring lion. I am poured out like water, and all my bones are out of joint; my heart is like wax; it is melted within my breast; my mouth is dried up like a potsherd, and my tongue sticks to my jaws; you lay me in the dust of death. For dogs are all around me; a company of evildoers encircles me. My hands and feet have shriveled; I can count all my bones. They stare and gloat over me; they divide my clothes among themselves, and for my clothing they cast lots. (Ps 22:12–17)

Exploring Negative Options on the Road to Healing

Part of the truthfulness of the laments is that they freely embody the disordered thinking of the one who is suffering within the structure of the Psalm. The Psalms contain all manner of responses to suffering. These include the desire to run away, to be on the verge of suicide, to strike down or curse enemies, and to refuse comfort.[20]

> Woe is me, that I am an alien in Meshech, that I must live among the tents of Kedar. Too long have I had my dwelling among those who hate peace. (Ps 120:5–6)

---

20. These examples and the observation is from Fred Gaiser, "The Emergence of the Self in the Old Testament: A Study in Biblical Wellness."

> There is no one who takes notice of me; no refuge remains to me; no one cares for me . . . Bring me out of this prison. (Ps 142:4, 7)

> I am shut in so that I cannot escape; my eye grows dim through sorrow . . . O LORD, why do you cast me off? Why do you hide your face from me? . . . I suffer your terrors; I am desperate . . . They surround me like a flood all day long; from all sides they close in on me. You have caused friend and neighbor to shun me; my companions are in darkness. (Ps 88:8b–9, 14, 15b, 17, 18)

> When he is tried, let him be found guilty; let his prayer be counted as sin. May his days be few; may another seize his position. May his children be orphans, and his wife a widow. May his children wander about and beg; may they be driven out of the ruins they inhabit. May there be no one to do him a kindness, nor anyone to pity his orphaned children . . . and may his memory be cut off from the earth. (Ps 120:7–10, 12, 15b)

> In the night my hand is stretched out without wearying; my soul refuses to be comforted. (Ps 77:2)

Each of these implies the consideration of a negative option for the one who is suffering. Nonetheless, expressing them to God and in community is a necessary step on the road to healing. Articulating the thoughts helps to order them within the framework of relationship to God and within the one who feels them.

"O My Soul" and Alienation

The Psalmist often laments with the expression, "O my soul."[21] This expression is used to indicate a person who is sick and alienated from God, the community, or his or her own self. The context of these cries of lament provides detailed descriptions of the person that has become sick. In Psalm 116 the lamenter begins by describing the distress of his illness.

> The snares of death encompassed me; the pangs of Sheol laid hold on me; I suffered distress and anguish. Then I called on the name of the LORD: "O LORD, I pray, save my life!" (Ps 116:3–4)

---

21. E.g., Pss. 42:5, 11; 43:5; 103:1, 2, 22; 104:1, 35; 116:7; 146:1; Heb. *nafshi*. The expression occurs 102 times in the lament psalms. Lamentations, Job, and Jeremiah also use it frequently.

He describes faith in the midst of his honest expression in suffering, and his alienation from other people.

> I kept my faith, even when I said, "I am greatly afflicted;" I said in my consternation, "Everyone is a liar." (Ps 116:10–11)

After his healing, he speaks to himself about his reintegration and return from the sojourn of his alienating sickness.

> Return, *O my soul*, to your rest, for the LORD has dealt bountifully with you. For you have delivered my soul from death, my eyes from tears, my feet from stumbling. (Ps 116:7–8)

"O my soul" (*naphshi*) has been described as "primarily a term of lament that emerges in anguish."[22] It refers to a "self" in isolation and turmoil. Since *the self* is defined in relation to the community, the expression "O my soul" expresses "the traumatic isolation of the soul" that longs to be in healthy relationship again. The term variously expresses a self's isolation from the community, from one's own self, and from God.[23]

Music, Art, and Lament

The Psalms are poems intended to be put to music, and this practice can add power to the lament. Secular music and other art forms (poetry, painting, and sculpture) are also used to express the dislocation and alienation of human experience. A scientist has noted that "humans suffer psychological exile; artistic creativity is fundamentally motivated by an urgent desire to relieve that misery . . . [In art] we can create order, structure, and meaning amid the frightening, chaotic vastness of self-aware existence."[24]

The music known as "the blues" is a secular adaptation of the laments of "spirituals."[25] The spirituals drew on biblical laments like Job and Habakkuk, affirming faith in the midst of suffering.[26] They recognized the "alienated, differentiated I" that accompanies suffering of all

22. Gaiser, "The Emergence of the Self," 8–9.

23. Approximation of the use of "O my soul" is as follows: isolation from the community (60 percent), from one's own self (20 percent), and from God (20 percent).

24. Kelly Bulkeley, *The Wondering Brain*, 106.

25. James Cone, *The Spirituals and the Blues*.

26. Ibid., 54–57.

kinds. The insight of these songs carried the same weight of separation from the community and from God present in the biblical tradition and most human experience. "The 'I' that cries out in the spirituals is a particular black person self-affirming both his or her being and being-in-community, for the two are inseparable."[27] The separation of members of slave families from each other may help to put this lamenting "I" in perspective. Jesus' isolation in his ministry and death provided a narrative for the "Lonesome Valley."

> I must walk my lonesome valley
> I got to walk it for myself,
> Nobody else can walk it for me,
> I got to walk it for myself.
> Jesus walked his lonesome valley,
> He had to walk it for himself,
> Nobody else could walk it for him,
> He had to walk it for himself.

The juxtaposition of a person's or a people's isolation and the parallel presence of Jesus' isolation in the song is the beginning of hope. In the midst of a lonesome valley of illness or other decentering experience, this kind of lament can re-center the self and reorder the chaos of one's alienation without denying its presence. Like the biblical laments, it brings a complaint into God's presence as an act of worship.

Leap Toward the Light

The fading of light expresses the reality of death and is a metaphor for alienated suffering. Similarly, Ecclesiastes notes the simple pleasure of seeing the sunshine, in reality and as a metaphor against dark days.

> My heart throbs, my strength fails me; as for the light of my eyes—it also has gone from me. My friends and companions stand aloof from my affliction, and my neighbors stand far off. (Ps 38:10–11)

> Light is sweet, and it is pleasant for the eyes to see the sun. Even those who live many years should rejoice in them all; yet let them remember that the days of darkness will be many. (Eccl 11:7–8)

27. Ibid., 61.

In the midst of suffering, choices are made for or against healing; to move toward or away from light and life. One possibility stands above the others: to move toward meaning in the midst of suffering. This requires a leap of faith toward someone. It may be a leap toward God or toward another who is a loving presence. It is a leap toward the light. It means believing that someone will care to listen to your lament and still remain. This is a risk, especially if loving acceptance and presence is not part of one's personal history. It is a risk because the outcome may be unknown to the one who suffers. One must rely on the testimony of others who have also suffered and made the leap. In the three-fold movement of growth noted in Psalm 13 (distress, trust, testimony) this is the second element of trust.

The healing of the reintegrated self begins when suffering is used as an opening to others.[28] Without this step of faith in the midst of suffering, suffering and its accompanying lament remains meaningless.[29] Before this step is taken, suffering is "useless, for nothing . . . basic sense-lessness," because pain "isolates itself . . . or absorbs the rest of consciousness."[30]

Our own suffering is "un-assumable," meaning that we cannot give our own suffering any meaning in isolation. Nor can anyone else suffer the illness we have, for us.[31] In order to find meaning we can decide to embrace our suffering in relation to other people or to God. For the move toward meaning, we must trust that our suffering can bear significance for another.[32]

Psalm 22: Trust and a Leap toward God

In the many Psalms of lament, the leap toward the light is always a leap toward God. They deal with extreme cases of isolation in which family

28. Cf. Frank, *The Wounded Storyteller*, 176.

29. It is meaningless and "an unhappy business" says the preacher in Eccl 4.7–8, to suffer only for yourself.

30. Emmanuel Levinas, "Useless Suffering," 158. Cited in Frank, *The Wounded Storyteller*, 176. Levinas was a philosopher and holocaust survivor.

31. Cf. Frank's reading of Levinas in Frank, *The Wounded Storyteller*, 177.

32. Levinas calls this the hope of the "half-opening." "Wherever a moan, a cry, a groan, or a sigh happen there is the original *call for aid, for curative help* . . . from the other . . . whose exteriority promises salvation; . . . a beyond takes shape in the inter-human." Levinas, "Useless Suffering," 158; cited in Frank, *The Wounded Storyteller*, 177. This "beyond" is the beginning of hope in relationship.

and friends have abandoned the one who suffers. God is the only refuge. In the first address to God in Psalm 22, we noted that God is the primary addressee (a total of thirty-two times in thirty-one verses). After crying out, "My God, my God, why have you forsaken me?" the lamenter reveals why he has trust enough to turn to this God that seems to have let him down.

Ps 22:1–5 remembers past answers to others' prayers. This association with others is the lamenter's first basis for a leap toward God.

> You are holy, enthroned on the praises of Israel. In you our ancestors trusted; they trusted, and you delivered them. To you they cried, and were saved; in you they trusted, and were not put to shame. (Ps 22:3–5)

In verses 9–10 he also remembers to God: "It was you who took me from the womb; you kept me safe on my mother's breast. On you I was cast from my birth." Here the past personal life of the lamenter provides a second basis for his leap. Finally, the primary request of the whole Psalm is given.

> But you, O LORD, do not be far away! O my help, come quickly to my aid! Deliver my soul from the sword, my life from the power of the dog! Save me from the mouth of the lion! (Ps 22:19–21a)

The presence of God is what the lamenter wants, at the very least. Many Psalms proclaim that the path to the road to healing for the isolated soul is the realization that God loves them.

- But surely, God is my Helper, the LORD is the upholder of my soul. (Ps 54:4)

- I cry aloud to the LORD, and he answers me from his holy hill. Selah. (Ps 3:4)

- I waited patiently for the LORD; he inclined to me and heard my cry. (Ps 40:1)

- My soul clings to God. (Ps 63:8)

- For God alone my soul waits in silence. From him comes my salvation. (Ps 62:1)

A disordered alternative is noted by the prophet:

> They do not cry to me from the heart, but they wail upon their beds; they gash themselves for grain and wine. (Hos 7:14)

A respite from anxiety and struggle is clear in the shortest psalm in Scripture.

> O LORD, my heart is not lifted up, my eyes are not raised too high; I do not occupy myself with things too great and too marvelous for me. But I have calmed and quieted my soul, like a weaned child with its mother; my soul is like the weaned child that is with me. O Israel, hope in the LORD from this time on and forevermore. (Ps 131)

A Communal Lament

Perhaps the most unexpected leap toward the light of God is in the book of Lamentations. In the midst of horrific devastation, a community preserved a graphic lament of starvation, siege, and slaughter in Jerusalem. This complaint of the exiled community, written during their captivity in Babylon, is unique in form and content, though it is one among many other communal complaints in Scripture.[33] Its uniqueness lies in our knowledge of the historical circumstances behind its poetry. It represents an unparalleled ferocity of hope that tells the truth, but believes in the presence of God and his love, in spite of the physical evidence.

Only a few thousand Israelites survived the devastation of Jerusalem in 586 BCE and the final deportation to exile in Babylon. The countryside had already been devastated by the Babylonian conquest. Now the city and temple were razed. Lamentations describes the destruction of their community.

> How deserted lies the city, once so full of people! How like a widow is she, who once was great among the nations! She who was queen among the provinces has now become a slave. Bitterly she weeps at night, tears are upon her cheeks . . . All her friends have betrayed her; they have become her enemies . . . Is it nothing to you, all you who pass by? Look around and see.

---

33. The book of Lamentations is a communal lament under the sub-category of "city lament" for a fallen city. Others include Pss 44, 60, 74, 79, 80, 137; Isa 15:1–16:14; 47:1–15; Jer 48:1–47; Amos 5:1–3, 16–20; Micah 1:2–16. For discussion se F. Dobbs-Allsopp, "Lament."

> Is any suffering like my suffering that was inflicted on me? . . .
> (Lam 1:1–3, 12)

In the second chapter the carnage and cannibalism of the siege is brought to the Lord.

> Look, O LORD, and consider: Whom have you ever treated like this? Should women eat their offspring, the children they have cared for? Should priest and prophet be killed in the sanctuary of the Lord? Young and old lie together in the dust of the streets; my young men and maidens have fallen by the sword. You have slain them in the day of your anger; you have slaughtered them without pity. (Lam 2:20–21)

In the fourth chapter this witness includes a description of those that fled Jerusalem who were hunted down.

> Men stalked us at every step, so we could not walk in our streets. Our end was near, our days were numbered, for our end had come. Our pursuers were swifter than eagles in the sky; they chased us over the mountains and lay in wait for us in the desert. (Lam 4:18–19)

In the final chapter, the reality of being prisoners is presented to the community and to God. Rape, torturous deaths, and slavery are the final historical context of the book.

> Women have been ravished in Zion, and virgins in the towns of Judah. Princes have been hung up by their hands; elders are shown no respect. Young men toil at the millstones; boys stagger under loads of wood. (Lam 5:11–13)

The book ends with the lamenting question that astoundingly still turns toward God, who has brought these events to the community for their rebellion.[34]

> Why do you always forget us? Why do you forsake us so long? Restore us to yourself, O LORD, that we may return; renew our days as of old unless you have utterly rejected us and are angry with us beyond measure. (Lam 5:20–21)

It is amazing that such descriptions are included as inspired Scripture. Even more amazing, however, is that the Jews who experienced this did

---

34. Lam 5:16.

not turn away from God, but believed in the goodness of the LORD in the midst of their suffering.

At the physical center of the book, is the heart of their amazing hope.[35] Within the historical context, the familiar song of verses 22–23 ought to be sung through gritted teeth. It expresses a ferocious hope.

> I remember my affliction and my wandering, the bitterness and the gall. I well remember them, and my soul is downcast within me. Yet this I call to mind and *therefore I have hope:* The steadfast love of the LORD never ceases; his mercies never come to an end; they are new every morning; great is your faithfulness. I say to myself, "The LORD is my portion; therefore I will wait for him." The LORD is good to those whose hope is in him, to the one who seeks him; it is good to wait quietly for the salvation of the LORD. (Lam 3:19–26)

This ancient text provides a demonstration of extraordinary resilience[36] under the stress of catastrophic violence, dislocation, and the decimation of a people that not only survives, but lives to thrive. The incredible faith of the book of Lamentations demonstrates what is possible in a community that believes in the steadfast love and promises of the LORD over the centuries, in spite of the immediate evidence. It represents, to the extreme, the movement toward God that is possible in the midst of adversity.[37]

Testimony

Testimony that emerges from suffering is the third movement of lament (distress, trust, testimony) toward hope and growth in the biblical tradition. A person who re-engages relationship in the community can

35. Each chapter of Lamentations is an *acrostic* (The first verse begins with *alef*, the first letter of the Hebrew alphabet and each of the following verses begin with the next Hebrew letter). The acrostics give structure to the grief. Each chapter has 22 verses (there are 22 letters in the Hebrew alphabet), except chapter three, which has 66 verses (three verses for each letter in the acrostic). This lends structural "weight" to the center of the book and its theme in 3:19–24.

36. "Resilience . . . allows an individual to bounce back, cope successfully, and function above the norm in spite of significant stress or adversity." M. Rutter, "Resilience: Some Conceptual Considerations," 626.

37. This resilience is also seen in the African-American church from the days of slavery to the present day.

become a witness to the vulnerability and the wonder of life, relationships, and God. Healing relationships are revealed in individual stories of struggle with injury, addiction, disability, chronic illness, or depression. Healing, even in the midst of suffering, involves becoming a witness to your own life and the relationships that sustain you in the midst of suffering, struggle, and weakness.

The Value of Testimony[38]

Giving witness to one's struggle in a community is a valuable gift. It is possible for one to waste their suffering; for it to remain meaningless. To become meaningful it must become be embodied in a story for others to hear. When a testimony is given, two gifts are given. First, the one who speaks grows and finds healing in the telling. Second, the community learns how to survive and thrive in future days.

The person who gives witness to suffering grows by doing so. He or she must recognize and name the meaningful events and relationships that have helped them to survive their particular trouble. A person comes to understand the significance of their own suffering by hearing their own testimony. Meaning is discovered in the telling as well as the hearing.

The benefits to the community that hears testimony are immeasurable. The survivor has something to teach, simply by relating the experience of survival. A survivor of multiple sclerosis observes that each person has abundances and each person is lacking.[39] This mutual recognition of need provides the context for sharing wisdom, struggle, and hope.[40] Writing about surviving breast cancer, one poet wrote, "I

38. "Narrative ethics" is the term used among healthcare practitioners to speak of testimony and witness in the field of medical ethics. Listening to a patient's narrative can "enhance medical caregivers' recognition of the complexity of treatment decisions." Frank, *Wounded Storyteller*, 155. See his excellent summary of medical doctor Rita Charon, "Narrative Contributions to Medical Ethics.

39. Nancy Mairs, *Ordinary Time*, 163; cited in Frank, *Wounded Storyteller*, 149.

40. Telling the story of one's suffering as a means to healing is a primary focus of the Center for Literature, Medicine, and Biomedical Humanities. Consider the Literature and Medicine Book Series, published by Kent State University Press. In this series, for example, titles include: Sayantani Das Gupta and Marsha Hurst, eds., *Stories of Illness and Healing: Women Write Their Bodies*; Jeanne Bryner, *Tenderly Lift Me: Nurses Honored, Celebrated, and Remembered*; Carol Donley and Maritn Kohn, eds. *Recognitions: Doctors & their Stories*; Jay Bauch, *Fourteen Stories: Doctors, Patients,*

had to remind myself that I had lived through it, already. I had known the pain, and survived it. It only remained for me to give it voice, to share it for use, that the pain not be wasted."[41] A woman who suffered for years with chronic pain related, "I am convinced only sick people know what health is. And they know it by its very loss."[42] Life is precious; live as if it *really matters.*

Biblical Testimony

The possibility of the afflicted person becoming a witness emerges in the praise sections of biblical laments. The Psalmist opens his imagination and anticipates the day when he has something to teach his community by giving testimony. Using the future tense, he imagines an end to his alienation from them.

> I will tell of your Name to my brothers and sisters; in the midst of the congregation I will praise you: You who fear the LORD, praise him! All you offspring of Jacob glorify him; stand in awe of him, all you offspring of Israel! For he did not despise or abhor the affliction of the afflicted; he did not hide his face from me, but heard when I cried to him. From you (LORD) comes my praise in the great congregation; my vows I will pay before those who fear him. The poor shall eat and be satisfied; those who seek him shall praise the LORD. May your hearts live forever! (Ps 22:22–26)

By rehearsing the words that he will use, the lamenter finds hope in the promise of his own, previously silenced, voice.

We see this pattern in large scale in the book of Job. Job sits in silence for many chapters as his friends foolishly try to convince him of his guilt before God. Job finally speaks in chapter 29[43] In these texts, new possibility emerges in the midst of suffering that begins to form a

---

and Other Strangers.

41. Audre Lourde, *The Cancer Journals*, 16; cited in Frank, *Wounded Storyteller*, 167.

42. A woman named Gail interviewed in Linda Garro, "Chronic Illness and the Construction of Narratives," 129; cited in Frank, *Wounded Storyteller*, 141.

43. Even after this Elihu repeats his strict doctrine of retribution. Job finally turns to God's presence (chs. 38–41) which is enough for him (42:2–6).

positive path of healing. Those on this path become a healing witness, for the sake of others.

In some cases, the person who suffers is so transformed that they become grateful in retrospect for their injury or illness. This is the case in of the Psalmist who experienced enlightenment through his affliction at the hands of others.

> The godless besmear me with lies, but with my whole heart I keep thy precepts; their heart is gross like fat, but I delight in thy law. It is good for me that I was afflicted, that I might learn thy statutes. (Ps 119:69–71; my translation)

The images of "besmear" and "fat" (KJV "fat like grease") refer to the unresponsive hearts, heavy ears, and shut eyes found in Isaiah 6:10: "Make the heart of this people fat, and make their ears heavy, and shut their eyes; lest they see with their eyes, and hear with their ears, and understand with their heart, and convert, and be healed."[44] They stand in contrast to the witness to his "delight" and "learning."

Habakkuk's lament begins with anguish over the systemic injustice in his community,

He emerges from suffering with astounding personal strength and faith. "O LORD, how long shall I cry for help and you will not listen? Or cry to you 'Violence!' and you will not save?" (Hab 1:2). When the Lord's response was that he will destroy Jerusalem for its injustice, Habakkuk was even more shaken.[45] His whole world was coming apart. His fear and trembling are clearly described.

> I hear, and I tremble within; my lips quiver at the sound. Rottenness enters into my bones, and my steps tremble beneath me. I wait quietly for the day of calamity to come upon the people who attack us. (Hab 3:16)

This terror is followed by a remarkable confidence in God.

> Though the fig tree does not blossom, and no fruit is on the vines; though the produce of the olive fails, and the fields yield no food; though the flock is cut off from the fold, and there is no herd in the stalls, yet I will rejoice in the LORD; I will exult in the God of my salvation. GOD, the Lord, is my strength; he

---

44. See also Ps 17:10.

45. See James Bruckner, *Jonah, Nahum, Habakkuk, and Zephaniah*.

> makes my feet like the feet of a deer, and makes me tread upon
> the heights. (Hab 3:17–19)

This witness provided others with an anticipation of the struggle that they would one day face. Habakkuk's willingness to suffer for corruption of the community in the advance of others and to emerge as a witness to a possibility beyond meaningless suffering was a prophetic task.

Paul's chronic illness became a witness to Christ. The Apostle Paul suffered some unknown chronic illnesses or disability. When his prayers for healing were answered with a "no," he became a witness to God's faithfulness within the suffering body of Christ. He reintegrated his experience with a strengthened faith.

> Three times I appealed to the Lord about this, that it would leave
> me, but he said to me, "My grace is sufficient for you, for power
> is made perfect in weakness." So, I will boast all the more gladly
> of my weaknesses, so that the power of Christ may dwell in me
> . . . whenever I am weak, then I am strong. (2 Cor 12:8–10)

When many people pray for healing, they are asking for independence in becoming the authors of their own story rather than becoming part of God's story. Paul prayed for healing for his "thorn in the flesh" three times and was refused that kind of healing by God.[46] He continued to turn toward God, and developed his theology of suffering with this chronic condition as his embodied experience.[47] He sought God's purposes regarding his illness and found an opportunity to testify to God's working through weakness. Rather than a lack of faith for a triumphant healing, Paul demonstrated a resilient faith in the midst of suffering. In the end, he considered it a gift for what he had learned about God.

The Testimony of Children

The further testimony of a group of children with kidney disease (see chapter seven) is also helpful for understanding the healing value of imagining the future positive outcomes of present suffering.[48] These

---

46. 2 Cor 12:7–10; cf. Phil 1:29.

47. Dozens of theories exist concerning Paul's "thorn in the flesh" including various disabilities, injuries, and chronic diseases. For a thorough examination of the proposals, see Wilkinson, *The Bible and Healing*, 195–235.

48. D. Bidwell and D. Batisky, "Identity and Wisdom," 1–25.

children deal daily with feelings of isolation and aloneness, generated by the intensity of their suffering experience. When asked, "What makes you more hopeful?" one set of answers indicated increased agency or empowerment when they could imagine possibilities for themselves for the future.

Remarkably, they were not escapist dreams, but a desire and calling to use the wisdom they gained *in suffering* to benefit others. Their "active connection with caregivers and other patients" were significant ways to create meaning in their illness. Some imagined that, in the future, they would be able to excel as health care providers themselves because they "went through this. I will know how to be present with patients who are suffering."[49]

They also spoke of their suffering in relation to God with two general interpretations: 1) "God did not cause my illness, but asked me to learn something from it in order to help others;" and 2) I feel blessed to have learned this from God.[50] This kind of healing in the midst of adversity and pain mirrors the concluding positive testimony of the lament Psalms in their vow-to-praise in the midst of the congregation.

This kind of testimony echoes the bond between witness and suffering found in the New Testament. The relationship between suffering and the credibility of witness is expressed both in the suffering of Jesus as a witness to the love of God for the world[51] and in the Apostle Paul's suffering to bring this message to the Gentiles. Paul knows that he witnesses through the suffering of his body. He brings others into the body of Christ by rendering his own body available to suffering.[52] This credibility helps us to distinguish between real hope and false hope.

Real Hope and False Hope

We began this chapter with the assertion that suffering can lead to despair or to hope and that practice of biblical lament forms a seedbed

49. Ibid.,18.

50. Duane Bidwell and Donald Batisky, "Abundance in Finitude."

51. "And just as Moses lifted up the serpent in the wilderness, so must the Son of Man be lifted up, that whoever believes in him may have eternal life. For God so loved the world that he gave his only Son, so that everyone who believes in him may not perish but may have eternal life." John 3:14–16; see also Phil 2:5–11.

52. Frank, *Wounded Storyteller*, 165.

for hope and healing in the midst of great illness or loss. We have seen that biblical lament is essentially relational. It begins when the one who suffers begins telling the story of sickness to someone he or she trusts. This is why Alcoholics Anonymous and related organizations are effective in producing hope. Recovering alcoholics begin, like the biblical laments, by acknowledgement of *distress*, *trusting* enough to turn to another in telling the truth about their struggle, and giving *testimony* to their hopes and helps for sobriety. They create *real hope* because the meetings are based on real relationships and real stories (relationality and narrativity) which are kept real by the twelve steps and the community of support.

Many priests and psychotherapists understand the problem of false hopes and the hopelessness and despair they create.[53] Believing in good feelings that everything will turn out all right is false hope because it is abstract and not founded in any relationship. Real hope is relative; it relies on relationships, external help, and response from others. That is why laments begin with crying out for response.[54]

Our national culture often assumes that hope is a deep inward and independent "self-sufficient absolute." This belief in absolutized hope also leads to hopelessness because it curses the ill to suffer alone. The mentally ill have real reason to despair of hope if this is true.[55] Real hope is relational, engaging the imagination of those in the community for strategies in the struggle for life.

Real hope transcends the present moment with a sense of the possible with the story and struggle of a community of help. The Christian witness is to real relationship with a real person who suffered, who died and who is God. The possibility of that hope requires a leap toward the light, in the company of others whose faith is cruciform. It is based in the story of Jesus' own embodiment of suffering as a witness to the love of God for the world.

> Let the same mind be in you that was in Christ Jesus, who, though he was in the form of God, did not regard equality with God as something to be exploited, but emptied himself, taking the form of a slave, being born in human likeness. And being

53. William Lynch, *Images of Hope.*

54. Ibid., 32.

55. Ibid., 39–40, 53. To believe in the potential of human perfection and omnipotence is the real source of anxiety and hopelessness. See p. 58.

found in human form, he humbled himself and became obedient to the point of death—even death on a cross. Therefore God
also highly exalted him and gave him the name that is above
every name. (Phil 2:5–9)

This is a story of suffering that begins with Jesus' lamenting cry
from the cross, "My God, My God, why have you forsaken me" and
continues in trust and witness. Can those who seek real hope ignore the
biblical tradition of lament?[56]

Considerations in the Use of Biblical Lament

If we can understand the following functions of biblical lament, laments can become a powerful source of hope and communion with
God, our healer.

- Laments are *not our primary sources* for a doctrine of God (theology). When the laments say "God is hidden," the lamenter
  (Psalmist) means, "It seems now, in my suffering, that God is
  hidden." This is not a metaphysical claim; it is a conversation
  with a God who is listening to the lamenter.

- No one *wants to feel or think* like the lamenters of the psalms.
  They help us to say what we are already thinking.

- Laments *keep the conversation* going.

- Laments *break down our isolation* in times of suffering. A lament expresses the hope that "I'm not crazy." Many in the Bible
  felt this way, too.

- Once we *can express* what is within, *and not be stopped*, healing
  can begin. We may then be prepared to hear the good news
  that God hears and will come to help.

- Jesus uses Psalm 22 on the cross. Jesus is *fully human*, as well
  as fully God. That means God *not only hears* the lament, "My
  God, why have your forsaken me," *but also that God has spoken
  the same experience* in Christ.

---

56. See Kathryn Greene-McCreight, *Darkness Is My Only Companion*.

Chapter Nine

Remembering God

Testimonies of Healing and Health

SCRIPTURE CONTAINS MANY TESTIMONIES to God's acts of health and healing.[1] These testimonies recall God's intervention in the past and witness to promises about God's healing in the future. They also provide a resource for the restoration of health in the present, as they model the practice of speaking of God's healing and life giving power using the past, present, and future voice.

Scripture texts that reflect on healing, rescue, or preservation in times *past* can bring healing to subsequent communities. In the book of Deuteronomy Moses reminds the people of God's acts of deliverance and healing in the wilderness, forty years after the fact. The Psalmist looks back hundreds of years to the same events and Isaiah draws on the same memories in the sixth century BCE to bring healing to the exilic community. Retelling the stories of God's deliverance is a transforming practice.

Many Psalms and prophetic oracles from God use the *present* tense and direct speech, making them timeless in their address. The Psalms especially speak with a voice that often seems contemporary, although all were written before the fifth century BCE.

Many key Psalms and other texts of comfort continue to offer relevant words of healing and *entre* to the healing presence of God.

Numerous texts also offer promises of *future* hope that creates hope for present situations. Isaiah offers many promises for the future of the

---

1. For a full treatment of texts of physical cures see Brown, *Israel's Healer*.

beleaguered and displaced Jewish community in the Diaspora which are yet to be fulfilled. "They shall beat their swords into plowshares, and their spears into pruning hooks; nation shall not lift up sword against nation, neither shall they learn war any more" (Isa 2:4). This text stands on a great monument in front of the United Nation's building today. It was embraced as a promise twenty-five hundred years ago, and is just as active today.

These three kinds of voices about past, present, and future healing acts of God are found throughout Scripture's testimonies. Besides offering resources that are used to great effect around the world, they form a paradigm for understanding the overarching narrative of human experience as one of whole life, whole lifetime health. Full healing in the present is contingent on remembering God by telling the truth about others' and our deliverance in the past. It is furthered by remembering God in speaking words of comfort and healing prayer for the sick in the present. Finally, remembering God's promises for the future given in biblical witnesses to the resurrection and in prayers for the dying gives hope for restoration, even in death.

Remembering and Retelling What God Has Done

Holistic healing involves the transforming practice of telling true stories about the God who has made, redeems, and sustains life on earth. These stories have the power to sustain health and bring healing.[2] The Bible retells its own stories, and the practice continues. Jewish and Christian communities of faith gather weekly to remember and retell

---

2. Health and healing are inculcated and retained by telling and retelling the past, shared, biblical story and by their ownership by members of faith communities. One OT scholar has identified three ways in which this transformation works: 1) Israel understood deliverance from Egypt as a gift of life-giving grace (Deuteronomy 26; Josh ua24). Its memory and retelling had the power to transform later generations (Deut 5:3); 2) Stories of transformation in the text invite the reader to similar transformation, to new life and new understanding in relation to others and to God. When Jacob is at the Jabbok crossing, he struggles with alienation from his brother, is given new name, and is reconciled to his brother (Genesis 44–45); 3) Unexpected results in stories can transform a reader. For example, the verdict in the case of Tamar and Judah forces the reader to reconsider assumptions about righteousness (Genesis 38). They invite the reader to think about complex relationships in which God has a stake and to consider that stake in relation to their own complexities of relation. See Bruce Birch, *Let Justice Roll Down*, 82–84.

the stories of a God who saves, delivers, redeems, and heals his beloved creation. This is practiced in regular worship services: public reading of Scripture; homilies that expound the stories of Scripture and reapply them in present terms; and celebrations of the primary stories of healing and restoration, e.g. Passover, Feast of Booths, Day of Atonement, Hanukkah, the Lord's Supper, Christmas, and Easter.

Three forms of remembering and retelling within Scripture illustrate the importance of story-telling for thriving communities and individuals:

- reapplying stories of God's deliverance in new situations.

- remembering God by means of his reputation/names as a provider of health, security, and healing.

- the practice of saying "thank you" in the form of the thank-offering (*todah*).

Remembering the Exodus

The most important foundational narrative of community deliverance and healing in Scripture is the exodus from Egypt: the protection from death offered in the blood of the Passover lamb; the pursuit by the Egyptian chariots, the despairing trap at the Red Sea; the unexpected defeat of the slavers swallowed in the sea of chaos; the LORD's victory and creation of a new people sung by the people on the shore in the songs of Miriam and Moses; and the new way of living established in the laws of Sinai (see chapter two). This story was told again and again in the Bible, and set a pattern for remembering, in detail, the past deliverance and faithfulness of the LORD. It established the Lord as *God of creation* through control of the elements of creation (the "plagues" and control of the sea); as the *redeemer* of an enslaved people from pharaoh's bondage; and as the *sustainer* of a new kind of community wandering in the wilderness.

This exodus narrative is paradigmatic for Israel's general societal health and identity, as well as its hope and healing in the midst of crisis. Throughout their history, whenever the Israelites encountered a societal change, they recalled God's acts of deliverance from Egypt. Jewish practice among those scattered around the world tells the Passover and Wilderness stories regularly for similar reasons. The pattern of retelling the story of the past for hope and healing of individuals and communities in the present has ancient roots. It is established as an inner-biblical pattern beginning with Moses and Joshua, continuing with Isaiah, and refitted in the New Testament to explain the death and resurrection of Jesus.

In Deuteronomy 26:1–12, Moses admonishes the person who experiences a good income to continue to hope in, trust, and worship the LORD by reciting the history of their deliverance by the LORD. This text was also vital in King Josiah's reforms against corruption in the seventh century BCE. In Joshua 24:1–18, the call to confirm familial values and identity relies, again, on the story of Exodus, as Joshua counsels the people to hope in the future on basis of God's past faithful protection and guidance. He calls upon them to choose to identify with a God who has and can continue to cause them to thrive as families and communities.

Several Psalms also recall the deliverance from Egypt for similar purposes. Psalms 77, 78, and 79 were important to the faithful community in the context of the Babylonian captivity (sixth century BCE). Through the remembrance of God's past deliverance, they worshiped and thrived in spite of their captivity. Psalms 104, 105, 135, and 136 also carried Exodus' remembrance into the heart of Israel's worship life.

The prophet Isaiah preached particularly to the exiles in Babylon using a similar method to build hope among the people and prepare them for their deliverance, which came in 539 BCE.

> I am the LORD, your Holy One, the Creator of Israel, your King. Thus says the LORD, who makes a way in the sea, a path in the mighty waters, who brings out chariot and horse, army and warrior; they lie down, they cannot rise, they are extinguished, quenched like a wick: Do not remember the former things, or consider the things of old. I am about to do a new thing; now it springs forth, do you not perceive it? I will make a way in the wilderness and rivers in the desert. (Isa 43:15–19)

Isaiah's pivotal move is expressed in the ironical, "Do not remember the former things." He teaches the proper use of "former" stories: they establish the power of God's presence to transform even the worst situation. The stories themselves carry the possibility (and therefore must be recalled), but must be reappropriated in every generation for a new situation. The prophets often recall the former exodus from Egypt as the paradigm to communicate the "new exodus" from Babylon.

> Was it not you who dried up the sea, the waters of the great deep; who made the depths of the sea a way for the redeemed to cross over? So the ransomed of the LORD shall return, and come to Zion with singing; everlasting joy shall be upon their heads; they shall obtain joy and gladness, and sorrow and sighing shall flee away . . . The oppressed shall speedily be released; they shall not die and go down to the Pit, nor shall they lack bread. For I am the LORD your God, who stirs up the sea so that its waves roar—the LORD of hosts is his name. (Isa 51:10–11, 14–15; see also Isa 40:11; 41:17–20; 42:10–11; 43:1–3, 9–10; 48:20–21; 49:7–12; 52:7–12; 55:12–13)

For Christians, this recitation necessarily includes a remembrance of the deliverance accomplished through the cross and resurrection of Christ.[3] In Acts 7, when Stephen is arrested and called to account to the high priest in Jerusalem for his evangelism, he begins with Abraham and uses the history of God's acts of past deliverance to explain his newfound hope in Jesus. The retelling of the exodus figures prominently as a foundation of the story of deliverance in Christ (Acts 7:9–38).[4]

Remembering God's Names

God is also remembered as a provider of security and healing by means of his reputation and names. God's names reflect stories in which God has established a reputation by bringing healing or deliverance to someone. Each of God's names or titles (appellations) comes out of a narrative context. As such, when subsequently used, they represent a witness to the event from which they came. Remembering God's reputation through his names in prayer or meditation on Scripture is a practice of health and healing, as it recalls the basis of trust in such a God.

God's one Name (imprecisely rendered *Yahweh*) is represented in English Bibles by the word "LORD" written in capital letters.[5] "The

---

3. Both Mark and Luke-Acts use the exodus as a paradigm for describing the Christian life. See David Pao, *Acts and the Isaianic New Exodus* and Rikki Watts, *Isaiah's New Exodus in Mark.*

4. The author of Hebrews works in a similar way to encourage and build up his readers, recalling the lives of faith of the distant past (Heb 11:1–39).

5. The "Name of the LORD" is the unpronounceable four consonant

Name" (Heb. *ha-shem;* or "his Name" *shemo)* is used as a shorthand for *Yahweh,* especially in the Psalms, recalling the revelation of God's personal concern and presence to Moses at Sinai in Exodus 3 (e.g., Pss 23:3, 25:11, 31:3; 106:8; 109:21; 111:9; 148:5, 13). This is the source of the name "I Am" which can be rendered "I will be who I will be." With God all things are possible. The LORD God (*Yahweh Elohim*) is the full expression of this Name (Exod 3:15–16).[6]

Many other descriptions are added to this Name (*Yahweh*) or to the word God (*'Elohim* or *'el*) throughout Scripture to create additional "names" or titles. "God sees me" (*'El-ro'i*) is the name Hagar gave God when she and her son Ishmael were rescued from death in the wilderness (Gen 16:3–16). "The LORD is my banner" (*Yahweh nissi*) recalls the miraculous defeat of the Amalekites who attacked the weakest in the wilderness (Exod 17:8–16). "The LORD is our healer" remembers the bitter water of Marah, which was made sweet for the people to drink (Exod 15:22–27; Deut 32:39). This incident is later recalled by the Psalmist and Jeremiah (Pss 30:2; 103:3; Jer 30:17).

"The Lord is my Shepherd" (*Yahweh ro'i*) also functions as a title of remembrance for David's early life as a tender of sheep which comes to be applied to all Israel (Pss 23:1; 78:52; 80:1). It has an earlier version in Jacob's blessing of his sons: "by the name of the Shepherd, the Rock of Israel" (Gen 49:24). The prophets carry it as a metaphor for God's tender care for his people (Isa 40:11; Jer 31:10; Ezek 34:11–12). In the New Testament, Jesus refers to himself as the "Good Shepherd" (John 10).

One of the most frequent titles for God is "Rock" (*tsur*).[7] When Moses sang a song of praise at the end of his life he began with a reference to God as the one who provided life-giving water from the rocks in an arid desert.

> For I will proclaim the name of the LORD; ascribe greatness
> to our God! The Rock, his work is perfect, and all his ways are

---

("tetragrammaton") Hebrew word rendered "Yahweh" given to Moses at Sinai (Exod 3:1–15). Jewish tradition "fences" the Name, which alternatively is articulated *hash-shem* or *adonai,* so that it was never spoken. See the discussion of the use of the Name of the Lord in the third commandment in chapter two.

6. Jesus was accused of blasphemy for claiming the Name when he said, "Before Abraham was, I Am" (John 8:58).

7. For "God is my Rock": see Pss 19:14; 28:1; 42:9; 62:1–2, 6–7; 71:3; 78:15, 20, 35; 89:26; 92:15; 95:1; 144:1–2.

just. A faithful God, without deceit, just and upright is he. (Deut 32:3–4; cf. verses 13, 15, 18, 30, 31, 37)

When David celebrated his deliverance from and defeat of all those who wanted to kill him, his song began,

The LORD is my Rock, my fortress, and my deliverer, my God, my Rock in whom I take refuge, my shield, and the horn of my salvation, my stronghold (Ps 18:2; Psalm 18 is repeated in 2 Samuel 22).

The later use of "rock" came to be associated with the refuge (*machseh*) that Jerusalem provided. God's gift of security against enemies and the water of Hezekiah's tunnel which provided water for the Assyrian siege of 701 BCE were attributed to God, the Rock and Refuge.[8] In the New Testament, Paul identifies Jesus with the rock of life-giving water that sustained the people in the wilderness.[9]

Remembering to Say "Thank You"

In our culture, we are taught them to say thank you and to write notes of thanks. It is good to be a thankful person. The ancient way of thanking, however, especially of thanking God, was a much more public expression which lifted up the details of the help received. The practice of the thank-offering and the thanksgiving psalms (*todah*) also illustrate the full healing potential of remembering God's acts of grace in the midst of sickness or distress.[10] A biblical *todah* was based on the Levitical commands to thank the Lord by bringing a peace offering to the temple and declaring what God had done in the midst of the worshiping community (Lev 3; 22:18–30).[11]

The practice of the thank-offering was in some ways similar to a modern barbeque, as families ate the meat together with the levites (the

8. For "God is my Refuge" see Pss 14:6; 27:5; 31:2–3; 46:1, 7, 11; 62:7–8; 91:2, 9; 94:22; 142:5; Ruth 2:12.

9. 1Cor 10:1–4; Jesus also described his teachings as a rock on which one would build one's life. See Matthew 7:24–29.

10. For more on Psalms of thanksgiving ("declarative praise") see Westermann, *Praise and Lament in the Psalms*, 18, 25–30.

11. Individual thanksgiving psalms include Psalms 9–11, 16, 30, 32, 34, 92, and 116. Community thanksgiving psalms include Psalms 65–68, 75, 107, 115, 118, 124, 125, and 129.

fat belonged to the LORD). Peace offerings (including thank offerings, vow offerings, and freewill offerings) were brought, the fat was burned as the meat was cooked and it was shared among the people who were there to worship. Then the one who had brought the offering stood and declared what the LORD had done. "I have been delivered from trouble, the Lord saved my life. I was sinking beneath the breakers and rollers but the Lord brought me up to the light."

In thanksgiving Psalms, it is important to note that God is made the subject of the sentence, in contrast to most contemporary forms of thanks, where the implied subject of the expression is "(I) thank you." In the formal genre of the Psalms, God is the subject: e.g., Ps 30: 11: "You have turned my mourning into dancing. You have loosed my sackcloth and girded me with gladness."[12] It is hard to overestimate the difference between ourselves as the subject of the sentence and God as the subject. The priority of the "I" is the first cause of sin in the Garden. Giving public thanks is transforming and healing precisely because it turns us from ourselves to our maker, the source of our life, restoration, and hope.

The second chapter of Jonah illustrates the *todah* in a specific narrative. It follows the traditional form of a psalm of thanksgiving, set in a dramatic context.[13] Jonah gives thanks to God for his deliverance *while still inside the belly of the fish* (Jonah 2:1). Here we see the distinction that medical cultural-anthropologists make between the *cure of disease* and the *healing of sickness*.[14] "Cure" is the elimination of a "disease" and is the goal of biomedical science. "Healing" is the value added solution to "illness" or "sickness." Illness and healing are not confined to science but always include personal, social, and cultural dimensions. One may be cured and healed, or cured and not healed. It is also possible that one may not experience a cure to their disease, but be healed in the midst of it. Jonah was healed but not yet delivered or "cured" of his terminal situation in the belly of the fish. He sang a song of his reconciliation with God and his deep gratitude for his life

12. Psalm 30 illustrates the four typical components of a psalm of thanksgiving: 1) 30:1–3 introduction; 2) 30:4–5 call to praise; 3) 30:6–12 a narrative account; vs. 6–7 crisis in retrospect; vs. 8 "I cried"; vss. 9–10 "you heard"; vss. 11–12a "You intervened"); 4) 30:12b praise/vow to praise.

13. For further discussion see James Bruckner, *Jonah, Nahum, Habakkuk, Zephaniah.*

14. John Pilch, *Healing in the New Testament*, 13, 24–25.

while his life is still at risk. Jonah was not expelled by the fish onto dry land (cured of his life threatening predicament) until he had been healed in relation to God, experienced overwhelming gratitude, and expressed praise for his deliverance from drowning.

Healing transcends biomedical categories because it addresses more than the disease. It is deeper than a cure because it restores relationships. Disease itself can become the occasion for more than a cure. It can become the agent, like Jonah's fish, of the healing one's deeper and relational alienations (which are sometimes the cause of the disease in the first place). Healing deals with self-identity, relationships with others, cultural values, and God. *Cure is temporary, since all die; but healing is forever.* Even without a cure, healing is the best restoration of health to the extent that many people, like Jonah, give thanks for the enlightenment they have received through their disease or chronic situation.

Thanksgiving and healing. The account of the cure of the ten lepers and the cure and healing of one illustrates the difference between cure and healing (Luke 17:12–19).[15] Jesus told the ten lepers to go, according to the law, to be examined by the priests. As they went they were cured of their skin disease. In going, all of them received the healing of restoration to the community as a value added to their cure from disease. They were free to be reintegrated into daily life.[16] But the one who returned to give thanks to Jesus demonstrated a deeper healing. Like the others he was cured (*iaomai*), but he was also pronounced "well" (*sozo*).

Three steps describe his additional healing: 1) "He saw that he was cured." He recognized the magnitude of what had happened to him and praised God in a loud voice; 2) "He turned back." His transformation and reflected gratitude led to a change in his direction and behavior in a way different from the other nine, who proceeded to the priests; 3) His identity was transformed. The narrative notes that he was an ostracized Samaritan. Here he becomes the one known by his faith in and praise of God. His faith was the cause of his healing in relation to God through Jesus.

Forgetting God precludes healing, even in those who are cured. We participate in the completion of our own healing by giving a testimony of thanks for God's healing work in us among our friends and

15. For a fuller account of the value added healing of the one leper see, Frederick Gaiser, "'Your Faith Has Made You Well': Healing and Salvation in Luke 17:12–19."

16. See Hector Avalos, *Health Care and the Rise of Christianity*, 23–27.

family. To say, "God has made me whole" is a speech-act; it *does* what it says; it completes the healing. It is healing to tell the truth about who God is and what God has done for us; ending silence, banishing forgetfulness. After the long struggle of his life Jacob warned his descendents, "You were unmindful of the Rock that bore you; you forgot the God who gave you birth" (Gen 32:18).

God Comforts and Heals in the Present

God is active in the processes of healing in many ways. As the Creator of intelligence and skill, God is active in the actions of the medical staff and the good work of those who labor in the healing arts to restore health. Scripture, however, offers additional resources for healing that are engaged by people of faith, as well as by most pastors, priests, rabbis, and chaplains. Among these healing practices are 1) bringing God's comfort through words of Scripture in the visitation of the sick; 2) bringing God's presence through prayers of healing for the sick.

Bringing God's Comfort with Words from Scripture

Words matter because they can create environments of healing and hope or of death and despair.[17] This power is a primary fact of the Bible: "And God said, 'Let there be light' and there was light;" and "God brought [the animals] to Adam to see what he would call them; and whatever Adam called every living creature, that was its name." Words change things. In fact, the Hebrew word for "word" (*dibber*) also means "action" or "deed." Some kinds of words are actually speech-acts.

One way of expressing the idea of the "speech–act" is that "words do what they say." Consider the effect of the words, "I love you" or "I forgive you." If your alienation is from God and you have confessed some sin, the following words may also bring you the experience of forgiveness: "In the mercy of God, you are forgiven." When Elisha said to Israel's enemy, the Syrian general Naaman, "Your healing is from God, not from me," something changed in Naaman's perception of the world, and perhaps in Elisha's as well.

17. Consider the effect of an oncologist's words on a patient who has decided to end chemotherapy: "I don't need to see you again." Consider the difference it could make to add, "May the Lord bless you and keep you."

Many biblical texts create verbal contexts for healing. This is the case especially when the direct speech of God is repeated to the sufferer by a caregiver. Then the healing potential is palpable. By speaking God's words through words of Scripture to the sick, an environment is created in which God's healing presence may be experienced.

Many shorter texts in the Bible are under-used in the practice of healing. These texts are best experienced when read out loud by a trusted family member or friend.[18] They include direct expressions of God's presence:

> For I am the LORD your God who upholds your right hand, who says to you, "Do not fear, I will help you" (Isa 41:13).

> For I will restore health to you, and your wounds I will heal, says the Lord (Jer 30:17a)

> My sheep hear my voice. I know them, and they follow me. I give them eternal life, and they will never perish. No one will snatch them out of my hand. (John 10:27–28)

Promises:

> For he has said, "I will never leave you or forsake you." So we can say with confidence, "The Lord is my helper; I will not be afraid. What can anyone do to me?" (Heb 13:5–6)

> But he was wounded for our transgressions, he was bruised for our iniquities; upon him was the chastisement that made us whole, and with his stripes we are healed. (Isa 53:5)

> And God is able to make all grace abound to you; that always having enough of everything, you may have an abundance for every good deed. (2 Cor 9:8)

Direct encouragement:

> Let not your heart be troubled; believe in God, believe also in me. (John 14:1)

> Be strong and let your heart take courage, all you who hope in the Lord. (Ps 31:24)

Expressions of confidence:

---

18. William Hume, known as the father of pastoral theology, suggested that we, his students, memorize these kinds of verses so that they might carry their full potential into meeting with those who were suffering.

> God is our refuge and strength, a very present help in trouble. Therefore we will not fear, though the earth should change, though the mountains shake in the heart of the sea; though its waters roar and foam, though the mountains tremble with its tumult. (Ps 46:1–3)

> I can do all things through Him who strengthens me. (Phil 4:13)

> But we have this treasure in jars of clay, so that it may be made clear that this extraordinary power belongs to God and does not come from us. We are afflicted in every way, but not crushed; perplexed, but not driven to despair; persecuted, but not forsaken, struck down, but not destroyed. (2 Cor 4:7)

Many of the one hundred and fifty psalms of the Hebrew Bible have provided those who suffer disease and illness with guidance into the healing presence of God. Tradition has identified those that are most helpful. These provide words for those who cannot find words of their own to speak, a common problem for those in pain. They also instruct us in the common experience of others who are ill in relation to God. Several of them serve as illustrations here.

Psalm 139 provides words for a person who experiences the isolation and alienation of illness with the first person assurance of God's presence. In the first six verses, the person speaks of God's personal acquaintance with them beginning with, "O LORD, you have searched me and known me. You know when I sit down and when I rise up." Verses 7–13 describe the distance experienced by a sick person, yet God's presence, even in death.

> If I make my bed in Sheol, you are there . . . If I say, "Surely the darkness shall cover me, and the light around me become night," even the darkness is not dark to you; the night is as bright as the day, for darkness is as light to you. (Ps 139:8b, 11–12)

The Psalm continues with an experience of wonder: the awareness that God has been present with them since before the person's birth, and will continue until the end.

> For it was you who formed my inward parts; you knit me together in my mother's womb. I praise you, for I am fearfully and wonderfully made. Wonderful are your works; that I know very well . . . In your book were written all the days that were formed for me, when none of them as yet existed . . . I come to the end— I am still with you. (Ps 139:13–14, 16b, 18b)

Psalm 91 declares protection from terror that many people face in illness which is known as intra-psychic suffering. This is the fear of the unknown future and the extreme inward alienation that compounds the actual pain of illness. The Psalm includes promises for those who hear or read and claim them.

> You who live in the shelter of the Most High, who abide in the shadow of the Almighty will say to the LORD "My refuge and my fortress, my God in whom I trust . . . He will cover you with his pinions, and under his wings you will find refuge; his faithfulness is a shield and buckler. You will not fear the terror of the night . . . nor the destruction that wastes at noonday . . . Because you have made the LORD your refuge the Most High your dwelling place, no evil shall befall you, no scourge come near your tent, for he will command his angels concerning you to guard you in all your ways. On their hands they will bear you up, so that you will not dash your foot against a stone. You will tread on the lion and the adder, the young lion and the serpent you will trample under foot. (Ps 91:1–2, 4–6, 9–13; see also Ps 121)

Psalm 73, probably first used in healing services at the temple, was written for the sick who live in integrity before God. In their sickness they struggle not only with sickness but possible death, in spite of their exemplary life. Yet they find goodness and strength in God as their refuge.

> All in vain I have kept my heart clean and washed my hands in innocence. For all day long I have been plagued, and am punished every morning . . . My flesh and my heart may fail, but God is the strength of my heart and my portion forever . . . But for me it is good to be near God; I have made the Lord GOD my refuge, to tell of all your works. (Ps 73:13–14, 26, 28; see also Ps 26:6–7)

Dozens of such Psalms have provided help and healing comfort and an experience of God's presence to the sick and dying.[19] Ten psalms are particularly recommended by Rebbe Nachman in his *Tikkun*.[20] He outlines the ways in which meditating on these psalms can aid in healing: Psalm 16 (God's protection); Psalm 32 (God's forgiveness); Psalm 41 (God heals illness); Psalm 42 (seeking God's presence); Psalm 59

19. For more examples see Pss 6, 30, 32, 38, 39, 41, 103, and 121.

20. Cited in David Freeman and Judith Abrams, eds. *Illness and Health in the Jewish Tradition*, 96.

(God's deliverance from enemies); Psalm 77 (a lament that remembers and praises God's past goodnesses); Psalm 90 (a wisdom psalm: "teach us to number our days"); Psalm 105 (praise to God for deliverance from Egypt); Psalm 137 (a lament and song of hope for restoration of what has been lost); Psalm 150 (pure praise of God).

The most familiar of all Psalms used to provide comfort may be Psalm 23. The structure, rhetorical features, and content of the psalm work together to bring healing.

> The LORD is my shepherd, I shall not want. He makes me lie down in green pastures; he leads me beside still waters; he restores my soul. He leads me in right paths for his name's sake. Even though I walk through the darkest valley, I fear no evil; for you are with me; your rod and your staff—they comfort me. You prepare a table before me in the presence of my enemies; you anoint my head with oil; my cup overflows. Surely goodness and mercy shall follow (lit. "pursues"; Heb. *radap*) me all the days of my life, and I shall dwell in the house of the LORD my whole life long. (Psalm 23)

The first feature is that the Name, the "LORD" begins and ends the Psalm. This typical poetic device (*inclusio*) creates a verbal environment of security and comfort on a subliminal level. The second is that the LORD a) leads, vss. 2–3; b) is "with" and provides the "comfort" of protection (rod) and guidance (staff), vss. 4–5; and c) "pursues me" with his goodness, v. 6. God begins in front, leading in order to show the way to "restore my soul" (lit. life). Then God comes alongside in the midst of the greatest dangers and struggle, to protect and sustain, even in the face of death. This accounts for the wide use of this psalm in the WWI trenches.[21] God's goodness pursues the reader, until the end of life.

The third and strongest rhetorical feature is the switch from third person language ("he") in verses 1–3 to the second person ("you") that indicates the LORD's presence in verses 4 and 5, just when the person enters the "shadow of death." The Psalmist begins by speaking *about* God, but the direct I-you address in the darkest struggle with death leads the reader to acknowledge the presence of God in the midst. The

---

21. When the soldiers in the World War I trenches recited "Even though I walk through the valley of the shadow of death, the Lord is with me," it is not likely that they were thinking of David in the eleventh century BCE. God's word is living and active.

reading, recitation, or memorization of passages such as this has been creating environments of hope for believers for thousands of years.

Bringing Healing

God is active daily through many congregations that pray weekly for the healing and comfort of those who are sick or injured. Many are cured and healed. Some cures can be explained bio-medically; for others, doctors just shrug their shoulders. In my home congregation the pastoral prayer names those who are in need and prays for their healing. A printed "prayer list" is provided to the congregation for prayers during the week. Some congregations use automated phone "prayer networks" with their active members to rapidly communicate urgent prayer needs. In another local congregation, the pastor names the infirm and prays for a cure and God's healing presence, "Heal them according to your will; but mostly keep them close to you." The practice of prayer and other support for the sick among congregations varies.[22]

Prayers for healing. Medical studies in the last twenty years have sought to explain the connection between prayer and healing. There are dozens of "well-designed and methodologically sound studies on the efficacy of one person's prayer affecting another person's health."[23] Several major features in *Time, Newsweek,* and other popular sources have featured studies and discussion of the relationship between faith and medicine.[24] The consensus is that there is a connection, but that it is a result of community support and relational factors. Positive results are also explained by "positive energy" directed toward or by the patient.[25] The fact remains that generally those who are praying are

22. See Susan Dunlap, *Caring Congregations,* for an ethnographic study of varying practices of mainstream Protestant church, an African American Pentecostal Holiness church, and the Hispanic sub-congregation of a Roman Catholic church, all in Durham, NC.

23. Bulkeley, *Wondering Brain,* 153; Bulkeley relies on a summary of research supporting intercessory prayer in Larry Dossey, *Healing Words.* He also cites neuroscience explanations of the efficacy of prayer from a Christian perspective represented in James Ashbrook and Carol Albright, *The Humanizing Brain.*

24. For example see *Newsweek*'s cover story, "God & Healing: Is Religion Good Science? Why Science is Starting to Believe" November 10, 2003. See also *Time*'s cover story on February 23, 2009.

25. Prayer by the patient for themselves is also established by neuroscience as a

directing their prayers to the God revealed in Scripture. Those who do not believe in God simply don't pray. The revealed text does not deny that God works through his community, but describes God's "positive energy," commonly known as the Holy Spirit, as mediated through the community of faith.[26]

For Christians, James 5:13–16 provides specific instructions regarding praying for the sick and anointing with oil. The instructions are "radically integral. Individual, social, and cosmic levels interpenetrate."[27] Individual alienation from the community and from God (through confession and forgiveness) is erased. Boundaries between rich and poor, physical and spiritual, present and future are dissolved.[28] Healing involves the body of Christ.

> Are any among you sick? They should call for the elders of the church and have them pray over them, anointing them with oil in the name of the Lord. The prayer of faith will save the sick, and the Lord will raise them up; and anyone who has committed sins will be forgiven. Therefore confess your sins to one another, and pray for one another, so that you may be healed. The prayer of the righteous is powerful and effective. (Jas 5:14–16)

"Elders" generally refers to faithful leaders in a church. In the ancient world, this stood in contrast to the professional healers located in temples.[29] In contemporary practice a pastor or priest often fulfills the function of visiting and praying for the sick. Pentecostal churches rely on congregational members.[30] In the Roman Catholic church, this text is the foundation of the sacrament of confession and recitation of "last

---

means of healing. "Contemplative practices genuinely transform the brain-mind system . . . the more energy one puts in to a contemplative practice the greater will be its transformational effects." Bulkeley, *Wondering Brain*, 165. He relies here on Eric Kandel, James Schwartz, and Thomas Jessel, eds., *Principles of Neural Science*.

26. The wide discussion of the power created in the human mind as an agent of healing the body is summarized in Thomas Dorege, *The Faith Factor in Healing* and Edgar Jackson, *The Role of Faith in the Process of Healing*.

27. Martin Albl, "'Are Any Among You Sick?' The Health Care System in the Letter of James."

28. Ibid., 143.

29. See the extended thesis that Christianity spread rapidly in the first two centuries in part because of this accessibility to health care. Christians made a practice of "house calls." Hector Avalos, *Health Care and the Rise of Christianity*.

30. See John Christopher Thomas. "Health and Healing: A Pentecostal Contribution."

rites." The text, however, calls for the "elders," generally meaning people of faith who know the one who is suffering. In churches with active healing ministries, at least one member will accompany a pastor to the bedside of one who has requested prayer for healing.

A recent study of pastoral care with persons who were dying dis-covered a very strong desire among Christians to receive biblical forms of prayer during their decline and at the time of death.[31] In this limited and self-selected group, the preference was for prayer with family mem-bers, Christian friends, pastors, and chaplains, *in that order.* The valued role of the family and community was clearly evident.[32]

The instruction to "confess your sins" sometimes raises the ques-tion of the relationship between sin and suffering (see this discussion in chapter seven).[33] The call, however, is not simply for the sick to confess their sins, but for the members of the congregation to "confess your sins to one another, and pray for one another, so that you may be healed." In the context of mutual confession of our pervading need for forgiveness, the corporate dimension of healing is in view. One person's illness is an occasion for all to experience God's healing presence. On more than one occasion, a member who has been praying for another's healing has experienced a healing of their own.

The regular confession of sins is practiced as a healing practice in many Christian congregations. One Protestant tradition uses the fol-lowing words, with reference to the *Shema.*

> We confess that we are in bondage to sin and cannot free our-selves. We have sinned against you in thought, word, and deed, by what we have done and by what we have left undone. We have not loved you with our whole heart; we have not loved our neighbors as ourselves. For the sake of your Son, Jesus Christ, have mercy on us. Forgive us, renew us, and lead us so that we may delight in your will and walk in your ways to the glory of your holy Name. Amen.

The regular reception of God's grace and forgiveness ("absolution") is participation in a real time story of deliverance. Loads of guilt are removed, anxiety released, and freedom and grace are declared.[34] This

---

31. Debra Gustafson, *Biblical Prayer in Relation to Dying.*

32. Ibid., iv–v.

33. See also Keith Warrington, *Healing & Suffering,* 57–60, 72–75.

34. Henri Nouwen writes that a Christian community is a healing community

healing absolution is offered with the quoting of biblical texts, often from the Hebrew Bible.

> For as the heavens are high above the earth, so great is his steadfast love toward those who fear him; as far as the east is from the west, so far he removes our transgressions from us (Ps 103:11–12).

> Though your sins are like scarlet, they shall be like snow; though they are red like crimson, they shall become like wool (Isa 1:18b).

> If we say that we have no sin, we deceive ourselves, and the truth is not in us. If we confess our sins, he who is faithful and just will forgive us our sins and cleanse us from all unrighteousness. (1 John 1:8–9)

Healing comes in many forms through prayer for sickness: mended relationships with family or with God; perhaps a new perspective on life, and involvement in community issues (e.g., cancer prevention). In faith, we are always healed, but not always cured of disease. Healing can include a cure; healing may come without a cure (see the discussion of Paul's faith and enduring chronic illness in chapter eight). Healing may come through death in the arms of the body of Christ and resurrection life. James instructs, "The prayer of faith will save the sick, and the Lord will raise them up."

Whether or not a cure is included, God still heals and instructs us to pray for healing.[35] The disciples are sent out to heal. However, our reading of the New Testament sometimes ignores the contours of life experience. Lazarus had to die twice. Bodies wear out. No one has the promise of perpetual good health. In the end, without physical access to the Tree of Life (Rev 22), death is the only door to complete healing. Resurrection and the promise of a new body, in the manner of the res-

---

because wounds and pains become occasions for new vision, not simply because wounds are cured. Mutual confession deepens mutual hope and shares burdens, and reminds us of God's forgiveness and coming new creation. Henri Nouwen, *The Wounded Healer*, 94.

35. For a discussion of the relationship between faith and healing, see NT scholar K. Warrington, *Healing and Suffering*, 27–39; and Warrington, *Jesus the Healer: Paradigm or Unique Phenomenon?*, 1–29; For an excellent study of the purpose of Jesus' miracles see Graham Twelftree, *Jesus, the Miracle Worker: A Historical & Theological Study*; and Audrey Dawson. *Healing, Weakness and Power: Perspectives on Healing in the Writings of Mark, Luke, and Paul.*

urrected Jesus, "the first born of the new creation" is the ultimate true healing. In the meantime, we are instructed to gather, confess our sins, anoint, and pray in the Name of the Lord for the healing of the sick.

The use of oil with prayers for healing has been interpreted in the history of the church in four ways, which are not necessarily mutually exclusive: 1) as an ancient form of medicine; 2) as psychological reinforcement of prayer; 3) as symbol of God's grace; and 4) as a means of God's healing touch (sacramental).[36] If the Hebrew Bible is taken as a significant background, anointing with oil is the outward means of demonstrating the presence of the God's Spirit. The association of anointing by God's Spirit and healing is seen most directly in Jesus' inaugural sermon in Luke 4, where he quotes and claims Isaiah 61: "The Spirit of the Lord is upon me, because he has anointed me to bring good news to the poor. He has sent me to proclaim release to the captives and recovery of sight to the blind, to let the oppressed go free, to proclaim the year of the Lord's favor." (Luke 4:18–19)

Death and Healing:
Hope in Resurrection is Health for Today

Prayer for healing (not cure) in the process of dying is also a valuable resource provided in Scripture. The experience of grief in the loss of a loved one to death will not be denied. Everyone dies. Separation and loss of relationship trigger recognition of how little control human beings have over their short lives.[37] For those who believe in Scripture's witness to bodily resurrection, healing prayer with the dying at the time of death is a valuable resource. Jesus' prayers to the Father during his decline, dying, and death are offered as a model of praying for healing while people are in the process of dying and at their death.[38]

Despair is not the necessary conclusion if grief and separation are temporary.[39] The testimony of the ancient text is that God has provided

36. See and compare Gary Shogren, "Will God Heal Us: A Re-examination of James 5:14–16a" and Kyle Schiefelbein, "'Receive this oil as a sign of forgiveness and healing': A Brief History of the Anointing of the Sick and Its Use in Lutheran Worship."

37. The fear of death is described as an enslavement from which one can be freed by relationship to Christ in Hebrews 2:14–18. See Gustafson, *Biblical Prayer*, 128–30.

38. Gustafson, *Biblical Prayer in Relation to Dying*, 130–39.

39. See the discussion of grief and hope in Joel Shuman and Brian Volck, *Reclaiming*

someone who does have control over death and life. In Christ's death and resurrection, God's love has ultimately overcome death. In some Christian traditions, funeral services are titled, "Witness to the Resurrection." The service is not triumphalistic, but acknowledges the hope and love that embraces grief and lament, and dismantles despair.

Freedom from Fear

Freedom from the fear of death while dying is possible in Christian hope. The fear of death is widely known and experienced by people without an overarching narrative or relationship with God. Death is an unknown, isolating future when the relationality and narrativity communicated in Scripture are absent. In the face of death, health and healing are still possible because of the promise of a continued relationship with God.

Freedom from fear allows for many kinds of healing at the end of life, so that some deaths may be described as "more healthy" than others. This "healthier dying" does not exclude anxiety, grief over what is being lost, or the pains of suffering. Yet, it frees the one dying and their loved ones from the commonly attending intra-psychic suffering concerning the future.

The Apostle Paul delineates the Christian witness based on more than five hundred witnesses to the bodily resurrected Jesus.[40] Paul himself testified that he saw and spoke with him.[41] Hope for the next life is based on relationship to Christ's resurrection by God. He begins with opposition to this hope.

> Now if Christ is proclaimed as raised from the dead, how can some of you say there is no resurrection of the dead? . . . If Christ has not been raised, then our proclamation has been in vain and your faith has been in vain. We are even found to be misrepresenting God, because we testified of God that he raised Christ. (1 Cor 15:12, 14–15)

---

the Body, 132–134.

40. 1 Corinthians 15:1–11; many testify that they saw, spoke with, ate, and touched Jesus. See, for example, Luke 24; John 21.

41. Acts 9:1–6; 26–29.

Paul testifies to the nature of God's triumph over the power of death for his human creation, based on the community's extraordinary experience of seeing the resurrected Christ.

> But in fact Christ has been raised from the dead, the first fruits of those who have died. For since death came through a human being, the resurrection of the dead has also come through a human being; for as all die in Adam, so all will be made alive in Christ. The last enemy to be destroyed is death. (1 Cor 15:20–22)

Paul also describes the transition between death and new life in terms of a new body. This "spiritual" (*pneumatikon*) body is a body that is enlivened by the Spirit (*pneuma*) of God who creates and sustains it.

> What is sown is perishable, what is raised is imperishable. It is sown in dishonor, it is raised in glory. It is sown in weakness, it is raised in power. It is sown a physical body, it is raised a spiritual body. (1 Cor 15:42b–44)

The amazing hope that birthed Christianity is a triumph over death that results in singing, even in the face of death. He quotes the impassioned words of God through Hosea the prophet, whose address to Death is a lament over God's decision to destroy the ten northern tribes.[42] Death's dominating monopoly over human life has been destroyed. Paul's conclusion soars in its exclamation like a song of joy.

> Listen, I will tell you a mystery! We will not all die, but we will all be changed, in a moment, in the twinkling of an eye, at the last trumpet. For the trumpet will sound, and the dead will be raised imperishable, and we will be changed . . . Then the saying that is written will be fulfilled: "Death has been swallowed up in victory. Where, O death, is your victory? Where, O death, is your sting?" (1 Cor 15:51–52, 54b–55)

Relational Hope

Hoping in "heaven" (a new heaven and new earth) has sometimes been criticized as an unfortunate "other worldly focus."[43] Even within recent

42. See Hosea 13 in which God struggles out loud concerning his decision to destroy Israel with the Assyrian army in 722. The ironic use of this dark text reverses the horror of the death of God's beloved community in a song of ultimate victory.

43. See Feuerbach's critique and the discussion of heaven in chapter five.

Christian traditions, many have objected to a focus on heaven. The movement known as Pietism is especially named as a culprit. A practical measure of this objection is the extent to which many songs about heaven have been removed from hymnals and Christian music.

A new assessment of Pietism, examining the work of the fathers of Pietism (Spener and Franke) demonstrates that hope in heaven actually fueled effective social reform for the most destitute. Pietists, at their best, were filled with hope and action for their communities *because of* their hope in heaven. Their visions of heaven filled their imagination with new possibilities for the present world.[44] This function is concomitant with the observation of neuroscience that curiosity, imagination, and wonder re-center and cause the growth of new neural pathways in the human brain.[45] (See chapter six.) Hoping in heaven helped Christians to imagine that the poverty, violence, and destitution of many communities could be transformed, when no one else could imagine it. Nonetheless, Christian hope, according to the biblical witness, is not exactly "in heaven," or only hope of a restored creation. It is described in Scripture as hope "in Christ" and "with Christ." It is tied to a story of relationship.

Relationship within a Continuing Story. The biblical resurrection hope is not "pie in the sky" nor the general feeling that "everything will be all right" but a relational continuance with a personal God.[46] The New Testament posits a personal, face-to-face meeting: "For now we see in a mirror, dimly, but then we will see face to face. Now I know only in part; then I will know fully, even as I have been fully known." (1 Cor 12:13) The Hebrew Bible's promise of God's coming peaceable kingdom is also made by a personal God who speaks in the first person through the prophet.

> For I am about to create new heavens and a new earth; the former things shall not be remembered or come to mind. But be glad and rejoice forever in what I am creating; for I am about to create Jerusalem as a joy, and its people as a delight. I will rejoice in Jerusalem, and delight in my people; no more shall the sound of weeping be heard in it, or the cry of distress. (Isa 65:17–19)

44. Michelle Clifton-Soderstrom, *Angels, Worms, and Bogeys*, 171–74.

45. See the discussion of experiences of wonder in chapter seven.

46. See the discussion of real hope and false hope in chapter eight; especially Lynch, *Images of Hope*, 32.

The wolf shall live with the lamb, the leopard shall lie down with the kid, the calf and the lion and the fatling together, and a little child shall lead them. The cow and the bear shall graze, their young shall lie down together; and the lion shall eat straw like the ox. The nursing child shall play over the hole of the asp, and the weaned child shall put its hand on the adder's den. They will not hurt or destroy on all my holy mountain; for the earth will be full of the knowledge of the LORD as the waters cover the sea. (Isa 11:6–9)

In the New Testament, the relational continuance of the narrative with a personal God is spoken in the first person, by Jesus. "I" go to prepare a place; and if I go, "I" will return and receive you.

Do not let your hearts be troubled. Believe in God, believe also in me. In my Father's house there are many dwelling places. If it were not so, would I have told you that I go to prepare a place for you? And if I go and prepare a place for you, I will come again and will take you to myself, so that where I am, there you may be also. (John 14:1–3)

Every Tear and Every Ethnicity. The final dimension of health and healing in human life is fundamentally relational. Just as the first human breath was breathed directly by God (Genesis 2), so the ancient text's witness is that the final creation will also be very personal.

The personal dimension of Christian hope in the new creation and human life to come is explicit and central in the New Testament. The ancient text uses the expression "with Christ" (Phil 1:23; 2 Cor 5:8) and "in Christ" (e.g., 1 Thess 4:16; 1 Cor 15:22) to express the relationship that preserves our personhood beyond death.[47] Yet, personal identity is not private. It exists within a story of human relation to God. "Who I am" exists beyond the grave to the extent that I am preserved in relation to God.[48]

The final words of the New Testament come from the resurrected Jesus, speaking from the throne. Often misquoted, it does not say passively, "every tear will be wiped away." Rather it is in the active voice: God will wipe away every tear.

And I heard a loud voice from the throne saying "See, the home of God is among mortals. He will dwell with them; they will be

47. Green, *Body, Soul, and Human Life*, 177–79.
48. Ibid., 180.

> his peoples, and God himself will be with them; he will wipe every tear from their eyes. Death will be no more; mourning and crying and pain will be no more, for the first things have passed away. And the one who was seated on the throne said, "See, I am making all things new." (Rev 21:3–5a)

"Who I am" also exists beyond the grave to the extent that God preserves me in relation to the many people groups in the world. The last word is that God's intention in this new earth and new heaven is to redeem the wounds between the cultures and ethnicities of the world.[49] It declares the healing of all the cultures.

> Then the angel showed me the river of the water of life, bright as crystal, flowing from the throne of God and of the Lamb through the middle of the street of the city. On either side of the river is the tree of life with its twelve kinds of fruit, producing its fruit each month; and the leaves of the tree are for the healing of the cultures (*ethnos*). (Rev 22:1–2)

The ancient narrative concludes with a vision of a healing multicultural community. The restoration of wholeness and health for all people groups is the Bible's *sine qua non*.[50] All people are made of dust and God's breath. All are made in the image of God. May this vision of the new creation inspire all who work in the healing arts and sciences to work toward this description of God's glory.

---

49. The word *ethnos* is routinely translated "nations" in English Bibles, a reflection of modern nation-state politics. It means "ethnicities" or "cultures." Something similar is the case in the English translation "nation" in the Hebrew Bible.

50. *Sine qua non*, roughly translates, "Without this, nothing else is possible."

Bibliography

Adler, Mortimer and Charles Van Doren. *How To Read a Book*. New York: Simon and Schuster, 1972.

Ashbrook, James and Carol Albright. *The Humanizing Brain: Where Religion and Neuroscience Meet*. Cleveland, OH: Pilgrim, 1997.

Avalos, Hector. *Health Care and the Rise of Christianity*. Peabody, MA: Hendrickson, 1999.

Barr, James. *The Garden of Eden and the Hope of Immortality*. Minneapolis: Fortress, 1993.

———. *The Semantics of Biblical Language*. Oxford: Oxford University Press, 1961.

Barth, Karl. *Church Dogmatics*. Edited by G. Bromiley and T. Torrance. Edinburgh: T & T Clark, 1958.

Baruch, Jay. *Fourteen Stories: Doctors, Patients, and Other Strangers*. Kent, OH: Kent State University Press, 2007.

Benoit, Pierre and Roland Murphy, eds. *Immortality and Resurrection*. New York: Herder and Herder, 1970.

Berkhof, Hendrikus. *Christian Faith: An Introduction to the Study of the Faith*. Translated by Sierd Woudstra. Grand Rapids: Eerdmans, 1979.

Birch, Bruce. *Let Justice Roll Down: The Old Testament, Ethics, and Christian Life*. Louisville: Westminster John Knox, 1991.

Braaten, Carl E. and Christopher R. Seitz, eds. *I Am the Lord Your God: Christian Reflections on the Ten Commandments*. Grand Rapids: Eerdmans, 2005.

van den Brom, Luco. *Divine Presence in the World: A Critical Analysis of the Notion of Divine Omnipresence*. Kampen: Kok Pharos, 1993.

Bromiley, G. ed. *Theological Dictionary of the New Testament*. Grand Rapids: Eerdmans, 1985.

Brown, F., S.R. Driver, and C.A. Briggs. *A Hebrew and English Lexicon of the Old Testament*. Oxford: Clarendon Press, 1951.

Brown, Michael L. *Israel's Divine Healer*. Grand Rapids: Zondervan, 1995.

Brown, William P. editor. *The Ten Commandments: The Reciprocity of Faithfulness*. Louisville: Westminster John Knox, 2004.

Bruckner, James. *Exodus*. Peabody: Hendrickson, 2008. Forthcoming edition from Grand Rapids: Baker, 2012.

———. *Implied Law in the Abraham Narrative*. JSOTS 335. Sheffield: Sheffield Academic, 2001.

————. *Jonah, Nahum, Habakkuk, Zephaniah.* The NIV Application Commentary. Grand Rapids: Zondervan, 2004.

Brueggemann, Walter. *Theology of the Old Testament: Testimony, Dispute, Advocacy.* Minneapolis: Fortress, 1997.

Bryner, Jeanne. *Tenderly Lift Me: Nurses Honored, Celebrated, and Remembered.* Kent, OH: Kent State University Press, 2004.

Buber, Martin and Walter Arnold Kaufmann. *I and Thou.* New York: Scribner, 1970.

Bulkeley, Kelly: *The Wondering Mind: Thinking about Religion With and Beyond Cognitive Neuroscience.* New York: Routledge, 2005.

Cassell, Eric. *The Nature of Suffering and the Goals of Medicine.* New York: Oxford University Press, 1991.

Catherine. *Purgation and Purgatory: The Spiritual Dialogue.* New York: Paulist, 1979.

Chester, Stephen J. *Conversion at Corinth: Perspectives on Conversion in Paul's Theology and the Corinthian Church.* London: T & T Clark, 2005.

Childs, Brevard. *The Book of Exodus.* Old Testament Library. Philadelphia: Westminster, 1974.

————. *Old Testament Theology in a Canonical Context.* Philadelphia: Fortress, 1985.

Christian Perspectives on Theological Anthropology: A Faith and Order Study Document. Faith and Order Paper 199. Geneva: World Council of Churches, 2005.

Clark, Chap. *Hurt: Inside the World of Today's Teenagers.* Grand Rapids: Baker Academic, 2004.

Clayton, Phillip. *Mind and Emergence: From Quantum to Consciousness.* Oxford: Oxford University Press, 2005.

Clifton-Soderstrom, Michelle. *Angels, Worms, and Bogeys: The Christian Ethic of Pietism.* Eugene: Cascade, 2010.

Cohen, Abraham. *Everyman's Talmud.* New York: Schocken, 1975.

Cone, James. *The Spirituals and the Blues: An Interpretation.* Maryknoll, NY: Orbis, 1991.

Cooper, John W. *Body, Soul, and Life Everlasting: Biblical Anthropology and the Monism-Dualism Debate.* 2nd ed. Grand Rapids: Eerdmans, 2000.

Crick, Francis. *Astonishing Hypothesis: The Scientific Search of the Soul.* New York: Simon and Schuster, 1994.

Cutter, R. William, ed. *Healing and the Jewish Imagination: Spiritual and Practical Perspectives on Judaism and Health.* Woodstock, VT: Jewish Lights, 2007.

DasGupta, Sayantani and Marsha Hurst, editors. *Stories of Illness and Healing: Women Write Their Bodies.* Kent, OH: Kent State University Press, 2007.

Davis, Ellen F. *Getting Involved With God: Rediscovering the Old Testament.* Cambridge: Cowley Publications, 2001.

Dawson, Audrey. *Healing, Weakness and Power: Perspectives on Healing in the Writings of Mark, Luke, and Paul.* Eugene, OR: Wipf and Stock, 2008.

Donley, Carol C. and Martin Kohn, eds. *Recognitions: Doctors and Their Stories: A Collection of Original Works in Celebration of the 10th Anniversary of the Center For Literature, Medicine and the Health Care Professions.* Kent, OH: Kent State University Press, 2002.

Dorege, Thomas. *The Faith Factor in Healing.* Philadelphia: Trinity, 1991.

Dossey, Larry. *Healing Words.* New York: Harper, 1993.

Douglas, Mary. *Purity and Danger: An Analysis of the Concepts of Pollution and Taboo.* London: Routledge and Kegan Paul, 1980.

Duchrow, Ulrich and Gerhard Liedke. *Shalom: Biblical Perspectives on Creation, Justice and Peace*. Geneva: WCC Publications, 1989.

Dunlap, Susan. *Caring Congregations: How Congregations Respond to the Sick*. Waco, TX: Baylor University Press, 2009.

Dyson, Michael E. *Pride*. The Seven Deadly Sins Series. New York: Oxford University Press, 2006.

Feuerbach, Ludwig and George Eliot. *The Essence of Christianity*. Buffalo: Prometheus Books, 1989.

Ford, David. *Self and Salvation: Being Transformed*. Cambridge: Cambridge University Press, 1999.

Frank, Arthur W. *The Wounded Storyteller: Body, Illness, and Ethics*. Chicago: University of Chicago Press, 1995.

Freeman, David and Judith Abrams, eds. *Illness and Health in the Jewish Tradition*. Philadelphia: Jewish Publication Society, 1999.

Fretheim, Terence E. *Exodus*. Louisville: John Knox, 1991.

————. *The Suffering of God: An Old Testament Perspective*. Philadelphia: Fortress, 1984.

Gaiser, Frederick. *Healing in the Bible: Theological Insight for Christian Ministry*. Grand Rapids: Baker Academic, 2010.

Gill, David W. *Doing Right: Practicing Ethical Principles*. Downers Grove, IL: InterVarsity, 2004.

Goldberg, Sylvie-Anne. *Crossing the Jabbok*. Berkeley: University of California Press, 1989.

Gonzalez, Michelle A. *Created in God's Image: An Introduction to Feminist Theological Anthropology*. Maryknoll, NY: Orbis, 2007.

Gove, Philip B., ed. *Webster's Third New International Dictionary of the English Language Unabridged*. Springfield, MA: Merriam-Webster, 1986.

Green, Joel. *Body, Soul and Human Life: The Nature of Humanity in the Bible*. Grand Rapids: Baker Academic, 2008.

Greene-McCreight, Kathryn. *Darkness Is My Only Companion: A Christian Response to Mental Illness*. Grand Rapids: Brazos, 2006.

Grenz, Stanley. *The Social God and the Relational Self: A Trinitarian Theology of the Imago Dei*. Louisville: Westminster John Knox, 2001.

Gunderson, Gary and Larry Pray. *Leading Causes of Life*. Memphis: The Center of Excellence in Faith and Health, 2006.

Gunderson, Gary. *Leading Causes of Life: Five Fundamentals to Change the Way You Live Your Life*. Nashville: Abingdon, 2009.

Gustafson, Debra. *Biblical Prayer in Relation to Dying: A Qualitative Study of Residents in a Christian Not-for-Profit Retirement Community*. Deerfield, IL: Trinity Evangelical Divinity School, Doctor of Ministry Thesis, 2008.

Hall, Douglas J. *Imaging God: Dominion as Stewardship*. Grand Rapids: Eerdmans, 1986.

Harrelson, Walter J. *The Ten Commandments and Human Rights*. Philadelphia: Fortress, 1980.

Harris, R.L. et al. *Theological Wordbook of the Old Testament*, 2 vols. Chicago: Moody, 1980.

Harrison, R.K. *Leviticus: An Introduction and Commentary*. Tyndale Old Testament Commentaries. Downers Grove, IL: InterVarsity, 1980.

Bibliography

Hauerwas, Stanley. *The Peaceable Kingdom: A Primer in Christian Ethics*. Notre Dame: University of Notre Dame Press, 1983.

Heilman, Samuel. *When a Jew Dies*. Berkeley: University of California Press, 2001.

Heschel, Abraham. *The Prophets: An Introduction*. New York: Harper and Row, 1969.

Hoekema, A. *Created in God's Image*. Grand Rapids: Eerdmans, 1986.

Hong, Edna. *Bright Valley of Love*. Minneapolis: Augsburg, 1979.

Hopkins, D.N. *Being Human: Race, Culture and Religion*. Minneapolis: Fortress, 2005.

Irwin, Lee. *Visionary Worlds: The Making and Unmaking of Reality*. Albany: State University of New York, 1996.

Jackson, Edgar. *The Role of Faith in the Process of Healing*. Minneapolis: Winston, 1981.

Jeeves, Malcolm. *Human Nature at the Millennium: Reflections on the Integration of Psychology and Christianity*. Grand Rapids: Baker Academic, 1997.

John Paul II. *Crossing the Threshold of Hope*. New York: Knopf, 1994.

Johnson, A.R. *The Vitality of the Individual in the Thought of Ancient Israel*. Cardiff: University of Wales Press, 1949.

Kandel, Eric R. et al., editors. *Principles of Neural Science*. New York: McGraw-Hill, Health Professions Division, 2000.

Kierkegaard, Soren. *Gospel of Our Suffering*. Translated by A.S. Aldworth and W.S. Ferrie. Grand Rapids: Eerdmans, 1964.

Kleinman, Arthur. *The Illness Narratives: Suffering, Healing, and the Human Condition*. New York: Basic, 1988.

Koestler, Arthur. *The Ghost in the Machine*. New York: Macmillan, 1968.

Köhler, Ludwig et al. *The Hebrew and Aramaic Lexicon of the Old Testament*. Leiden, Netherlands: Brill, 1994.

Kreeft, Peter. *Everything You Ever Wanted to Know about Heaven . . . But Never Dreamed of Asking*. San Francisco: Ignatius, 1990.

Laytham, D. Brent, ed. *God Is Not . . . Religious, Nice, "One of Us," an American, a Capitalist*. Grand Rapids: Brazos, 2004.

Levin, Jeff. *God, Faith, and Health: Exploring the Spirituality-Healing Connection*. New York: Wiley, 2001.

Levison, John R. *Filled With the Spirit*. Grand Rapids: Eerdmans, 2009.

Lourde, Audre. *The Cancer Journals*. San Francisco: Spinsters, 1980.

Louw, J.P. and E.A. Nida, eds. *Greek-English Lexicon of the New Testament: Based On Semantic Domains*. New York: United Bible Societies, 1988.

Lynch, William. *Images of Hope: Imagination as Healer of the Hopeless*. Notre Dame: University of Notre Dame Press, 1965.

Luther, Martin. *Luther's Works*, vol. 28, J. Pelikan, editor. St. Louis: Concordia, 1958.

MacIntyre, Alasdair C. *Dependent Rational Animals: Why Human Beings Need the Virtues*. Chicago: Open Court, 1999.

Mairs, Nancy. *Ordinary Time: Cycles in Marriage, Faith, and Renewal*. Boston: Beacon, 1993.

McDannell, Colleen and Bernhard Lang. *Heaven: A History*. New York: Vintage, 1990.

McKnight, Scot. *The Jesus Creed: Loving God, Loving Others*. Brewster, MA: Paraclete, 2004.

Mendenhall, G.E. *Law and Covenant in Israel and the Ancient Near East*. Pittsburgh: Biblical Colloquium, 1955.

Miller, Patrick D. *Character and Scripture: Moral Formation, Community, and Biblical Interpretation*. Grand Rapids: Eerdmans, 2002.

Moreland, James Porter and Scott Rae. *Body and Soul: Human Nature and the Crisis in Ethics*. Downers Grove, IL: InterVarsity, 2000.

Murphy, Nancy. *Bodies and Souls, or Spirited Bodies?* Cambridge: Cambridge University Press, 2006

Niebuhr, Reinhold. *The Nature and Destiny of Man*. New York: Scribners, 1943.

Nielson, W.A. ed. *Webster's New International Dictionary of the English Language*. 2nd edition Springfield, MA: Merriam, 1947.

Nouwen, Henri. *The Wounded Healer: Ministry in Contemporary Society*. Garden City, NY: Doubleday, 1979.

Olyan, Saul. *Disability in the Hebrew Bible: Interpreting Mental and Physical Differences*. Cambridge: Cambridge University Press, 2008.

Pao, David. *Acts and the Isaianic New Exodus*. Tubingen: Mohr Siebeck, 2000.

Park, Jong Chun. *Crawl with God, Dance in the Spirit*. Nashville: Abingdon, 1998.

Pedersen, J. *Israel: Its Life and Culture*, vols. 1–2. London: Oxford University Press, 1926.

Peterson, Gregory. *Minding God: Theology and the Cognitive Sciences*. Minneapolis: Fortress, 2003.

Pilch, John. *Healing in the New Testament: Insights from Medical and Mediterranean Anthropology*. Minneapolis: Fortress, 2000.

Pinker, Steven. *How the Mind Works*. New York: Norton, 1997.

Plaskow, Judith. *Sex, Sin and Grace: Women's Experiences in the Theologies of Reinhold Niebuhr and Paul Tillich*. Washington D.C.: University Press of America, 1980.

Plaut, W.G. et al. *The Torah: A Modern Commentary*. New York: Union of American Hebrew Congregations, 1981.

Preuss, Julius. *Biblical and Talmudic Medicine*. Translated by Fred Rosner. New York: Sanhedrin Press, 1978.

Ramsey, Paul. *Basic Christian Ethics*. New York: Scribner's Sons, 1950.

Reynolds, T.E. *Vulnerable Communion: A Theology of Disability and Hospitality*. Grand Rapids: Brazos, 2008.

Rogerson, John. *A Theology of the Old Testament: Cultural Memory, Communication, and Being Human*. Minneapolis: Fortress, 2010.

Rosner, Fred. *Medicine in the Bible and Talmud: Selections from Classical Jewish Sources*. The Library of Jewish Law and Ethics, vol. V. New York: KTAV, 1977.

Russell, Jeffrey Burton. *A History of Heaven: The Singing Silence*. Princeton: Princeton University Press, 1997.

Ryle, Gilbert. *The Concept of the Mind*. New York: Barnes and Noble, 1949.

Shuman, Joel James and Brian Volck. *Reclaiming the Body: Christians and the Faithful Use of Modern Medicine*. Grand Rapids: Brazos, 2006.

Simundson, Daniel. *Where Is God in my Suffering?* Minneapolis: Augsburg, 1983.

Stendahl, Krister. *Immortality and Resurrection: Four Essays by Oscar Cullman, Harry A. Wolfson, Werner Jaeger, and Henry J. Cadbury*. New York: Macmillan, 1965.

Tillich, Paul. *Systematic Theology*. Chicago: University of Chicago Press, 1967.

Twelftree, Graham. *Jesus, the Miracle Worker: A Historical and Theological Study*. Downers Grove, IL: InterVarsity, 1999.

Van Gemeren, Willem, ed. *New International Dictionary of Old Testament Theology and Exegesis*. Grand Rapids: Zondervan, 1997.

Van Harn, Roger, ed. *The Ten Commandments for Jews, Christians, and Others*. Grand Rapids: Eerdmans, 2007.

Bibliography

Warrington, Keith. *Healing and Suffering: Biblical and Pastoral Reflections.* Eugene, OR: Wipf and Stock, 2005.

———. *Jesus the Healer: Paradigm or Unique Phenomenon?* Eugene, OR: Wipf and Stock, 2000.

Watts, Rikki. *Isaiah's New Exodus in Mark.* Grand Rapids: Baker, 2000.

Westermann, Claus. *Genesis 1-11: A Continental Commentary.* Minneapolis: Fortress, 1984.

———. *Praise and Lament in the Psalms.* Translated by K. Crim and R. Soulen. Atlanta: John Knox, 1981.

White, H.C. *Shalom in the Old Testament.* Philadelphia: United Church Press, 1973

Wilkinson, J. *The Bible and Healing: A Medical and Theological Commentary.* Grand Rapids: Eerdmans, 1998.

Wolff, H.W. *Anthropology of the Old Testament.* Translated by M. Kohl. Philadelphia: Fortress, 1974.

Wright, Christopher J. H. *Deuteronomy.* Peabody, MA: Hendrickson, 1996.

Wright, N.T. *Surprised by Hope: Rethinking Heaven, the Resurrection, and the Mission of the Church.* New York: HarperOne, 2008.

P. Yoder. *Shalom.* London: Hodder and Stoughton, 1989.

Yoder, P. and W. Sawatsky, eds. *The Meaning of Peace: Biblical Studies.* Louisville: Westminster John Knox, 1992.

Articles

Adler, Rachel. "Those Who Turn Away Their Faces: Tzaraat and Stigma." In *Healing and the Jewish Imagination: Spiritual and Practical Perspectives on Judaism and Health*, edited by R.W. Cutter, 142–59. Woodstock, VT: Jewish Lights, 2007.

Albl, Martin. "'Are Any Among You Sick?' The Health Care System in the Letter of James." *Journal of Biblical Literature* 121.1 (Spring 2002) 123–43.

Arnold, Bill. "Soul-Searching Questions about 1 Samuel 28." In *What about the Soul? Neuroscience and Christian Anthropology*, edited by Joel Green, 75–84. Nashville: Abingdon, 2004.

Ayala, Francisco J. "Biological Evolution and Human Nature." In *Human Nature*, edited by M. Jeeves, 46–64. Edinburgh: The Royal Society of Edinburgh, 2006.

Barr, James. "The Image of God in the Book of Genesis—A Study in Terminology." *Bulletin of the John Rylands Library* 51 (1968–69) 11–26.

Beck, A.T. "Cognitive Therapy." In *Encyclopedia of Psychology*, vol. 2., edited by A.E. Kazkin, 169–72. Oxford: Oxford University Press, 2000.

Bertram, G. et al. "Psyche." In *The Dictionary of the New Testament*, vol. 6, edited by G. Kittel and G. Friedrich, 608–66. Grand Rapids: Eerdmans, 1974.

Bidwell, Duane and Donald Batisky. "Abundance in Finitude: An Exploratory Study of Children's Accounts of Hope in Chronic Illness." *Journal of Pastoral Theology* 19/1 (2009): 38–59.

———. "Identity and Wisdom as Elements of a Spirituality of Hope among Children with End-stage Renal Disease." *Journal of Childhood and Religion* 2/5 (2011) 1–25.

Bird, P. "Male and Female He Created Them: Genesis 1:27 on the Context of the Priestly Account of Creation." *Harvard Theological Review* 74 (1981) 129–59.

Brown, Francis, et al. *The New Brown, Driver, Briggs, Gesenius Hebrew and English Lexicon: with an Appendix Containing the Biblical Aramaic.* Peabody, MA: Hendrickson, 1979.

Brown, Warren. "Human Nature, Physicalism, Spirituality, and Healing: Theological View of a Neuroscientist." *Ex Auditu* 21 (2005) 112–27.

Bruckner, James K. "A Theological Description of Human Wholeness in Deuteronomy 6." *Ex Auditu* 21 (2005) 1–19.

———. "Boundary and Freedom: Blessings in the Garden of Eden." *The Covenant Quarterly* 57 (February 1999) 15–35.

———. "Ethics." In *Dictionary of the Old Testament: Pentateuch*, edited by T.D. Alexander and D.W. Baker, 224–40. Downers Grove, IL: InterVarsity, 2003.

———. "Health." In *Dictionary of Scripture and Ethics*, edited by Joel Green, 385-87. Grand Rapids: Baker Academic, 2011.

———. "Health." *Ex Auditu* 18 (2003) 124-32.

Brueggemann, W. "Healing and Its Opponents." In *I Am the Lord Who Heals You: Reflections on Healing, Wholeness, and Restoration*, edited by G.S. Morris, M.D, 1–6. Nashville: Abingdon Press, 2004.

Caragounis, C. "Kingdom of God/Kingdom of Heaven." In *Dictionary of Jesus and the Gospels*, edited by Joel Green and Scot McKnight, 417–30. Downers Grove, IL: InterVarsity, 1992.

Chamblin, J. "Psychology." In *Dictionary of Paul and His Letters*, edited by Ralph P. Martin et al., 766. Downers Grove, IL: InterVarsity, 1993.

Charon, Rita. "Narrative Contributions to Medical Ethics: Recognition, Formulation, Interpretation, and Validation in the Practice of the Ethicist." In *A Matter of Principles: Ferment in U.S. Bioethics*, edited by E. DuBose, 260–64. Valley Forge, PA: Trinity International Press, 1994.

Clifton-Soderstrom, Karl, "When Self Takes Center Stage." *The Covenant Companion* 67 (2009) 12–15.

Clines, D.J.A. "The Image of God in Man." *Tyndale Bulletin* 19 (1969) 53–103.

Conradie, Ernst. "Resurrection, Finitude, and Ecology." In *Resurrection: Theological and Scientific Assessments*, edited by T. Peters et al., 277–96. Grand Rapids: Eerdmans, 2002.

Dobbs-Allsopp, F. "Lament." In *Eerdmans Dictionary of the Bible*, edited by D.N. Freedman, 784–85. Grand Rapids: Eerdmans, 2000.

Donahue, J.R. "Biblical Perspectives on Justice." In *The Faith that Does Justice*, edited by J. Haughey, 68–112. New York: Paulist, 1977.

Duffy, Stephen J. "Anthropology." In *Augustine Through the Ages: An Encyclopedia*, edited by Allan Fitzgerald, 26. Grand Rapids: Eerdmans, 1999.

Fabry, H.J. "*leb, lebab.*" In *Theological Dictionary of the Old Testament*, edited by Johannes Botterweck and Helmer Ringgren, translated by John Willis, 14 vols, 425. Grand Rapids: Eerdmans, 1974.

Fawver, J.D. and Overstreet, R. Larry. "Moses and Preventative Medicine." *Bibliotheca Sacra* (July-September 1990) 270–85.

Foreyt J.P. and G.K. Goodrick. "Cognitive Behavior Therapy." In *Encyclopedia of Psychology*, 2nd edition, edited by R.R. Corsisni, vol. 1, 245–48. New York: Wiley, 1994.

Fredericks, D.C. "*nepes*" in *New International Dictionary of Old Testament Theology and Exegesis*, 5 vols. Edited by W.A. Van Gemeren, 3:133–34. Grand Rapids: Zondervan, 1997.

Fretheim, Terence. "Salvation in the Bible versus Salvation in the Church." *Word and World* 13.4 (1993) 363–72.

Bibliography

Gaiser, Frederick. "The Emergence of the Self in the Old Testament: A Study in Biblical Wellness." *Horizons in Biblical Theology* 14 (June 1992) 1–29.

———. "'Your Faith Has Made You Well': Healing and Salvation in Luke 17:12–19." *Word and World* 16.3 (Summer 1996) 291–301.

Garro, Linda. "Chronic Illness and the Construction of Narratives." In *Pain as Human Experience: An Anthropological Perspective*, edited by Byron Good, 129. Berkeley: University of California Press, 1992.

Hefner, P. "The Human Being." In *Christian Dogmatics* vol. 1, edited by C.E. Braaten and R.W. Jenson, 333–35. Philadelphia: Fortress, 1984.

Johnston, Philip. "Humanity." In *New Dictionary of Biblical Theology*, edited by T.D. Alexander and B. Rosner, 564–65. Downers Grove, IL: InterVarsity, 2000.

Katz, Sheri. "Person." In *Augustine Through the Ages: An Encyclopedia*, edited by Allan Fitzgerald, 648. Grand Rapids: Eerdmans, 1999.

Kedar-Kopfstein, B. "*me'od.*" In *Theological Dictionary of the Old Testament*, edited by G. J. Botterweck et al., 8:39–41. Grand Rapids: Eerdmans, 1974.

Kim, Grace Ji-Sun. "In Search of a Pneumatology: Chi and Spirit." *Feminist Theology* 18.1 (2009) 117–36.

Kittel, G. and G. Friedrich, eds. "Basileus" and "Baileia." In *Theological Dictionary of the New Testament*. Translated by G. Bromiley. Abridged in one volume by G. Bromiley, 97–102. Grand Rapids: Eerdmans, 1985.

Kobasa, S.C. "Stressful Life Events, Personality and Health: An Inquiry into Hardiness." *Journal of Personal Social Psychology* 37.1 (1979) 1–11.

Lawson, Karen. "Spirituality in Medicine: What is its Role, Today and Tomorrow?" *Word and World* 30.1 (2010) 71–80.

Laytham, Brent D. "Keeping the Commandments in Their Place." *United Methodist Reporter* (November 26, 2003) 1–2.

Levinas, Emmanuel. "Useless Suffering." In *The Provocation of Levinas: Rethinking the Other*, edited by R. Bernasconi and D. Wood, translated by R.A.Cohen, 158. London: Routledge, 1988.

Luc, Alex. "lev," in *New International Dictionary of Old Testament Theology and Exegesis*, vol. 2. Edited by W. A. Van Gemeren, 749–54. Grand Rapids: Zondervan, 1997.

Luther, Martin. "Lectures on Galatians." In *Luther's Works*, edited by J. Pelikan and H. T. Lehmann, translated by J. Pelikan, vols. 28–29. St. Louis: Concordia, 1986.

Lysaught, M.T. "Vulnerability Within the Body of Christ: Anointing of the Sick and Theological Anthropology." In *Health and Human Flourishing: Religion, Medicine, and Moral Anthropology*, edited by C. Taylor and R. Dell'Oro, 159–82. Washington, D.C.: Georgetown University Press, 2007.

Maslow, A.H. "A Theory of Human Motivation." *Psychological Review* 50:4 (1943) 370–96.

Meyer, Carol. "Wellness and Holiness in the Bible." In *Illness and Health in the Jewish Tradition*, edited by David L. Freeman and Judith Z. Abrams, 127–33. Philadelphia: Jewish Publication Society, 1999.

Miller Jr., Patrick. "The Place of the Decalogue in the Old Testament and Its Law." *Interpretation* 43 (July 1989) 229–42.

Moberly, R.W.L. "Did the Serpent Get It Right?" *Journal of Theological Studies* 39 (April 1988) 1–27.

Mogensen, Bent. "*Sedaqa* in the Scandinavian and German Research Traditions." In *The Productions of Time: Tradition History and Old Testament Scholarship*, edited by Knud Jeppesen and Benedikt Otzen, 67–80. University of Aarhus: Almond Press, 1984.

Muilenburg, James. "Imago Dei." *The Review of Religion* (May 1942) 392-406.

Newsweek, editorial staff. "God and Healing: Is Religion Good Science? Why Science is Starting to Believe." *Newsweek,* November 10, 2003, 44–56.

Pinker, Steven. "How to Think about the Mind." *Newsweek,* September 27, 2004, 78.

Pollock, Susan E. "The Hardiness Characteristic: A Motivating Factor in Adaptation." *Advances in Nursing Science* (January 1989) 53–62.

Powe, Barbara. "Psychosocial Support." In *All-in-One Care Planning Resource: Medical-surgical, Pediatric, Maternity, and Psychiatric Nursing Care Plans,* edited by Pamela L. Swearingen, 74–80. St. Louis: Mosby Elsevier, 2008.

Rad, Gerhard von. "Israel's Earliest Creed." In *The Problem of the Hexateuch and Other Essays.* Translated by E.W. Trueman Dicken. New York: McGraw-Hill, 1966.

Rutter, M. "Resilience: Some Conceptual Considerations." *Journal of Adolescent Health* 14 (1993) 626–31.

Schiefelbein, Kyle. "'Receive this oil as a sign of forgiveness and healing:' A Brief History of the Anointing of the Sick and Its Use in Lutheran Worship." *Word and World* 30 (Winter 2010) 51–62.

Schwarz, Hans. "The Content of Christian Hope." In *Christian Dogmatics,* vol. 2, edited by C. Braaten and R. Jenson, 555–74. Philadelphia: Fortress, 1984.

Schweizer, Eduard. "Body." In *Anchor Bible Dictionary,* vol. 1, edited by D.N. Freedman, 767–72. New York: Doubleday, 1992.

Schweizer, Eduard and F. Baumgartel. "*Soma.*" In T*he Dictionary of the New Testament,* vol. 7, edited by G. Kittel and G. Friedrich, 1024–94. Grand Rapids: Eerdmans, 1974.

Seebass, H. "nepes" in *Theological Dictionary of the Old Testament,* 15 vols. Edited by G.J. Botterweck and H. Ringgren; translated by J.T. Willis, 9:497–519. Grand Rapids: Eerdmans, 1974–2011.

Seybold, K. "khalah" in *Theological Dictionary of the Old Testament,* 15 vols. Edited by G.J. Botterweck and H. Ringgren; translated by J.T. Willis, 4:399–409. Grand Rapids: Eerdmans, 1974–2011.

Shogren, Gary. "Will God Heal Us: A Re-examination of James 5:14–16a." *Evangelical Quarterly* 61 (April 1989) 99–108.

Simundson, Daniel. "Health and Healing in the Bible." *Word and World* (Fall 1982) 330–39.

Smelik, Klaas. "The Witch of Endor: 1 Samuel 28 in Rabbinic and Christian Exegesis till 88 A.D." *Vigiliae Christianae* 33.2 (1979) 160–79.

Teske, Roland, "Soul." In *Augustine Through the Ages: An Encyclopedia,* edited by Allan Fitzgerald, 808. Grand Rapids: Eerdmans, 1999.

Thomas, John Christopher. "Health and Healing: A Pentecostal Contribution." *Ex Auditu* 21 (2005) 88–107.

Tusaie, Kathleen and Janyce Dyer. "Resilience: A Historical Review of the Construct." *Holistic Nursing Practice.* (January/February 2004) 3–8.

Van Pelt, M. et al. "ruach" in *New International Dictionary of Old Testament Theology and Exegesis,* 5 vols. Edited by W.A. Van Gemeren, 3:1073–78. Grand Rapids: Zondervan, 1997.

Verhey, A. "Health and Healing in Memory of Jesus" *ExAuditu* 21 (2005) 24–48.

Bibliography

White, Lynn Jr. "The Historical Roots of Our Ecological Crisis," *Science*, 155 (1967) 15–31.

White, S.A. "Afterlife and Immortality." In *The Oxford Guide to Ideas and Issues of the Bible*, edited by Bruce Manning Metzger and Michael David Coogan, 7–10. Oxford: Oxford University Press, 2001.

————. "Human Person." In *The Oxford Guide to Ideas and Issues of the Bible*, edited by Bruce Manning Metzger and Michael David Coogan, 207–8. Oxford: Oxford University Press, 2001.

World Council of Churches Faith and Order Paper 199. *Christian Perspectives on Theological Anthropology: A Faith and Order Study Document.* Geneva: WCC, 2005.

Wright, C. "Old Testament Ethics: A Missiological Perspective." *Catalyst* 26.2 (2000) 5–8.